The Place of the Ideal Community
In Urban Planning

The Place of the Ideal
Community in Urban Planning

THOMAS A. REINER

Research Associate
The Institute for Urban Studies
University of Pennsylvania

Philadelphia

University of Pennsylvania Press

To Lewis Mumford

Utopian in Quest
Of an Ideal Urban Environment
In a World of Peace

Preface

This study is the first volume of a city-planning series which is being published by the University of Pennsylvania Press for the Institute for Urban Studies. Succeeding works, to be issued intermittently, will examine other aspects of urban structure and processes of interest both to city planners and other students of urban life.

Throughout history, men have envisioned ideal communities. The more significant of these, however, were concerned primarily with the reorganization of social and economic institutions and only incidentally, if at all, with the physical form of the cities in which activities take place. Whether in the classic tradition of Plato, the Christian tradition of St. Augustine, or in the more secular perspectives of More, Rousseau, and their successors, the good life was envisaged largely in political, religious, moral, social, or economic terms. During the nineteenth century, however, both the deterioration of the conditions of urban life and the possibility of an ever rising standard of living occasioned by the industrial revolution, led to an increasing emphasis upon the physical as well as the social environment. Thus Fourier, Owen, Buckingham, and Howard emphasize the physical environment. Bellamy deals in some degree with it, and George built a philosophy upon observations of the economic effects of urban growth.

This outpouring of utopias is testimony to the optimism, and the faith in progress, which characterizes the nineteenth century, and utopian writing at least until Huxley. This makes all the more striking the singularly static quality of most utopias, their lack of a sense of evolution. Of course, Darwin was not widely read until late in this period, and ecological concepts were apparently not applied to urban areas until well into this century, notably by Geddes. Thus the scientific, as well as the philosophical, perspectives for an evolutionary and ecologically consistent set of utopias have emerged only

[7]

in recent years, and past utopias have not been analysed systematically in these terms.

If the world is spared the holocaust of war, our enormous potentials for economic growth, and the urbanization which will result from such growth, make it essential that we understand the reciprocal effects of physical relationships, economic development, and social values upon each other. Thomas Reiner, lecturer in city planning and research associate at the Institute, here considers the nature of a number of plans for ideal communities and their implications for the practice of city planning. In so doing, he undertakes the analysis suggested by such noteworthy critics of utopian thought as David Riesman, in "Some Observations on Community Plans and Utopia", and Martin Meyerson, in "Utopian Traditions and the Planning of Cities."

The Institute wishes to express its gratitude to the Ford Foundation, which made this study possible.

WILLIAM L. C. WHEATON
DIRECTOR

Foreword

The field of urban planning is deeply concerned with questions of attaining an improved environment. It seems worthwhile, then, to study those ideals already expressed and to give some thought to the way they have been constructed. This is the theme of this work.

Conducted as part of the research program of the Institute for Urban Studies of the University of Pennsylvania, this study owes much to the support given it by William L. C. Wheaton, Director of the Institute, and to Robert B. Mitchell, Chairman of the University's Department of City Planning. In the course of the book's preparation, many people have commented on the subject and helped the writer to complete the project. In particular, thanks are due Herbert Gans, Lewis Mumford, and, again, William Wheaton. At an earlier stage of this study, when it was the subject of a thesis presented to the Department of City and Regional Planning of the Massachusetts Institute of Technology, Burnham Kelly, Kevin Lynch, and other members of the M.I.T. Planning faculty gave much needed assistance. Since then, Edward Gruson persuaded me to develop the subject further.

The graphic work in Chapter III was done by Michael Rubenstein and Ibrahim Jammal. Grace Milgram gave considerable time to the task of preparing this study for publication. Compilation of the bibliography (Chapter VI) was greatly facilitated by the assistance received from the Library of the Graduate School of Design of Harvard University and the Library of the School of Fine Arts of the University of Pennsylvania. Janet Scheff Reiner lent her critical abilities and her understanding of the subject; that the study came to print is largely due to her continuous help and enthusiasm.

To all these and to the many others (for few are the planners who fail to have strong feelings on the topic of Ideal Communities) I would like to express my gratitude, but also my apologies for not having written just as they would. For one of the most challenging and characteristic features of the Ideal Community is that, in the last analysis, it is a quite personal document. No two are alike, and no two critics will leave an Ideal Community with the same impression and conclusions. Consequently, while the thought and aid of others is very much a part of this work, the traditional disclaimer of shared responsibility is perhaps especially appropriate here.

T. A. R.

Contents

CONTENTS

I

Introduction

THIS MONOGRAPH is, first, an analysis of an urban-planning idea, and, second, a presentation in an organized fashion of the efforts which have been undertaken as the concept has been developed. As the title suggests, the substance of the study is the belief that an over-all model of an ideal neighborhood, city, or larger urban area is a valid, useful, and significant tool in urban planning. The importance of Ideal Communities[1] extends beyond the confines of the field of urban planning, for such designs appear to be among those achievements by which outsiders identify and assess urban planning.

The Ideal Community format shows a solution to contemporary urban problems by means of an interrelated scheme of general propositions. This depicts all those aspects of the urban environment the author thinks relevant. Thus, its creator produces a highly personal document focusing on those elements which are felt to be necessary and sufficient to determine the particular Ideal Community.

Most characteristically, the planner's Ideal Community is a mapped representation of the total urban environment, showing proposed uses of the land, a circulation scheme, and the distribution of certain public facilities. Supporting textual and statistical materials describe the scheme in greater detail. Ideal Communities are found in a wide range of format and degree of detail. The establishment of logical and useful boundaries for the class of proposals we label *Ideal Communities* was a difficult task. At most, those schemes listed in the appended Bibliography can be grouped by means of operational definitions.

The Ideal Community is deduced from basic assumptions about the good life, but only occasionally are these explicitly stated. Often, the Ideal Community hinges on methods to be employed to achieve that goal. It may

[1] *Community* is here defined as a generic term which includes neighborhood, town, city, and metropolis.

[15]

involve considerations originating in such fields as sociology, economics, architecture, and the public welfare professions, as well as in the bodies of knowledge more central to urban planning. In the latter category are resource management, housing, land use, and similar areas of concern.

Attention will center on those Ideal Communities designed in the last seven decades, predominantly products of the twentieth century. These are the schemes which are concerned with resolving the problems of our times, our physical environment, our society, and our economy. They would build for a tomorrow keyed to an understanding of a present which we find recognizable.

It is the physical aspects of the designs which will receive the lion's share of the emphasis. It is not this writer's wish to deny the primacy of the social or economic facets of urban existence. Yet a parallel analysis of nonphysical aspects of Ideal Communities must wait for another occasion. Though we shall concentrate on physical planning considerations, we shall nevertheless point out some of their broader implications.

IDEAL COMMUNITIES AND UTOPIAS

Ideal Communities are part of a larger group of creations which can be termed *utopias*. In most general terms, utopias are anticipations of an improved environment for man, from the Greek word *topos* ("place") and a pun on *eu* ("good") and *ou* ("not"). A utopia is a relatively complete picture of a situation which it is desirable to reach. It may have physical, institutional, and spiritual aspects. Utopia is set up as a contrast to the contemporary, inadequate world with its characteristic imperfections. It represents a goal situation.[2] The Ideal Communities which are the subject of this study are those utopias which incorporate description and analysis of the physical environment. Among the other categories of utopias, one will find proposals for communal reorganization of society, revolutionary tracts, and novels taking place in imagined surroundings which stress mankind's rising above contemporary limitations.

It is possible to distinguish in the bulk of what is traditionally identified as city-planning literature a predominant interest and concern with the physical aspects of the environment. Furthermore, much of planning has been involved with the means necessary to reach predetermined goals rather than with developing a methodology for evaluating alternative ends or with proposing such alternatives. By virtue of the very emphasis on place, goal

[2] As Buber has written (1949,* p. 7), the crucial element is the triumph of the human will driven by a social morality toward "what should be."

* Dates in parentheses refer to the Bibliography, beginning p. 163.

aspects, while present, have been poorly developed conceptually. This is so even though propositions regarding human nature and society or its institutions are the bases of the assumptions from which physical considerations are generally deduced. On the other hand, a utopia other than an Ideal Community frequently has its place, or physical form, outlined most dimly. The physical representations of such utopias, when made, are at best plausible and very roughly sketched contingent possibilities based on the goals and assumptions which prompt the authors to speculate. But, often utopia is not even this. The design of the environment may remain only a poorly conceived extension of one or another major point (such as the work relationships which give rise to a factory scheme), or the physical representation may be altogether lacking. This is unfortunate, because even if the primacy of nonphysical considerations is granted, an attempt to envisage more fully the physical consequences of utopia could show whether the scheme has any practicability or not or what modifications would be appropriate. In any event, the more general utopia can rarely be put into planning terms, and few of these can be analyzed meaningfully with the tools of planning as these exist today. In short, while Ideal Communities have emphasized the *place* aspect of the phrase "good, place," the other utopian writings have been concerned with the *good*.[3]

While Ideal Communities do differ in this respect from other types of utopias, this should not becloud the essential unity of all such concepts. Ideal Communities share an interest with other utopias in the improvement of man's surroundings. They spring out of the same intellectual,

[3] There exist many writings which evaluate utopias. The interested reader is referred to the following; many other sources are cited therein.

On the general topic of utopias, *see* Mumford (1922), Mannheim (1934, 1936), Riesman (1947), Buber (1949), and Negley and Patrick (1952). Mannheim stresses the total societal aspects, Buber the communal, Negley and Patrick the political, and Riesman some of the planning implications. Mumford attaches importance to their impact on all institutions, but to some extent so do the other writers. Negley and Patrick's work is an anthology with explanatory and interpretive chapters.

Parrington's survey (1947) attempts to cover the extensive American writings; the "English Utopia" is analyzed by Morton (1952). Wilson (1940) is one of many writers who emphasize the close relationships between socialism and utopias. Morgan (1946) stresses the historical roots of utopian writings.

Hertzler's work (1923) studies first the sociological conditions depicted in the utopias. In turn, he presents the sociological context in which they were written and their subsequent impact on society. A special emphasis is given the Hebrew prophets. Berneri's book (1950) includes extensive reprints from the original works. The author stresses the authoritarian and power aspects which characterize most of the utopian writings. She thus pinpoints (as did Mumford) their inapplicability to physical planning: the quest for symmetry, pattern, predictability results in an environment that, if nothing else, is too artificial and "planned" for much (urban) planning to take place. Ross's (1938) is a somewhat lighter and briefer survey. He does share, however, the same antiauthoritarian interpretation. Both Ross and Berneri include extensive bibliographies.

political, and moralist soil. And, though far from being identical concepts, interaction and relationships between Ideal Communities and other utopias do exist and do deserve some thought.

Effects of utopias on the environment

Each of the utopian trends in its own right has had effects on our society, directly or indirectly. Utopian communities have been built,[4] as have other types of enterprises which first came to public attenion by means of utopias. Our environment has been changed through the realization of objectives first voiced in one or a series of utopias. So long as these are a part of our landscape, they do deserve the planner's attention; insofar as men still build with utopian "idola"[5] uppermost in their minds, the utopias of yesteryear are the facts of today and very possibly the problems of the future. Table 1 suggests some of the many interactions which have been noted.

Utopian elements in planning

Just as the planner must deal with consequences of actions having their foundations in utopian concepts, twentieth-century planning itself has incorporated, albeit often indirectly, many of the ideas which first found expression in utopian literature. And even as some wellsprings of planning thought can be traced through such source fields as architecture, social work, or law, so have utopias contributed to planning concepts. Some of the ideals which planning shares with utopian writings include the concept that in the first instance it is possible and worthwhile to manipulate the environment, that the good man is a reflection of a decent and healthy environment, that a work-oriented neighborhood or town is desirable. It may very well be possible to trace the descent of concern with the neighborhood and neighborliness from anarchosyndicalist and yet earlier origins.

[4] Utopian communities are that perhaps surprisingly large number of voluntary and relatively isolated settlements which are dedicated to some religious, political, or at times economic ideal. They have flourished in the United States, France, Israel; in fact, all over the world. Many were created in response to a call first voiced in utopian writings.

Utopian communities have been subject to detailed analysis. For European experiments, see Wilson (1940, especially part 2, chaps. 2, 3, and 4) and Buber (1949, chap. 7). Holloway's survey of American communities (1951) points to their European antecedents. Calverton (1941), Hine (1953), and Holloway deal at length with the experience of some of the more significant communities in the United States. Briefer descriptions will be found in Tunnard (1953, part 3) and in Parrington (1947, passim). (The latter is an extended treatment of American utopian thought.) Israeli experience is interpreted by Buber (1949, "Epilogue") and studied by Spiro (1956). For a contemporary if somewhat personal set of articles, see the special issue of Liberation: "Community: A Symposium" (1957).

[5] Idolum: a term coined by Mumford (1922) to describe the world of goal-directed ideals, with a stress on their interactions.

Table 1. Impact of Utopian Thought*

Utopia	Form which Utopia Takes	Examples of Consequences of Interest to Planners
Religious	Religious community	The religious and utopian community's purposes or practices may run athwart standards or laws of the jurisdiction in which it is located.
Utopian	Sectarian community	
Reformist	Housing, recreation movements	Pressures for and construction of public housing, parks, and all the consequent satisfactions and problems.
Economic	Movements for just or efficient distribution of resources	Attempts to apply to the municipal environment the concept that unearned increment should revert to the community.
Political	Political reform movements	Plans to establish neighborhood size in relation to size of politically active group; the full range of problems that deal with equitable decision making.
Communal	Community movements	School-centered neighborhoods, citizen participation in planning decisions.
Conservation	Park and conservation movements	Metropolitan pressures and attempts to obtain regional parks.

* In addition, one can note such further factors, as the military paradigm, which have influenced city building since antiquity. This has played a most conscious role in civic design: from the time of Renaissance schemes, such as that of Palmanova, through construction and replacement of the bastions which ring metropolises such as Paris and Vienna, to the interest shown in the very recent past in attempts to reduce urban vulnerability to atomic attack.

One must also consider specifically the utopian novel. Bellamy's *Looking Backward* (1888) has had profound effects on men of many persuasions and in numerous fields, including planning. The utopian novel has presented to wide audiences new ranges of possible human environments and new goals for contemporary society and has suggested paths to their achievement. In a similar vein, such a novel as A. T. Wright's *Islandia* (1942) points out how much that is regarded by our society as timeless and given need not in fact be so. At the same time, Wright recognizes with considerable astuteness the permanent, human qualities. The lasting value of such works lies at least partly in their suggestion of a flexible and relativistic view of social institutions and of that which is called *human nature*.

General observations on utopia

Obviously, utopias themselves are but one form taken by concern with the ideal environment. A far greater literature of a didactic, propagandist, or prophetic nature has, for centuries, urged, exhorted, and threatened man with the possibility and the need to improve himself and his surroundings. Like many other contemporary disciplines, planning owes as much to this literature as it does to utopia.

Utopia building, and utopian thinking, is part of a liberal education of planners, as it is of all educated people. Therefore, familiarity with utopias and similar endeavors has a place in the planner's education (for an elaboration of this point, *see* Riesman, 1947). But the peculiar nature of his vocation demands more of the planner in this respect. The responsibilities of the urban planner include those of the technician and visionary charged with anticipating and charting alternative courses to achieve goal situations. In view of these particular functions, thorough grounding in all utopian approaches would seem to be a prerequisite of the planner's training.

CATEGORIES OF IDEAL COMMUNITIES

Ideal Communities reflect differences in the way authors of such schemes interpret the relation between the proposal and the existing society. A design can either serve to support an existing social order or it may urge a radical departure. (For elaboration of this point, *see* Mannheim, 1934, pp. 201 ff., and 1936, chap. 2.) It should be added that writers vary in the degree to which they show awareness of this dimension to their plans. With this in mind, one can detect three major approaches to the creation of Ideal Communities:

1. The Ideal Community as a solution within the framework of the currently expressed goals of the residents. The Ideal Community in this instance is a reordering, a tidying up. Adams's scheme for a residential city (1934) is an example. No fundamental societal innovations are suggested. The design calls for an ordered replacement of the chaos characterizing the land-use distribution in urban areas along lines suggested by successful, stable suburban home districts.

2. The scheme which incorporates major revisions of the environment so as to achieve a better life, but one which still is in accord with the fundamental wishes of the community, as these are understood by the author. Justement's proposal (1946) for the reconstruction of the national-capital area would fall in this category. This calls for institutional changes of a more basic nature.

[20]

3. An Ideal Community which requires a reconstructed outlook on the part of the public. The author either himself urges such a fundamental change or assumes that such a reorientation lies just below the surface. Given the opportunity, new ways will characterize human behavior and society as a whole. This may involve a program to remove impediments to the assertion of the new life. The proposal by Goodman and Goodman (1947) for a communal reorganization of urban society is of this type.

The term *Ideal Community* perhaps needs further clarification with regard to the intent of the author to direct himself to specific, real, and immediate problems. The following categories of Ideal Communities indicate the variation in this respect, particularly so far as land use and physical planning considerations are concerned.

1. Idealized designs (including the physical representations of the literary utopias) with only incidental consideration of land use and physical planning elements. Renaissance ideal cities are of this type; their rigid patterning exemplifies the imposition of will on the environment.[6]

2. Idealized schemes with definite concepts of land use in the plan. The spatial demands of activities and their locational interrelations are given explicit consideration. Howard's *Garden Cities of Tomorrow* (1898) is an example of the writings in this class.

3. Schemes with hypothetical sites in mind and meeting imagined but re-

---

[6] Rosenau's recently published book (1959) presents an extended review of such designs and visions of the perfect order. The title, *The Ideal City in Its Architectural Evolution,* is misleading only in that Dr. Rosenau does not limit herself to such a narrow perspective. The major emphasis is given to contributions made roughly between 1500 and 1900, but briefer sections present ideals from antiquity and some modern schemes. She traces the gradual transition to today's emphasis on social concepts; prior to the Enlightenment, religious and geometrically formal ideals dominated.

For an analysis of such designs from classic times to the past century, *see* Lang (1952). This well-written article unfortunately approaches the topic too narrowly for our purposes: the emphasis is on the visual arts. Nevertheless, there are some gemlike insights: the author justifies her critique of philosophy's domination of town planning by pointing out that the late eighteenth- and nineteenth-century Rousseauian influence led to ridiculous schemes, placing a premium on "an endless expanse of vegetable allotments" (p. 101).

For a planner's historical survey of urban ideals, with a stress on economic and social forces, *see* Blumenfeld (1943). Tyrwhitt (1950) gives a more extended planner's review of pretwentieth-century proposals. Like Blumenfeld, she also analyzes the archetype urban environment of a number of historical periods. These too have served as inspiration for the creation of ideal urban forms.

As noted above, utopian writings tend to be sketchy in their description of the physical environment. It is not surprising, therefore, that the works mentioned in footnote 3 discuss what might be called physical planning considerations only parenthetically. Riesman's article (1947) stands of course as a notable exception.

Ingersoll (1959) in parts 1 and 2 of her bibliography lists numerous original and evaluative works falling in the category of idealized designs.

alistic obstacles to their realization. Wright's Broadacre City (1945)[7] is built on a section of terrain typical of large portions of Midwestern U.S.A.

4. An Ideal Community which selects as a working basis a real site but is not particularly concerned with the actual problems the area faces economically or socially. Garnier's Cité Industrielle (1918) pays this kind of limited attention to the realities of the site.

5. A scheme which develops a plan for a site but where the author does not feel constrained by limitations usually placed on the area's officially responsible planner. Justement (1946), for example, presented such a proposal for the Washington area. This was more a scheme designed to develop principles of general applicability than it was a plan designed to serve in a particular planning context. Considerations of acceptance do not really limit the proposal.

6. Master plans which are prepared to serve an actual clientele but are clearly intended to represent a new departure. The MARS plan for London (*see* Korn and Samuely, 1942) is of this nature.

The Ideal Communities studied in this monograph lie in the second, third, fourth, and fifth categories. An analysis of physical-planning concepts can proceed fruitfully from a review of such proposals.

THE USE OF IDEAL COMMUNITIES

As a model

Ideal Communities are but one form of presenting goals regarding the environment. However, they specifically deserve attention insofar as they are used to show how and what planning principles of general applicability are developed. Much of the field's exploration and creativity has been part and parcel of the design of Ideal Communities. This way of assessing the validity of propositions corresponds both to the use of the ideal firm in economic analysis and to the study of aerodynamic principles in a wind tunnel. In the course of this monograph, we shall see how successfully this pattern has been followed. Further reasons why Ideal Communities form an important part of planning and should play a role in the planner's education can be summarized as follows.

As typical of the planning approach

At its best the Ideal Community is composed of interrelated proposals giving a synoptic view of the urban environment. It is therefore quite appropriate to a field which stresses the breadth and interconnection of ele-

[7] Schemes for a Broadacre City have appeared in numerous of Wright's works. Although the earliest full description is contained in *The Disappearing City* (1932), perhaps the most extensive presentation is found in *When Democracy Builds* (1945).

ments. Although the approach is not faultless, it is susceptible to reformulation to the point where it can handle the full range of problems and techniques of an enriched urban planning.

Urban planning has a tradition of thinking in Ideal Community terms. As has been suggested, this reflects to some degree ties with other fields. As a consequence, this is an area of contact with those outside the planning profession, for the Ideal Community format (if not its content also) is one which can communicate to others the findings, as well as the aims, of the field. Similarly, Ideal Communities can serve to crystallize basic policy alternatives for the public and other clients of the planner.

The planner in this connection has two other functions. First, the Ideal Community (as well as such other proposals as master plans which stress factors of interrelation and mutual consistency) shows the impact on each other of the various findings of the specialists in nonplanning fields. Secondly, the planner, perhaps more than practitioners in other fields, sees his unique function, contribution, and skills to lie in the direction of applying to the future such findings and values as are drawn from today's experience. The conclusions of others working in the substantive areas in which planners also work are rarely so presented.

As an essential part of planning history

A sequence of efforts benefits from joint review. Both the critic and the student should have available the full scope of a field's achievements. In urban planning, however, this is hard to come by. Yet a periodic review of achievements would assure that worthwhile contributions are not lost. It is easy even for rather sophisticated urban-planning schemes to all but disappear, as has happened to a number of proposals. Such is the fate, for example, of Fritsch's new-town design (1896). In its consideration of growth possibilities and in its other innovations, this was far ahead of its time.

It is more than just a matter of who was first or a question of meting out justice. An important measure of a field's maturing is the degree to which succeeding generations of theorists build on the body of earlier ideas and experience. Similarly, the extent of the application of accumulated knowledge by its practitioners is a clue to the discipline's progress. As in other fields, it is wasteful to ignore significant previous efforts.[8]

[8] It is important to recognize, however, that a certain portion of planning thought either holds no relevance to the present or is woefully inadequate methodologically. In such cases there should be honest and clear abandonment of earlier efforts. The field of planning seems prone to carry a number of historical albatrosses. This study will serve its purpose if it helps the planner evaluate historical antecedents and judge if they really do satisfy today's more rigorous requirements or are relevant to contemporary problems. The rest, without much loss, do deserve to be abandoned. As Merton (1957, p. 5) notes, other fields labor under similar conditions.

Familiarity with Ideal Community proposals also suggests a range of approaches and solutions, and the breadth and creative richness which planning can offer. The student in the planning laboratory as well as the practitioner may benefit from the use of a catalog of ideal approaches which, even if not exhaustive in scope, often exceeds the individual's experience, recollections, or imagination.

As an indication of areas of agreement

Considerable interest has been expressed in attempts to establish areas of substantive agreement in the field of urban planning. Higgins has called on planners to formulate, review, and, in concert, accept a set of shared principles and has offered (1949) a set as a stimulus to thinking and discussion. The American Institute of Planners, the planners' professional organization, is currently involved in similar activities. It is hoped that this will serve to structure and identify the profession, prove to be an aid to its clients, and communicate planning's basis to related professions. Other fields, given the areas of agreement, would be better able to utilize the findings and proposals of the field of planning and could direct their own researches to the evaluation and validation of propositions originating in it. A careful study of the Ideal Community literature can go a long way toward identifying such areas of agreement and at the same time point out where basic differences exist.

As ideals with practical consequences

Knowledge of ideal schemes contributes to an understanding of some of the more practical endeavors of planners. A work such as *Garden Cities of Tomorrow* directly influenced the construction of the English Garden Cities and later the New Towns. Thomas Adams, Le Corbusier, and Clarence Stein, to mention only three of many influential writers, have been involved in significant planning enterprises and have left their mark indirectly on countless other projects. A better understanding and more fruitful critique of a large portion of the field's achievement, therefore, will rest on familiarity with Ideal Community proposals, as these may with greater directness present their authors' intent.

As elements in the development of criticism

Planning does not have a systematic body of critical literature. But a field or art which lacks a technique for accumulation of criticism lacks vitality and potential for growth. There is a false sense of achievement when works are indiscriminately praised. What is attempted here is a *critical* review of Ideal Communities and of the propositions propounded by means of the Ideal Community form. It is hoped to suggest some further steps in the direction of systematic appraisal. It is also hoped that this work will stimulate others to apply their critical faculties to the classic master plans, such as those for Chicago, San Francisco, London, Copenhagen, or Moscow, and to the plans and studies emanating in growing numbers from planning offices.

To suggest areas of research

Study of Ideal Communities will also prove to be helpful if it furthers research which expands planning theory and substantive knowledge. The fruitful hypothesis (as well as research program) is that which can be validated and, even better, is a step to further research and development of theory. In other words, one of the aims of this monograph is to assess and reformulate some of the propositions offered in the Ideal Community literature in order that their validity may be established or that they be disproved. Far too little testing has been done.

A word of caution

The Ideal Communities discussed here represent writings and designs of urban planners (though sometimes the writers became recognized as such largely by virtue of these same products). While the schemes are an indication of the field's progress, achievements, and substance, they do not cover the work of all those who express concern with the substance of various aspects of urban planning. Experts from other fields, many of which are more directly concerned with a particular issue at hand than is planning, may very well come to conclusions which differ qualitatively and quantitatively from the findings of urban planners. Furthermore, a competence in these other fields frequently leads to a more rigorous approach. Thus, the social psychologist or sociologist approaches the neighboring and mutual-aid question from a more exacting (though rarely normative) point of view than does the planner who is designing an Ideal Community.[9] Of course, it is incumbent on the planner to utilize the findings from these neighboring fields. But it should not be overlooked that the planner does make a contribution by his very willingness to explore and be creative precisely where the current angels of research and academic endeavors fear to tread.[10]

[9] *See* Festinger (1950) and Foley (1952) as two significant works in this respect.

[10] This kind of courage, possibly foolhardy, is only justified where the proposals are made in a form where verification is possible and significant enough to merit undertaking.

II

Physical Planning Principles
in Ideal Communities

ONE OF THE VALUES of Ideal Communities which led to this study is their usefulness in developing planning principles. We will, in Chapter IV, deal with the content. Let us first consider the types of statements, what kind of principles are involved, how they are used, and what they tell us about the author and his work.

Some of the propositions presented in Ideal Communities are very broad indeed, while others are confined to much narrower ranges of circumstances. It is often left to the reader to determine exactly the level of applicability which is intended or is appropriate. But before he can make such an analysis, a more difficult though still preliminary step faces him. Often, the real meaning of an Ideal Community, the principles that the author seeks to convey, are far from self-evident. These the reader must clarify.

When the propositions are not set forth explicitly, they must be deduced from the body of the work. This may require calculations from a set of stated propositions, as when density proposals are derived from area and population standards. This will be necessary when the author shows no particular concern with the problem under consideration. Another type of situation arises where the critic probes further below the surface for the author's convictions in the absence of a direct and explicit presentation of the propositions. For example, this may involve study of the distribution of work places in relation to residential areas and consideration of the implied understanding of man's various needs and activities. It may well be, however, that a certain view ascribed to a writer is not one to which he would subscribe were he pressed, particularly by a critic with the benefit of historical hindsight. But the critic, as user of a plan or of an Ideal Community, is entitled to delve as deeply as he can and to conclude that in any given scheme particular precepts dominate. Thus, Sanders and Rabuck (1946), by virtue of ring elements in their design, imply it is possible to predetermine city size as well as to hold the population within these limits. It is legitimate for the critic to ascribe such a planning approach even though nowhere in the work is there an outright assertion to this effect. The user of this scheme would either have to accept this interpretation or be prepared to modify the proposal. It may be added that one of the advantages of selecting physical planning propositions for detailed analysis is that these, more than others, tend to be discussed with relatively greater explicitness.[1]

SOURCES OF PROPOSITIONS

Just as the Ideal Communities themselves, the propositions they embody come from several sources. They may be developed in response to a planning situation with planning techniques in mind. Stein's Radburn and Greenbelt schemes (1951) would be excellent examples of this type of work. Or the propositions may have resulted as a consequence of, or a deduction from, an ideal outside the field of planning. Often this may be reformist in nature (the various English new-town proposals may be cited as examples), or it may stem from the transfer of standards from other professions (such as the school-size considerations which formed one of the bases of Perry's original Neighborhood Unit formulation, 1929).

At the level of the all-encompassing theories, both urban planning in general and Ideal Communities in particular lean heavily on the social sciences. At the other extreme, operational principles are borrowed or adapted from a great number of disciplines, among them economics, demography, public administration, engineering, anatomy, and others. The glaring inadequacies but also some leavening effects of the Ideal Community schemes tend to be observed at levels of excessive generality or specificity: here there is reliance on neighboring professions. Unfortunately there often is an inadequate in-

[1] It is sometimes difficult to distinguish an author's ideal from the givens, the assumptions on which he bases his schemes. For example, an Ideal Community may be designed so as to maximize each family's opportunity for horizontal mobility and to provide each household with a garden. If the author believes this need can only be satisfied by means of low structures with gardens abutting, then obviously this becomes an important element in the final picture. We would further conclude that the writer thinks in terms of a relatively isolated but close-knit family unit with patterns of leisure and domestic values not unlike those we often note today in middle-class suburbs in the United States and England. But it may very well be that the author's intention is far from wanting to preserve such a way of life. He may simply be bringing into the picture what he considers a necessary element of the better life as he defines it and be unconscious of some of the implicit consequences of the plan he presents. In this example, the framework of the future society is shown as excessively tied to the characteristics of today's environment.

tellectual foundation and a failure to keep abreast of developments in these other fields.

TYPES OF PROPOSITIONS

The first major categorization with which we will deal is that which would distinguish goals from instrumentalities. The propositions formulated in Ideal Communities are usually tools to achieve ends but are not ends themselves. The discovery of the ends, as was suggested above, is only one of the critic's duties; the analysis of the tools as they serve to reach these is the other portion of his task. This is a matter which must be approached relativistically.[2] Just as the total scheme is instrumentative to a yet larger design, so the propositions themselves can become ends, as for the duration of the political struggle for their acceptance.

The most significant difference among the propositions would seem to be the extent to which each is descriptive or normative. The first form which this takes is how much the propositions *propose* or *expose*. Some are clearly directed towards establishing principles which disclaim reliance on existing patterns, seeking instead to build up new forms. Such a work would be Howard's *Garden Cities* (1898), at least insofar as there are contrasts between the then-existing trends toward urbanization in England and his scheme for dispersal.[3] The other extreme is found in writers who essentially try to reduce to basic elements the observed conditions under study. Hoyt's (1939) and Burgess's (1923) attempts to identify fundamental urban forms by studying existing cities may be taken as prototypes of this approach. The former, a specialist in real-estate economics, maintains that the city necessarily has a sectorial pattern. This reflects the outward push of the wealthy; the structure is largely expressed in terms of rent categories of residential areas. Reasoning that is in a sense not too dissimilar leads Burgess, a sociologist, to conclude that mobility and growth pressures give an essentially ring form to the city. It is interesting to note that these two writers, both relying on empirical evidence, nevertheless offer quite contrary interpretations of urban form.[4] Other writers who support theories of size, form, or other elements of city structure with data obtained from the contemporary

[2] Among others, Kaplan (1958) has pointed out that there is a hierarchy of propositions down from broad criteria which establish the bounds to public activity, through goals, more immediate objectives, and then to specific programs.

[3] Of course, to the degree that Howard strived to provide a continuity to the English way of life, preserving it by offering a more amenable and viable environment, his work is one which attempted to isolate the essential elements of a culture and maintain them—a conservative, nonutopian endeavor.

[4] Hoyt in particular has been criticized for his failure to indicate the process by which the regularity in urban form was shaped (Rodwin, 1950, and also Firey, 1947).

urban scene do so at levels of lesser generality. Propositions from this latter group of expository works tend to be more specific. Since propositions and schemes current in the field do vary in the degree to which they are bound to existing conditions, it is helpful to bear this distinction in mind.[5]

In terms of a fact-value dichotomy, few of the propositions or schemes are totally bereft of value elements and implications. Even the most empirical observations and proposals exist in a perspective-giving framework having value content. To place these values beyond the pale of evaluation and criticism would limit analysis of Ideal Communities to a most rudimentary and insignificant level. And to maintain that the proposals or planning work itself should steer clear of value considerations would so restrict planning as to render progress impossible. Therefore, rather than attack the value-laden features of Ideal Communities as such, a careful value analysis should be incorporated in each critique. The identification of stated and implicit values is not the least important part of a scheme's analysis. What an author may hold to be fact may actually be a highly normative statement. What seems eternal may only apply to a restricted set of circumstances.

Mannheim's thoughts (1936) are particularly illuminating in this context. When an approach serves to bolster the existing order, with only palliative improvement suggested, Mannheim maintains one is dealing with concepts that are "ideologies." But if the design is for the genuine reconstruction of society and environment, with little regard for present institutions when these impede the achievement of the good life, then a truly "utopian" proposal is at hand. The trouble is, of course, that writers are not explicit or even aware of the reconstructionist nature of some of their recommendations; or, on the other hand, there are instances where new physical forms may cloak the perpetuation of tradition though this is not recognized by the proponent.

The dimension of realizability of utopias in general and Ideal Communities in particular has been discussed in Mumford's (1922) and Riesman's (1947) writings. Mumford distinguishes between (a) Utopias of Escape, which stress the immediate release from difficulties without asking the necessary basic questions, and (b) the Utopias of Reconstruction, which are defined as realistic reconstitutions of the social and physical environment, keyed to particular goals and to basic human needs. Riesman's dichotomy distinguishes between irrational systems of belief not in the holder's interest and schemes which are both rational and achievable and in the long-run

---

[5] Interestingly, one of the few areas in which one uniformly finds a high degree of normative writings is functional land-use differentiation. The authors rely on existing city patterns, if at all, only to determine size or general location requirements of land uses and facilities. But the very quality of land use and facility intermixture so characteristic of most urban areas today is rejected by these proposals.

interest of the holder.[6] The former are labeled "ideology," and only the latter, Riesman writes, can be defined as "utopian." One might add that an irrational system of belief could not be in the holder's interest (e.g., the City of God concept). Plausible schemes to his disadvantage (such as Orwell's *1984* and Huxley's *Brave New World*) are implicitly considered as ideologies.[7] It would seem, however, that to limit utopias, Ideal Communities, and planning propositions only to those that are realizable is overly restrictive. Yesterday's "impossible" often is but today's challenge and tomorrow's realization. The only qualification that is needed in a planning context is that each proposal contain appraisals of the immediate and long-range practicability of a scheme and its elements.

As with many such analyses, "ideology" and "utopia" do not form a dichotomy but rather are at opposite ends of a continuum. Portions of a proposal may fall at one end, portions at the other, or they may be at some distance along the way. This continuum from utopia to ideology suggests variation in the degree to which reliance is placed on so-called given factors or the degree to which all is questioned. Parsons (1949) notes that, in general, we see in our environment "conditions" (over which we have no control) and "means" (which represent that part of our surroundings which can be changed). The ability to distinguish properly such "means" from "conditions" may be precisely the kernel of genius in the field of planning. Often what separates the good scheme from the bad are those qualities of imagination and temerity which question one or another aspect of society —unchanged within memory—and realize that modification, in fact, *is* possible in a particular instance and that controls are appropriate. The dramatic and creative ideal is based on expanding areas of human control, although the scheme may show an inadequate appreciation of the little that we do know of human nature and behavior. On the whole, as Riesman has trenchantly shown, planners have leaned in the direction of writing conservative ideologies. Those in related professions, but writing as planners, often go even beyond utopia and meander, as cultists, in the paths of excess.

[6] A similar feeling is expressed by those writers (Blumenfeld, 1949, for example) who maintain that planners and plans, to serve and to survive, must be consonant with long-term trends of the particular society they serve. It is not possible to thwart history. As one examines designs such as Comey's (1923) (justified on similar grounds and not entirely without resemblance to Blumenfeld's sketch), one is made painfully aware that the line between the wish not to "thwart history" and *laissez-faire* renunciation of responsibility is indeed a thin one.

[7] Such analyses raise numerous other questions. For example, how is the "long-run interest" to be measured, and by whom? What if the client's short-run interests, or his admittedly limited interests, clash with the ascribed long-run interest? And what about that human nature which cannot be violated—it is far from understood, yet probably much less inflexible than one is led to believe. Can human nature be a serious base for critique?

In general, the proposals which we shall analyze in Chapter III do fall into two categories resembling Mannheim's distinction between "ideology" and "utopia." There are those which envisage a society which is a radical departure from the current environment, and others which suggest a life essentially similar to that surrounding us, with perhaps some of the more obvious kinks straightened out and the worst impediments removed. It is interesting that the most conservative (i.e., "ideology" laden) proposals do not seem to require any less physical modification of today's urban structure than do the more "utopian" ones. If anything, the opposite would seem to hold. For example, the physical aspects of the Goodmans' second scheme (1947) (which must be classified as highly "utopian") suggest, with only relatively minor modifications, precisely those bleak, confused areas of our cities which most irritate traditional planners and those more enlightened elements in the business community who support urban redevelopment programs. On the other hand, far greater expenditures and changes in the physical environment on a vast scale would be involved in many conservative "ideological" proposals. In this latter group would fall such a deification of the contemporary commercial society as that of Ferriss's Metropolis (1929) or the perpetuation and extension of upper-class suburbia, which is the essence of many neighborhood unit designs and new-town proposals. A detailed analysis could fruitfully be undertaken to see which approach, "utopian" or "ideological," would, in reality, cost more and to evaluate the implications of such a finding.

PROPOSITIONS AND PRINCIPLES

The distinct reluctance in this chapter to use the word *principle* to describe normative statements or recommendations for the planner's use remains to be explained. It seems important to distinguish between the broad class of assertions which refer to goals or means to achieve these and those more restricted group of propositions which are verified and of very definite and explicit applicability. It is for the latter group that the term *principle* should be reserved. The words *planning principles* carry with them an understanding of finality absent in the more general propositions and imply that certain steps have been taken to insure their validity. A principle of this type resembles, say, the laws discovered in mechanics, although in the less-exact social sciences, they are better expressed in probabilistic terms.

The propositions which receive the most attention in Ideal Communities are presented by their authors with conscious intent to affect public policy and to change the form and substance of the city. Yet it must be conceded that only a few are buttressed by any empirical evidence. To the extent that

[31]

they remain in this tentative state, the propositions should be labeled *hypotheses,* with the term *principle* reserved for those relatively rare examples where some form of proof exists and rigorous evaluation of the statement's validity is presented. The formulation of refutable hypotheses is a first step in research activity.

Lying at the foundation of any science or aspiring science are a series of postulates. These are the premises from which, in a given context, a chain of reasoning or a study will start. To the degree that a postulate is a veiled value statement and not of general acceptance, the premise lacks the quality of self-evidence and hence is not a true postulate. A classic example of a postulate from economics is the proposition that an individual can arrange his preferences for goods along some scale. From this base, some of the most elaborate analyses in the study of consumer behavior proceed. With the selection of such a set of self-evident postulates the field of planning will have made a substantial forward step.

One final category of propositions can be found in Ideal Communities. Such statements, although possibly cloaked in wording suggesting their self-evident or even definitional quality, still express the beliefs and preferences of the author and must be analyzed in their given social context. In terms of the logical structure of Ideal Communities, these terms may serve as postulates in a given argument, in the sense that the reasoning is based on them. They obviously vary in the importance of their subject matter. They are rarely phrased so as to permit easy verification or evaluation subject to more general criteria. As such, these statements possess what sometimes is another meaning given the word *principle*: when one speaks of these as the ultimate values or bases. Value statements abound in great numbers in Ideal Communities. Their analysis constitutes the most challenging part of a critique. They must first be identified, then only can one establish their relationship to a broader set of criteria, found within or outside the given work.

The following are examples in these categories:

1. *Hypotheses*
    a. A school-oriented neighborhood, as compared to one which is based on other foci, will provide the greatest degree of community cohesiveness.
    b. When work areas and residential areas are located together, there is a reduction in commuting.
2. *Principles*
    a. Physical limitations preclude more than X vehicles from using one lane of a highway per hour at a given speed.
    b. If children are to walk to school within Z minutes (the value state-

ment), then schools in residential areas should be spaced no more than Y miles apart.

3. *Postulates*

    a. A city's government is faced with the task of organizing a limited amount of space for a variety of uses.

    b. An increase in population has as a concomitant either a greater density or a need for expansion of the developed area, or both.

4. *Value Statements*

    a. The city should reflect to the maximum the residents' needs and desires.

    b. Wage earners should not live more than X minutes' travel time from their jobs.

III

A Prospect of Ideal Communities

IN THIS CHAPTER, twenty Ideal Communities are each briefly discussed. They are subject to a uniform critique, although at times the desire to present parallel reviews proved to be a trifle restrictive.

No justification on strictly methodological grounds can be presented for the selection of this particular group of Ideal Communities, save the writer's belief that, as a group, they serve to give an adequate picture of the breadth and periodic depth that the proposals in general achieve. It is quite likely that no two readers would have made the same choice. Some would hesitate to omit those well-known proposals not listed here: where, for example, is Hilberseimer's *New City* (1944)? Others will criticise the failure to include such worthy and detailed schemes as those by Stein (1951). Still others will puzzle over the apparent favoritism shown the Corbusier (ASCORAL) linear city (1945) over, say, that designed by planners in the Soviet Union a decade earlier. To all these questions there lies but one reply: that this writer found the twenty examples selected representative of the several hundred existing Ideal Communities. The important and the forgotten, the cultist and the wise, the early and the contemporary, and the alien and the domestic are represented in the following pages.

The Ideal Communities are presented in the chronological order in which they were first published. Reference to the many others will be found in the Bibliography, Chapter VI.

With each analysis, there is also presented a map showing key features of the scheme. These drawings have been edited to permit comparison from scheme to scheme. A uniform legend is used throughout (*see* page 35). Since the areas covered by the scheme vary widely, it was necessary to use three standard scales: 1 in. = 4 miles, 1 in. = 1 mile, and 1 in. = ¼ mile.

[34]

LEGEND

1-5 dwelling units per gross residential acre

6-20 dwelling units per gross residential acre

21-30 dwelling units per gross residential acre

31-50 dwelling units per gross residential acre

51 + dwelling units per gross residential acre

commerce

industry

institutions

open space

T. FRITSCH, DIE STADT DER ZUKUNFT, 1896

1. Context of Proposal

A product of the last decade of the nineteenth century, *Die Stadt der Zukunft* ("The City of the Future") is mainly directed at the excesses brought on by the Industrial Revolution. It precedes other town-planning works focusing on those problems. The author, apparently a German publicist or journalist, was very much concerned with his country's standing and strength and the role of cities in this regard. It is an item of reformist literature, published as one of a series of tracts devoted to contemporary problems.

2. Summary of Proposal

A ring city of parallel land-use bands should be constructed. These well-defined bands should be started along a base radius; the origin may be an existing town. Growth is by more or less simultaneous addition to each of the rings. In the long run, these bypass the original center and the city assumes something of a spiral form.

3. Content Analysis

a. Assumptions: Cities and technology are harbingers of a new life but so far have served largely to create chaos and add to misery. Fritsch felt most strongly that rational decision making rather than chance should control cities' growths and destinies. Order and rationality are boiled down to the contention that different land uses should be kept separated. While his is a quest for rationality, Fritsch, paradoxically, was shocked by destruction caused by adherence to commercial or economic criteria of worth: there is an antiquarian streak in the man. It is justified by reference to the need to conserve what already exists in the face of change. This fits his definition of organic growth. While the city should be an efficient production and trade center, it must also serve higher ends, such as aesthetic and creative satisfactions. Social stratification is accepted as a given factor.

b. Form: The city is the sum of parallel bands of distinct land uses, whose widths vary as changing area demands arise. Related zones are placed next to each other: high and middle-income housing, commerce and factories, etc. The aim is to introduce order, reduce traffic, and enhance the appropriateness of surroundings. Shafts of open land periodically pierce the city. The width of the green is proportional to density. Since the high-prestige center is devoted to low-density houses, there is little public open space near the inner

T. Fritsch, 1896.

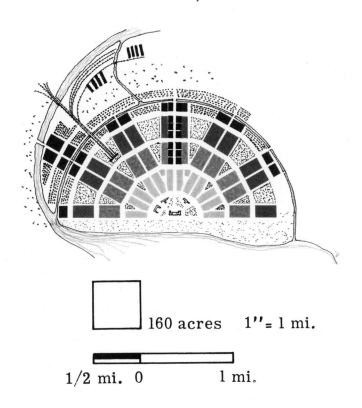

160 acres   1''= 1 mi.

1/2 mi. 0   1 mi.

Based upon drawing in Die Stadt der Zukunft.

rings. The surrounding country is easily accessible to those who need it the most: the poor, unhealthy masses.

c. Circulation: The ring and radial road system is supplemented by a railroad loop. Streets are designed to discourage heavy traffic from entering noncommercial precincts. An underground truckway network is proposed. Pedestrian paths are provided, linking the various public open spaces, some of which lie inside high-density residential superblocks.

d. Population: This is a plan for growth, and no design size is offered. It is evident that the author thought in terms of cities in the 100,000 to 1 million range.

e. Density: No specific standards are offered, but private ownership of land is cursed as a cause of overcrowding. Under the proposed system of public land ownership, the residential belts are rigidly classified according to wealth of household and, therefore, by housing type. The inner zone is designed for one-family house densities on the order of four to ten dwelling units per residential acre and succeeding belts to some thirty to forty dwelling units. No innovations are offered here; rather, the best of existing site-planning practice is presumed.

f. Consideration of future growth: This new city, by virtue of its spiral form, can meaningfully exist almost from its inception. As it grows to metropolitan scale, it envelops, so to speak, the original growth and thereby an ancient core for the city is created. A sharp break with existing urban patterns is required to start the city, although an already built-up core can be accommodated.

4. Evaluation

The proposal's main virtue lies in its strong presentation of the case for land-use and traffic differentiation. Although these are offered as matters of conviction rather than the results of research, in this respect they do not differ much from today's writing on these topics. The proposal is also strong and imaginative in its treatment of the manner in which a city can accommodate growth pressures.

While we must take issue with the scheme's class-differentiating bands, there is at least the recognition that low-income people should have the least distance to travel (or is the high-density area a buffer between the wealthy and the factories?). The diagrammatic representation of the proposal is supposedly schematic, yet the balance of areas seems unrealistic. In view of the expressed scorn for the materialistic aspects of urban life, the disproportionately large areas set aside for industry seem particularly perplexing. Finally, while public ownership of land may, temporarily, control development, the expectation that the lowest densities will be maintained at the core seems unduly optimistic.

This work deserves attention if for no other reason than its being the first of the realistic critiques of the urban environment from a physical planning viewpoint. It sought not to abolish the city[1] but to rationalize it. In the attempt, several of the most pervasive themes found in the Ideal Community literature first find published expression.

Bibliography

FRITSCH, THEODOR. *Die Stadt der Zukunft.* Leipzig: Hammer, 1896. 2nd. ed. 1912.

E. HOWARD, GARDEN CITIES OF TOMORROW, 1898

1. Context of Proposal

An innovational approach to those already recognized and highly inter-related problems afflicting the modern city, living conditions therein, and its functions, this work was written at a time when excesses of the Industrial Revolution were still at their peak. Although intended to be of general applicability, the focus of the study is the wish to decant London's high and growing population. The proposal also shows evidence of Howard's experiences in the United States Middle West. No reliance on other town planners can be detected but the work indicates an awareness of movements aimed at preventing unearned increment (Henry George), Buckingham's 1849 Industrial Town Model ("Victoria"), proposals for land nationalization (Spence, and others), plans for systematic colonization overseas, and the suggestion by the economist Alfred Marshall that London's population could be reduced by moving whole neighborhoods as a unit to the country. In its form this is a popular tract seeking to gather support for a movement to be dedicated to the decongestion of metropolitan centers and the provision of a salubrious environment.

2. Summary of Proposal

Towns of predetermined size (32,000 population) are the solution to the fundamental problem of our society: overcrowded cities. The towns are

---

[1] A subsequent edition (1912, p. 30) points to the very poor regenerative capacity of cities, the low birth rate and poor health records of residents, and states that national interest demands small cities, keeping most of the people on the land.

E. Howard, 1898. The garden city.

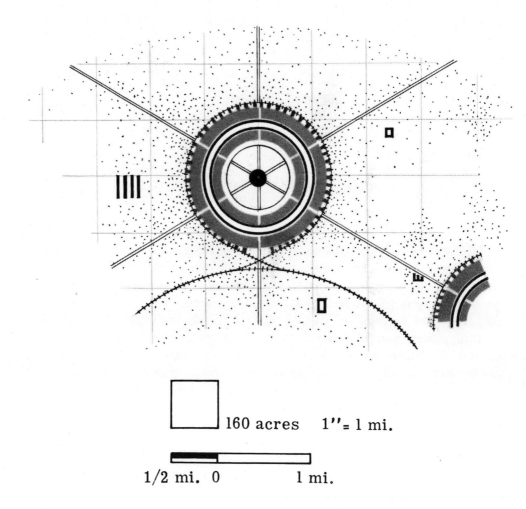

160 acres   1''= 1 mi.

1/2 mi. 0   1 mi.

Based upon drawing in Garden Cities of Tomorrow.

E. Howard, 1898. The ward.

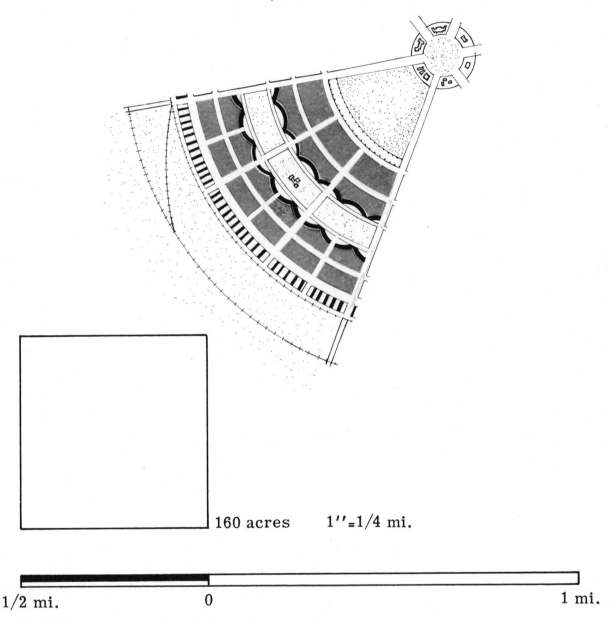

160 acres   1″=1/4 mi.

1/2 mi.   0   1 mi.

Based upon drawing in <u>Garden Cities of Tomorrow.</u>

to be separated from each other by inviolate greenbelts devoted to agricultural, institutional, recreational, and certain other specialized activities. Each town is equipped for the full economic, social, and cultural daily life of its citizens and shows a highly developed sense of neighborhoods. A system of unified land ownership and leaseholds maximizes both the public interest and individual choice.

3. Content Analysis

a. Assumptions: A tone of moderation pervades the work: consider the size of a town, reformism without control or cultism, some municipal action rather than socialism or dogmatic *laissez faire,* and town and country synthesis rather than either in isolation. Man is seen as amenable to cooperation, though this condition may have to be fostered, since man is also highly individualistic. The long-term solution to problems caused by the industrial revolution must rest on restoring people to the land which itself has been modified and improved. City development is financed by means of public use of the increment in land value, collected by rentals instead of taxes.

b. Form: The town is the sum of a fixed number of neighborhoods. A sector-concentric form at the town scale is combined with a polynucleated metropolis of coequal units surrounding a core city (which presumably already exists). These are all closely linked by road and railroad.

c. Circulation: A radial-ring system of streets is established; the town is surrounded by a railroad to serve the country-oriented industries. Heavy traffic is thus kept to the outside. A pedestrian scale of accessability is created.

d. Population: Thirty-two thousand persons form the Garden City. Except as a plausible example, the choice of this figure is not defended. The metropolis ("Social Cities") is of unspecified size.

e. Density: Residential areas contain about twenty dwelling units per net acre. Town-wide densities are about eight dwelling units per acre. Again, these are not defended, but, like the population estimate, they come from the judicious weighing of incomes, land value, and other considerations.

f. Consideration of future growth: The city is to be built as one effort. Further growth is by establishment of new Garden Cities. Modification of the internal pattern is not considered.

4. Evaluation

The proposal shows no internal inconsistencies, though certain omissions are noted (for example, a failure to discuss clearly the functional difference between Garden Cities and the central core of the Social Cities). Control of future growth by an industrial and a rail belt seems unwisely rigid. The desired end might be otherwise achieved. On the whole, this work, which has had profound effects on the thinking of the planners who followed, shows remarkable perception of the way cities work.

Howard's permanent contributions to the field of city planning lie in pointing out the advantage of planned development and growth of cities at a time when most thinkers felt this to be beyond the ken and skill of our civilization, in suggesting that the size of a city was a legitimate area of control, and in establishing the groundwork of the neighborhood concept. Of equal significance are his efforts to popularize these ideas and to interrelate them with many other themes. His service as a prime mover in the development of Welwyn and Letchworth Garden Cities in the first decades of this century cannot be overlooked. *Garden Cities* stands among the earliest systematic treatments of zoning of land uses, the ideal of low density, and the preservation of inviolate green areas around towns.

Bibliography

HOWARD, EBENEZER. *To-morrow; A Peaceful Path to Reform.* 1st ed. London: S. Sonnenschein, 1898.

————. *Garden Cities of To-morrow.* 2nd ed. London: S. Sonnenchein, 1902.

————. *Garden Cities of To-morrow.* New edition, ed. by F. J. OSBORN, with an introductory essay by LEWIS MUMFORD. London: Faber & Faber, 1946.

Many words have been written about Howard and his contributions; no text book on planning fails to discuss his work. The following are two of the numerous citations:

OSBORN, FREDERIC JAMES. *Green-belt Cities.* London: Faber & Faber, 1946. Chap. 1.

PURDOM, CHARLES BENJAMIN. *Building of Satellite Towns.* 2nd ed. London: J. M. Dent, 1949. *Passim.* (The first edition, dated 1925, carries an essay by Howard.)

E. CHAMBLESS, ROADTOWN, 1910

1. Context of Proposal

This is an approach to the solution of urban problems by a gadget-minded "dealer in patents." The proposal was prompted by Chambless's disgust with the American environment at the turn of the century, which arose in part because of his stock-market losses. The author lacked knowl-

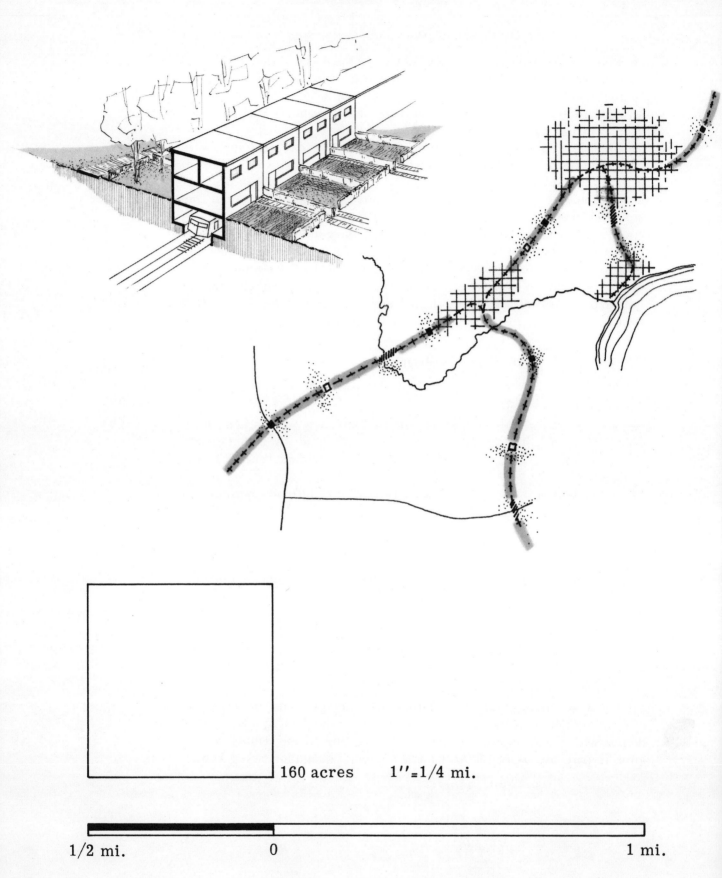

E. Chambless, 1910.

160 acres   1''=1/4 mi.

1/2 mi.   0   1 mi.

Based upon drawing in Roadtown.

edge of planning outside the United States. No reference is made to the Spanish Linear City which somewhat resembles Roadtown. He apparently had little expertise in any field related to planning. Evidence by outside consultants is submitted, however, in support of the plan's economic and circulation aspects. The book is a frank effort to obtain financial backing for the proposal which, the author asures the reader, is a realistic and readily achievable cure for society's ills.

2. Summary of Proposal

The form of the future urban milieu is that of indefinitely extended lengths of row houses. Monorail transit operates in the structures' basements. This is the basic circulation facility. Civic, commercial, and industrial buildings are interspersed among the residential. Agricultural uses and gardens lie alongside Roadtown. The author asserts that a most welcome urban-rural synthesis arises in the immediate environs of each home. Not only is the "town" resident's house set in open land, but the farmer too lives in Roadtown. Various other political, public health, and related reform proposals are added on the strength of the basic proposal.

3. Content Analysis

a. Assumptions: Contemporary society, most specifically in its characteristic of "bigness," prevents man, an essentially cooperative and creative being, from expressing himself. His immediate environment must be reconstructed so that work, exchange, and intellectual endeavor can be conducted at close hand. While the scheme is very much home-oriented, there are proposals for the communal provision of cooking and other services. There is an almost puritanical zeal expressed for the elimination of waste, be it in the form of middlemen's profits, effort expended in travel, or nonproductive household chores. There is a great appreciation throughout of technological advances and the application of mechanisms which make the lot of the people "easier." A syndicalist view of society underlies the suggestion that only those affected by a measure are entitled to vote on a particular issue.

b. Form: Vehicular circulation, sheltered space, and pedestrian walkways are superimposed on each other in one contiguous row of 21-ft. by 20-ft. houses. Nonresidential uses are interspersed in an unspecified pattern, with factories, trading centers, and communal enterprises housed in separate structures. Home industry and agriculture constitute part of the activity of the typical household. Farming and recreational areas are found in the surrounding open land.

[45]

c. Circulation: There is almost exclusive reliance on monorail transport and transit to which each structure is accessible and intimately tied. This system is the scheme's main *raison d'être.*

d. Population: No optimum size is given. About 100 families are considered the necessary minimum. This is equivalent to a Roadtown one-half mile in length.

e. Density: Two hundred fifty families per mile is the standard. This is derived by calculating house width and allowing for nonresidential structures. There is no explicit consideration of minimum lateral separation. Presumably it is considerable, measured in miles.

f. Consideration of future growth: A Roadtown can begin in any metropolitan suburb. Interim lengths between one-half mile and a continental network are considered appropriate. Since buildings are structurally standardized, internal use of buildings can, apparently, be changed at will as, for example, demands for manufacturing space increase.

4. Evaluation

Essentially, the weakness of this scheme lies in the attempt to maximize all goals through use of only one rigid form. The author does not realize that in this manner other problems are created: for example, the choice among services that any individual finds at his disposal is far more limited than if he were surrounded by activity. There is an implicit and unresolved conflict, furthermore, between the manifest desire to see a largely self-sufficient household and the provision of an elaborate transportation system. The latter either generates, by its very convenience, traffic and travel disruptive of the home or becomes an expensive and underutilized liability to the community. Another paradox arises from the failure to realize that normally spaced transit stops are required for the operation of an efficient transit system, yet these would tend to create clustering of houses. One must also question whether the wish to break up bigness ("the trusts") is not inconsistent with the almost pathological reliance on the products of mechanization. Finally, Chambless fails to show why the better and more coherent society *necessarily* follows from the structural scheme he envisages: do not the improvements, to a large extent, flow from reform proposals of a more general nature?

Roadtown has value as a relatively well-thought-out extreme solution of some aspects of the relation between circulation and modern life. As such, it points out, unwittingly at times, the consequence of an excessive reliance on circulation-based solutions.

Bibliography

CHAMBLESS, EDGAR. *Roadtown.* New York: Roadtown Press, 1910.

A PROSPECT OF IDEAL COMMUNITIES

A. Comey, REGIONAL PLANNING THEORY, 1923

1. Context of Proposal

This is an American "Reply to the British Garden City Challenge," written after World War I by a planner grounded in landscape architecture. No explicit recognition is given to related planning ideas, though familiarity with at least the garden-city literature can be presumed. This essay appeared first as a magazine article written as a challenge to what the author felt was the unwarranted growing popularity of English planning concepts, particularly the idea that population movement and size of towns are subject to control.

2. Summary of Proposal

Central commercial areas are located at the intersection of major regional highways. Ribbons of industrial development with a backbone of transportation arteries extend from these cores. The factory areas are encased within residential districts, which are interspersed with community and local shopping facilities. Ample agricultural and other open lands separate the ribbons from each other and penetrate almost to the heart of the city.

3. Content Analysis

a. Assumptions: Growth is essential to metropolitan health and should not be stifled. In fact, it cannot be prevented or even much retarded. The function of city planning is to guide the inevitable development more or less along the lines of its "natural" tendency. This tendency has its optimum expression in close relation to transportation, for circulation routes give value to land and so determine its uses. City form is thus a function of the communication network, which in itself reflects regional linkages. The life envisaged is simply a more rational version of the suburban environment held desirable in America in 1923.

b. Form: Star-shaped centers of urbanization have commercial and industrial cores, whose location is based on transportation facilities and accessibility. Proximity to open land is seen to enhance the quality of surrounding linear residential areas. Commercial and community facilities are distributed throughout the residential area in a hierarchical pattern.

c. Circulation: The regional grid is presumed to consist of a triangular

A. Comey, 1923.

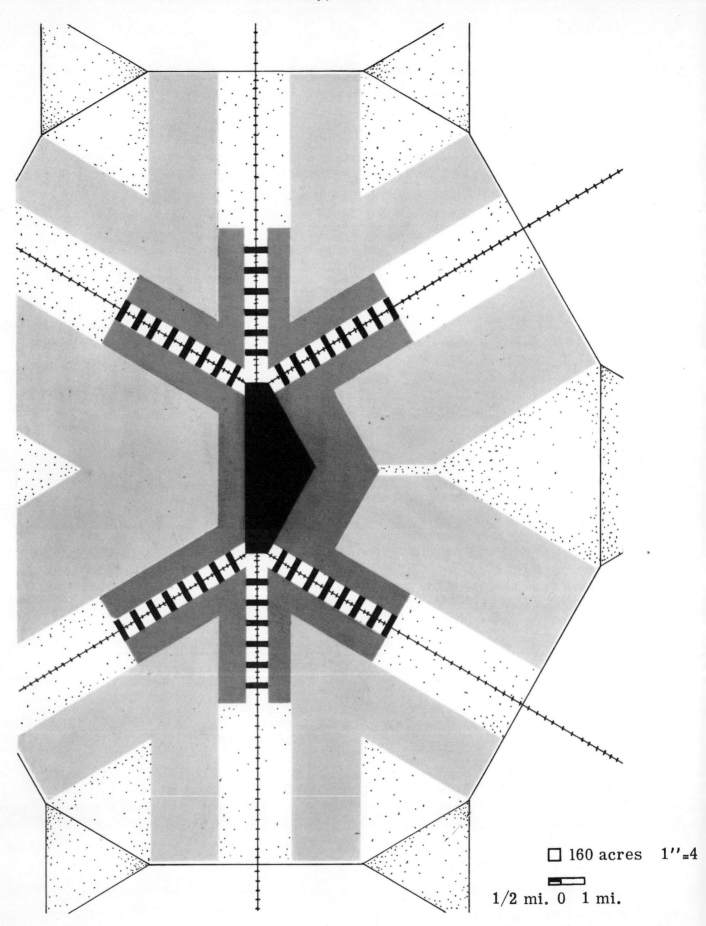

☐ 160 acres 1''=4

1/2 mi. 0 1 mi.

Based upon drawing in ''Regional Planning Theory,'' <u>Landscape Architecture</u>, January, 1923.

network interconnecting all major centers of activity. Consequently, numerous spokes extend from each major intersection. Interurban rail transit and highways play a key role. This network gives form to development throughout the region. Within urbanized areas, a spine-and-rib system of major roads is supplemented by a local street system which is not described. Routes are differentiated by size to reflect their function.

d. Population: Ten to thirty thousand inhabitants constitue the lower range of optimum city size. This is not further elaborated. With interest in growth, no maximum is suggested either for the towns or for the aggregates of towns which together make up a metropolitan area.

e. Density: Density levels are, presumably, those of the better garden suburbs, although calculation from the drawings yields very low densities. No attempt, apparently, was made to relate the residential areas to the capacity of the transportation network, the size of the central business district, or to employment opportunities.

f. Consideration of future growth: Since this Ideal Community is designed for growth, interim lengths of the ribbon development are considered satisfactory. One can presume that existing urban centers would be appropriate starting points for the ideal shown. No consideration is given to questions of modification of the final pattern or subsequent growth.

4. Evaluation

It is hard to justify such a complex and evidently expensive transportation system when the aim is solely to serve relatively self-contained communities ("self-contained" on the grounds that work, trade, recreational, and community facilities are placed close to residential districts). Growth is the keynote, yet the core central business district is apparently of a fixed size. It is assumed that all factors along the arterial spine would grow together, yet this is unlikely. The use of a ribbon development, especially in commercial areas, leaves much to be desired. In actuality, congestion would surely arise at intersections.

The intention to allow for growth is laudable and is strongly put, though the criticism of the Garden Cities is not carefully detailed. The proposal is a good example of the often met recognition of the need to plan for a hierarchy of facilities and of the desirability of preserving real open space near the city—and of the problems arising from planning in this fashion.

Bibliography

COMEY, ARTHUR. "Regional Planning Theory: a reply to the British challenge." *Landscape Architecture,* XIII (January, 1923), 81–96. Reprinted, *ibid.,* Augusta, Me.: Printed by C. E. Nash, 1923.

E. GLOEDEN, DIE INFLATION DER GROSS-STÄDTE, 1923

1. Context of Proposal

The proposal contained in *Die Inflation der Gross-Städte* (The Inflation of the Large City") came out of a generation which saw great advances in municipal enterprises and administration, but which also witnessed defeat in war and a devastating inflation. It is small wonder, then, that the work looks to the peaceful if distant past, as well as hopefully to a future where present problems will have been resolved with the undertaking of social and economic innovations. It appears that the aim was to galvanize public opinion at a crucial juncture of German urban history—as if the author felt that indeed a new era was beckoning.

2. Summary of Proposal

A metropolis consists of a number of identically sized cells of 100,000 inhabitants. Each of these units is designed to perform a characteristic function in the larger whole, yet all are coequal and self-contained to a large degree. They are linked by an extensive interurban railway system and are served by major public facilities set in the surrounding greenbelts.

3. Content Analysis

a. Assumptions: The overriding consideration in planning an ideal urban environment is the linkage of home and work sites. No laborer and no school child should have to walk more than the fifteen minutes traditional in European agricultural communities. Time spent traveling is time lost. Stability, homogeneity, and permanence are highly valued. Thus, all residents of a cell share common skills, concerns, and destinies; ideally these would be passed from generation to generation.

b. Form: Each cell is no more than 1½ miles in diameter; the size is set by reference to a maximum fifteen minutes' walk to the center. The core is composed of a variety of establishments and services appropriate to a central business district. This is surrounded by a circle of work places which characterize the unit, such as factories, commercial enterprises, offices, or government bureaus. Apartment houses ring the work center; in turn, a band of lower density, one-family structures forms the outer edge of the unit. Individual cells are separated from others in the honeycomb by a greenbelt in which are located large-scale communal facilities, transportation operations, and nuisance uses. The cells stand about 2 miles center to center.

[50]

E. Gloeden, 1923. The metropolitan area.

☐ 160 acres   1″=4 mi.

▬▬
1/2 mi. 0 1 mi.

Based upon drawing in Die Inflation der Gross-Städte.

E. Gloeden, 1923. The cells.

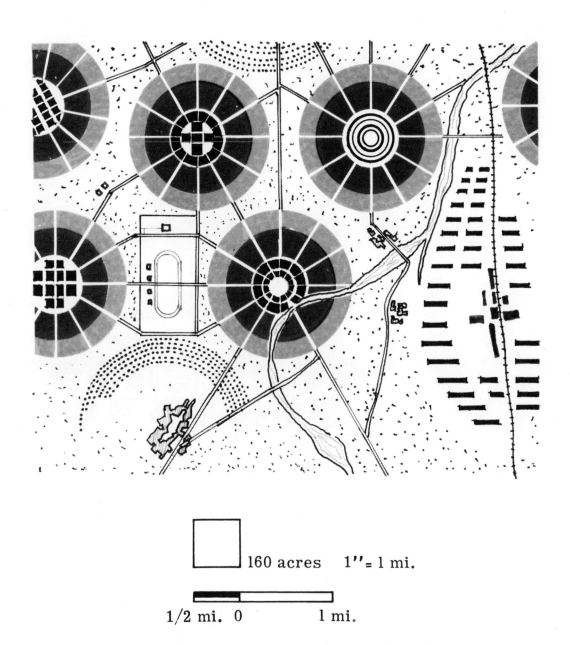

160 acres   1″= 1 mi.

1/2 mi. 0   1 mi.

Based upon drawing in Die Inflation der Gross-Städte.

c. Circulation: Aside from long-distance rail transport, only interurban rapid transit is shown. This network constitutes a series of triangular grids linking all centers. Within the cells, designed to house a walking population, there appears to exist no public transit, and even private vehicles, it is anticipated, will be kept to a minimum.

d. Population: The units are limited to 100,000 people. This is a figure derived from the evaluation of unspecified aesthetic, public health, and economic factors, and considerations of client size for cultural and communal facilities. There appears to be no optimum for the aggregate of cells.

e. Density: Combining the optimal area and population, the writer obtains the density for the residential zone. Comparison with existing metropolises and with some experimental settlements leaves him satisfied with the density levels he derives: about one hundred people per acre, less at the edge, more toward the center. He feels he justifies this relatively high figure by banishing the host of industrial and commercial uses which typically reduce the livability of residential precincts.

f. Consideration of future growth: Each metropolis could grow by adding more and more cells. Individual units, designed on a simple ring basis, are expected to reach their final size through the addition of pie-shaped sectors. While the constituent parts are to have a definite limit, the entirety can grow apparently without bounds. Accretion to existing small-town cores may, the author holds, be a feasible starting point for the individual units. No consideration is given to the possible and required future modification of either the cells or the metropolis.

4. Evaluation

This plan is feasible only to the extent the specialization of the cells is practicable. Whether or not diversity contributes to a more viable economic base has not yet finally been settled. There is no reason whatsoever to suppose, however, that the optimum levels are uniformly such as to maintain populations of 100,000. When to this is added the restrictive feature that employment is to be found within the cell, we have further grounds for skepticism. However, the design bears within itself the tools for its own destruction. The extensive transport network would surely contribute to a wider job market. It would also lead to a more realistic solution for families with several job seekers.

This work is an early example of a polynucleated approach which has appealed to numerous planners in more recent years. The absence of a clear focus for the metropolis identifies this proposal as an alternative to the satellite town approach such as Howard's (1898). It differs from Garden

Cities in other ways, too, as in the significantly narrower greenbelts. Insofar as the proposal stresses a walk-to-work ethos, it forecasts a number of designs; however, the issue of traffic is never really met.

Bibliography

GLOEDEN, ERICH. *Die Inflation der Gross-Städte und ihre Heiligungsmöglichkeit.* Berlin: Der Zirkel, 1923.

LE CORBUSIER, THE CITY OF TOMORROW, 1924

1. Context of Proposal

This is an early essay into planning by the famous French architect. It is implicitly concerned with Paris, the scene of the dramatic core renewal forged by Baron Haussmann half a century earlier. *The City of Tomorrow* was written just after World War I, when the automobile's potentials were first felt and when skyscrapers and garden suburbs began to affect French urbanist thought. It is an outgrowth of notes and exhibits presented at the 1922 Paris design exposition.

2. Summary of Proposal

The high-density core is composed of green-set and highly accessible skyscrapers intended for the conduct of business, communication, and administrative activities. These are surrounded by in-town residential areas. In turn, these are bounded by a greenbelt. Beyond lie industrial areas and residential garden cities. A premium is placed on smooth communications and efficiency in the city's operation.

3. Content Analysis

a. Assumptions: There is a frequently expressed desire to appear "reasonable" and to show the plan's "rationality." The author emphasizes order, convenience, and efficiency as instrumental to this end. To cite one example, these considerations lead him to design a circulation system consisting only of straight roads. Le Corbusier is highly impressed with mechanical artifacts: much of the plan is intended as an accommodation of the city to the automobile. While this work speaks with revolutionary fervor, claiming at the same time to be value neutral, Le Corbusier designed the city with a middle-class clientele in mind and in some ways was quite conservative.

b. Form: A skyscraper center of very high density but low coverage pro-

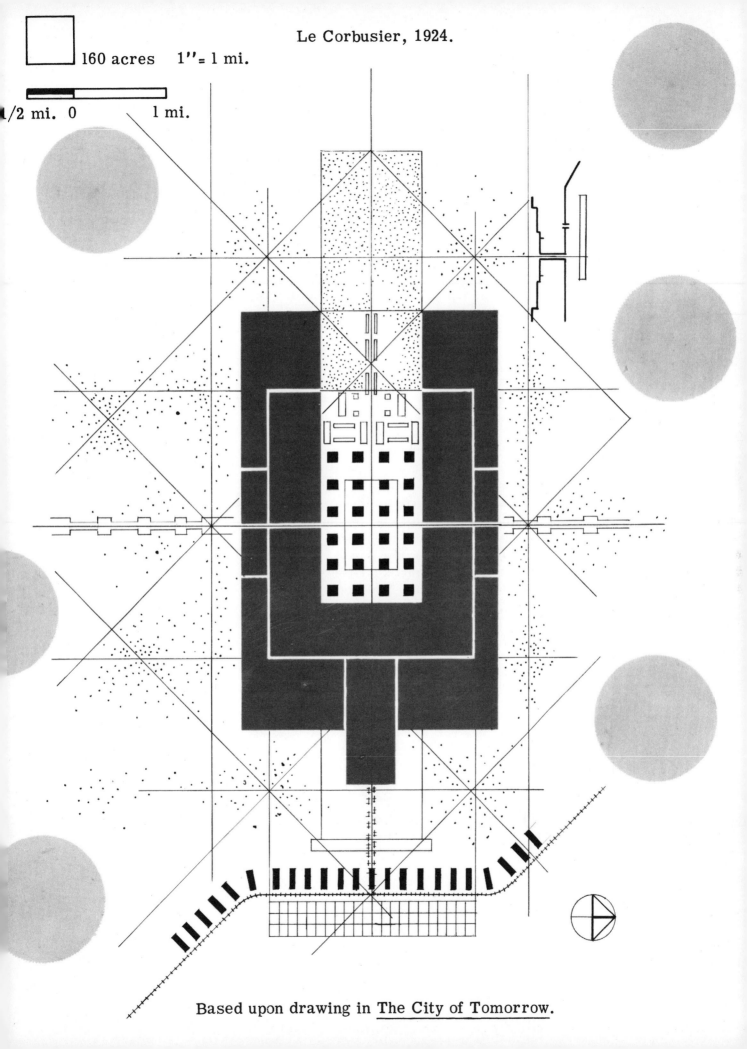

Le Corbusier, 1924.

160 acres   1″= 1 mi.

1/2 mi.   0   1 mi.

Based upon drawing in The City of Tomorrow.

vides the concentration of job opportunities consistent with the aim of reducing effort spent in walking. The inner district is surrounded by residential zones. These are of two housing types, and, as in the case of the core, both show a wish to introduce open space into the city. One of these is designed for middle-class residence, the other for a higher income and more sophisticated clientele. The bordering greenbelt is used for institutions and recreational areas. On the horizon, and subject only to the most limited discussion, are found factory districts and garden towns.

c. *Circulation:* The superblock scale is tied to the maximum distance pedestrians are presumed to be willing to walk and to the proposal that underground rapid-transit stops be located at each street intersection. This gives a rectangular grid composed of 200 by 400 meter blocks. Areas of heavy traffic are provided with multilevel circulation facilities. The entire network focuses on the center of the city and on the major structures located there.

d. *Population:* The population is set at 3 million, presumably to resemble Paris. The superblocks vary in size, but here, too, no justification is given for the 3,000 to 4,000 population figure. Though the blocks appear to have some of the quality of communities, the population size is a product of architectural considerations within the given superblock dimensions.

e. *Density:* In both types of inner residential district, approximately fifty dwelling units per residential acre are proposed. There is no discussion of the garden cities where 2 million people, the mass of the industrial workers, would live. Densities in the downtown office core are raised to the maximum, 1,200 workers per acre.

f. *Consideration of future growth:* To achieve the ideal city, renewal of existing centers must proceed. Great emphasis is placed on the viability of central business districts. While structural replacement is anticipated, no great sophistication is shown so far as means are concerned. Future changing conditions are sparsely treated. Certain residential uses, it appears, can expand into the greenbelt if the need arises.

4. Evaluation

Although Le Corbusier correctly notes the differing site demands of commerce and industry, a solution which so separates office from factory areas leaves something to be desired. When one notes that most of the downtown workers will be commuters from the garden cities, the separation appears to be even less justified. It is also highly dubious whether the downtown concentration would not prove to be self-defeating, even with twenty-lane highways, multitrack subways, and many-leveled streets. Further, there is no recognition of the automobile's centrifugal force.

As the ideal city of commerce, and one that most emphatically does not turn its back on the *city*, this proposal has had considerable influence. Kern's, Ferriss's, and Goodmans' first schemes reflect the same approach. Its shortcomings are the failure to substantiate most claims and a reluctance to spell out more adequately the economic and, particularly, the social goals and consequences of the plan.

Bibliography

Le Corbusier (C. É. Jeanneret-Gris). *Urbanisme*. Paris: G. Crès, 1924. Among the several editions of the English translation:
————. *The City of Tomorrow and Its Planning*. New York: Payson and Clarke, 1929.

H. Ferriss, the metropolis of tomorrow, 1929

1. Context of Proposal

The Metropolis of Tomorrow is the creation of an architect-delineator at work in major cities of the United States. It was written at the peak of the construction boom of the 1920's just as the first results of building bulk and height regulations were becoming known. Although the author shows cognizance of city planning and its legal, economic, and social aspects, no specific connection with other planning works is apparent. It remains fundamentally an aesthetician's approach. A work of self-expression, it also shows the wish to popularize and lend meaning to the new zoning concepts and to emphasize the psychological and symbolical impact of aesthetic factors.

2. Summary of Proposal

The proposal is for a densely built-up metropolitan center. Three imposing building clusters dramatically signal the focusing of business, art, and scientific activity. These surround a hollow core; it is not possible to tell whether this is a park or serves as an immense traffic interchange. Each of the skyscraper groups stands at the apex of a sector devoted to related activities, with the intensity of development decreasing outward.

3. Content Analysis

a. Assumptions: City structure must show that it is a product of man's will, and therefore it should be patterned. Nevertheless, growth of urban areas cannot be arrested. At most it can be channeled. A plan is, therefore,

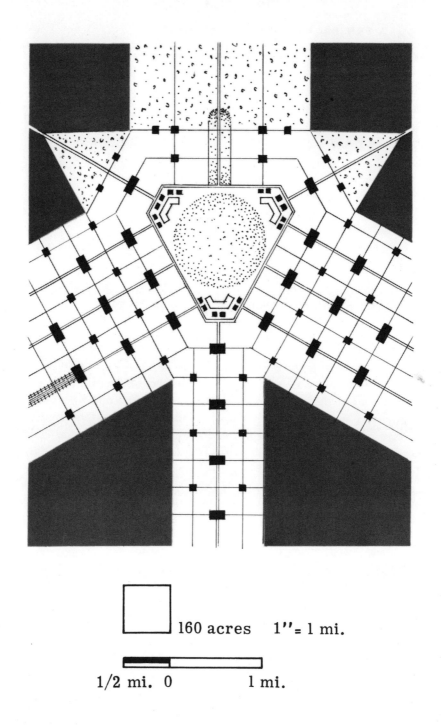

160 acres   1'' = 1 mi.

1/2 mi. 0   1 mi.

Based upon drawing in Metropolis of Tomorrow.

a forecast of trends already in evidence. The city is seen to be largely an instrument for communication and exchange; little consideration appears to be given other functions. These major activities deserve recognition and should be vested with the dignity and beauty given by awe-inspiring skyscraper architecture.

b. Form: The form is basically a sector city, with increasing activity as the center, short of the hollow core, is approached. Each sector is devoted to a major use: business, which is slightly larger than the others, arts, and sciences. Within the sector, intensity of development is peaked at traffic intersections. Major skyscrapers are placed at half-mile intervals not only to give aesthetic emphasis but also to simplify the movement of people. Where two land uses merge, a creative synthesis occurs: thus, the university is found between the arts and the sciences districts. Residential uses predominate in intervening, pie-shaped districts, but, like industrial, recreational, and other uses, are not subject to any analysis.

c. Circulation: A ring-and-radial system of circulation for wheeled traffic is proposed. Grade separations are envisaged at points of high traffic intensity, but no concept of measuring or otherwise accommodating congestion is presented. Other forms of circulation appear to play a secondary role, although it must be inferred that the densities envisaged would require major reliance upon subsurface mass transit.

d. Density and population: Little actual consideration is given these, but gross residential densities approaching fifty dwelling units per acre would predominate. The center of the city is designed so as to concentrate the labor force in tall buildings. Ferriss states that such structures give the most efficient distribution of interior space. No evidence is given in support of this contention.

e. Consideration of future growth: Only in the most general terms does this proposal incorporate trends evident at the time of writing. How the ideal would be reached is not spelled out, although it is evident that Ferriss thought of the proposal as along the same continuum as the development brought about by zoning. Growth within the scheme can easily be accommodated by extension of use areas along radials.

4. Evaluation

A city with "arts" and "sciences" precincts of the magnitude shown would be of truly gigantic proportions. The approximate equality of these districts with the business sector is, likewise, grounds for skepticism. The sea of low buildings and of the residential portions of the city is sketched all too vaguely. Activities housed in any but the major structures receive scant

[59]

attention. The plan is somewhat reminiscent of Le Corbusier's contemporary *Plan Voisin* for central Paris. In both works little attention is paid to problems of execution.

On the surface, this is a work which suggests several uses of skyscrapers for their symbolic impact and gives insight into a prevalent line of imagination. There is, in addition, the suggestion that variation in the distribution of building bulk affects the city's efficiency as well as its attractiveness. The problem, of course, is to put this concretely so that the validity of the contention can be tested. The concept that certain activities thrive when located at boundaries of land uses similarly has merit.

Bibliography

FERRISS, HUGH. *The Metropolis of Tomorrow*. New York: Ives Washburn, 1929.

C. PERRY, THE NEIGHBORHOOD UNIT, 1929

1. Context of Proposal

The Neighborhood Unit formula grew out of Perry's concern with the absence of improvement in the physical and social conditions in metropolitan areas of the United States during the first quarter of this century. Perry was considerably influenced by the zoning, settlement house, and various other reform movements. His work also reflects the increasing interest shown in rationalizing municipal services such as schools. The original essay was written as part of the Regional Plan of New York, as a guide to development in new suburban areas. It was subsequently adapted by the author to already built-up areas.

2. Summary of Proposal

The neighborhood, which is defined as dwellings together with their surroundings, should be so organized as to restrict the increasingly disturbing influence of motor traffic. The Neighborhood Unit should contain only dwellings and ancillary services such as an elementary school, parks, and local stores. The layout would be governed by the following considerations:

Size: Not more than one-quarter to one-half mile radius from the school; total area is a function of density.

Boundaries: Arterial streets sufficiently wide to permit bypassing of through traffic and also to serve to identify the area.

C. Perry, 1929.

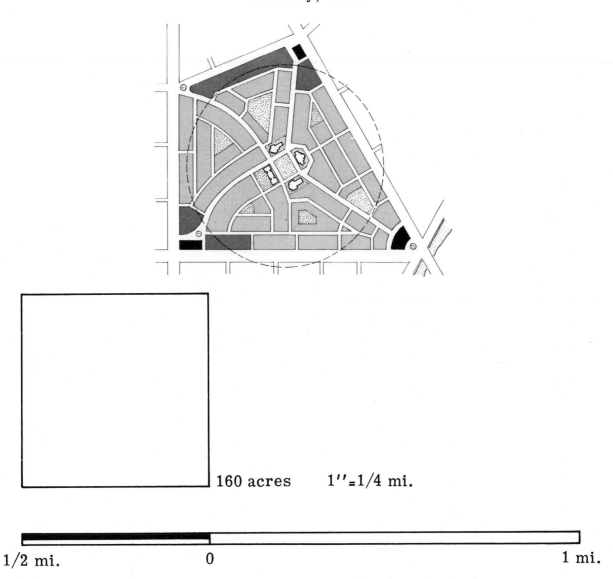

160 acres   1''=1/4 mi.

1/2 mi.   0   1 mi.

Based upon drawing in "The Neighborhood Unit," Regional Survey of New York and Its Environs.

Open spaces: These should be provided to equal 10 per cent of the
total area.

Institutions: Those serving only the Unit should be grouped together
at the center.

Stores: Those serving a larger area should be grouped at the circumference near stores of other Units.

Internal street system: It should be designed so as to discourage through
traffic, with individual streets of a size which reflects the loads they
should carry.

3. Content Analysis

a. Assumptions: Vehicular congestion, slum dwellings, and social breakdown are the worst evils of our urban society; these must be combated by
means of improvements in the physical surroundings. A causal relationship
between the type of environment and the type of society and individual
behavior is explicitly posited. Referring to findings of the social sciences,
Perry maintains that group life is essential to man, is desired by him, and
is a prerequisite to social education and order. Organization of the environment on a neighborhood basis is an essential vehicle for the exercise of group
life; it also serves to preserve the most significant values of our society.

b. Form: A neighborhood is a well-defined residential district up to
1 square mile in area. A school, other public buildings, and recreation space
are located near the center, commerical facilities along the arterial streets
which surround the unit. Apartment houses also are more appropriately
placed on the edge; the typical Neighborhood Unit is predominantly composed of freestanding one-family houses.

c. Circulation: The explicit aim is the reduction of traffic within the
unit. A hierarchy of circulation routes is proposed: arterial through streets
forming the Unit's boundaries, major and minor streets in the interior.
The latter are designed so as to discourage through traffic and only to bear
the number of vehicles necessary to serve the immediate vicinity.

d. Population: The number of residents is keyed to the population which
can most efficiently support one elementary school: 5,000 to 9,000 people.

e. Density: The prototype area submitted with the New York Regional
Plan shows a gross density of about five one-family houses per acre. This is
derived from a standard residential lot 40 by 100 feet. Some range in densities as well as in structural types, Perry holds, is consistent with the proposal but would result, in view of the dependence on the school plant,
in a greater or lesser geographic spread.

f. Consideration of future growth: The proposal suggests that a plan of strategic location of public facilities could convert the present city into one of neighborhoods. In general, however, the formula is written in terms of newly built areas. Perry does not suggest or consider the possibility or desirability of making provision for further change in the future.

4. Evaluation

Essentially, the approach is eclectic, taking suggested standards and empirical evidence from a wide range of fields pretty much at face value. The Neighborhood Unit formula combines a compatible selection of these, but this means that other schemes could also satisfy similar conditions. And when the initial data themselves are questioned or modified, a greater range of proposals would be appropriate. Thus, if more critical use were made of census and historical data, the proposed norms would not simply reflect existing conditions. The normative suggestions boil down to a plea to keep traffic out of residential areas and to place supporting facilities more strategically. The sharpest criticism has focused on the degree to which modern urban society can, even under optimum circumstances, resemble the neighborly, closeknit group Perry pictures. And, if it can, is this compatible with other goals of a democratic society? Opponents have pointed to the excessively homogeneous and parochial society which results and have also questioned the assumption that the Unit should be limited to one-school-oriented areas.

With some or considerable modification, this seminal essay has continued validity, especially where it formulated the first realistic protection from the automobile. Its influence is evident in the work of most planners active today, and it has stimulated a relatively extensive body of amplifying and critical literature, both within and outside the field of planning.

Bibliography

PERRY, CLARENCE ARTHUR. "The Neighborhood Unit," *Regional Survey of New York and Its Environs.* VII, 22–140. New York: Committee on Regional Plan of New York and Its Environs, 1929.

———. *Housing for the Machine Age.* New York: Russell Sage Foundation, 1939.

DAHIR, JAMES. *The Neighborhood Unit Plan, Its Spread and Acceptance; a selected bibliography with interpretative comments.* New York: Russell Sage Foundation, 1947.

BAUER, CATHERINE. "Good Neighborhoods," *Annals of the American Academy of Political and Social Sciences,* CCXLII (November, 1945).

Isaacs, Reginald. "The Neighborhood Theory," *Journal of the American Institute of Planners,* XIV (Spring, 1948), 15–23.

———. Statement in "Symposium: Frontiers of Housing Reform," *Land Economics,* XXV (February, 1949), 73–78.

T. Adams, design of residential areas, 1934

1. Context of Proposal

This is an English town planner's study, written during several years' residence in the United States and association with Harvard University. While the full impact of the Depression is not noted in the book, the excesses of the 'twenties receive considerable attention. The work is at least partly directed to the problem of growth. Adams seeks to relate his ideas to the infant sciences of land economics and sociology. Most of the proposal seems to stem, however, from experience in suburban design and site planning. As one of the Harvard City Planning Series, this work appears to have had as its purpose the provision of reasoned support for the protagonists of zoning and of land-valuation reform. The purpose of this reform is to link land's earning capacity more closely to its supposed real value.

2. Summary of Proposal

The ideal town is a rather compact, urbanized mass with clearly distinguished land-use areas. Residential districts, divided into a hierarchy of communities, almost surround the city's central business district. Parks, parkways, and commercial areas are distributed throughout the residential portion of the city. The nonresidential areas, however, receive but scant attention.

3. Content Analysis

a. Assumptions: The ideal environment, that is, one that brings about a good society, is characterized by homogeneous neighborhoods of owner-occupied one-family dwellings set in gardens. Stability of use and of value and a clear patterning and segregation of activities are the hallmarks of a good city. Throughout the work, one detects a note of moderation and conservation.

b. Form: The proposal is one for a massed city, with civic and commercial belts surrounded by a major residential sector and, on one side, by a smaller industrial area. Green spaces, with circulation routes, interpenetrate

[64]

T. Adams, 1934. The city.

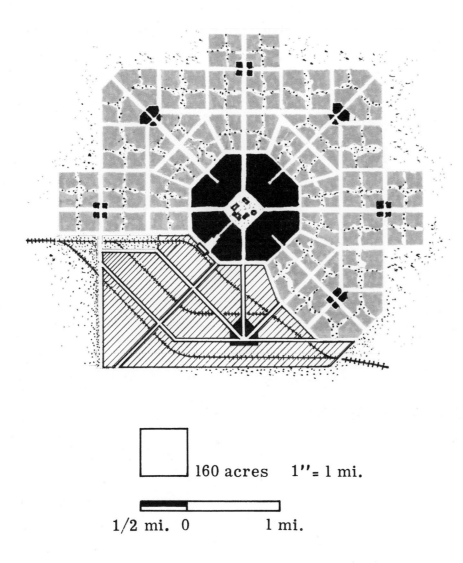

160 acres   1″= 1 mi.

1/2 mi. 0   1 mi.

Based upon drawing in <u>Design of Residential Areas.</u>

T. Adams, 1934. Residential Area.

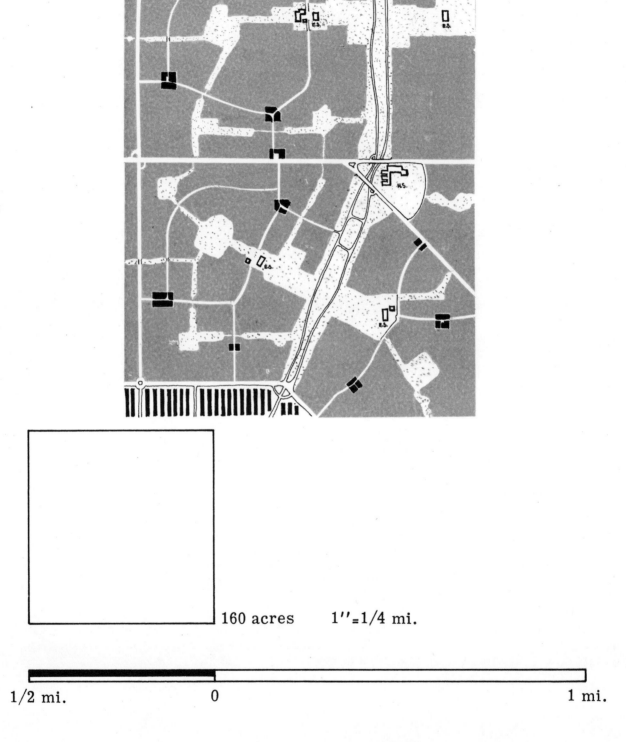

160 acres   1''=1/4 mi.

1/2 mi.   0   1 mi.

Based upon drawing in <u>Design of Residential Areas.</u>

the residential areas. Residential neighborhood units resemble Perry's design, and each focuses on its one school. Optimum land-use distributions, by per cent of total area, are suggested. This, incidentally, is a rare example of such specificity in these models.

c. Circulation: The roadway pattern is a combination of (*a*) an over-all radial-circumferential system and (*b*) a rectangular grid serving to define neighborhoods. An avowed goal is ease of communication between sections of the city. Parkways are shown encased in green rights of way which also connect schools, parks, and similar facilities. The plan shows internal streets as loosely drawn, reflecting the topography.

d. Population: Optimum total population is considered only as a function of area and density. Neighborhood population, some 6,000 people in 100 to 200 acres, reflects housing density, family size, and the walk-to-school formula.

e. Density: In order to achieve the desired environment of good homes, a ceiling on densities must be rigidly enforced. No more than twelve houses per gross acre can be tolerated; about six per gross acre is the optimum.

f. Consideration of future growth: In general, the ideal neighborhood unit is seen as a new development; the ideal city, though, is recognized as somehow evolving from today's conditions. The problem of change is not given much emphasis, but expansion of residential areas by the addition of further units can be accommodated and, indeed, is expected.

4. Evaluation

The design for a rather constricted, predetermined business and civic center is inconsistent with provision for growth by expansion of residential areas. Were real green wedges, rather than parkways, provided to break up the sizeable mass of residential land use, business and public expansion could take place if circumstances so warranted. It should be said that the open land problem is a matter of distribution, not of quantity: fully one-half the city's surface area is allocated to streets and public open space. More generally, there are grounds to question the wisdom of an approach expressed in terms of averages derived from today's environment, when it is precisely this environment which the author seeks to ameliorate. Finally, it is interesting to note that the same aims, with some freedom to grow as an added bonus, could be satisfied equally well with a linear scheme. This suggests the danger of limiting one's sights; it also points out the flexible nature of forms of the city.

This scheme is an excellent and, for its time, advanced prototype. In intervening years, such concepts have become accepted by and expected from practising planners. Though today's reader may find it somewhat conservative, many of the plans prepared since then bear close resemblance to this scheme.

Bibliography

ADAMS, THOMAS. *Design of Residential Areas*. Cambridge: Harvard University Press, 1934. Especially, pp. 122–146.

R. NEUTRA, RUSH CITY REFORMED, 1934

1. Context of Proposal

Rush City Reformed is an architect's vision of the city of growth, designed in California during the 'twenties. The formulation of the proposal shows considerable reliance on demographic statistics. It bears little evident relation to other planning works. It is not only an expression of ideal city life and environment, it is also a vehicle for the presentation of architectural experiments and solutions.

2. Summary of Proposal

The ideal city has a central business district linked by limited-access superhighways to numerous neighborhoods located along these roads. These are larger than other authors' neighborhoods. The residential units can be attached to each other indefinitely by virtue of the internal land-use distribution. Residential areas are divided into districts of similar houses designed to shelter families of a given structure. In order to reduce commuting and traffic between and within neighborhoods, areas of light industry are provided in each unit. Major thoroughfares are designed to serve as area boundaries.

3. Content Analysis

a. Assumptions: Neutra feels that for both economic and social reasons, the major job facing the planner is to foster neighborliness. Consequently, he believes families which are at the same stage of development should be grouped together in relatively standardized houses. The liberal provision of clubhouses in residential areas is an indication of the belief that an increasing number of domestic and other functions can best be met socially. As is evident in the detailing of residential areas, the scheme expresses the hope

R. Neutra, 1934.

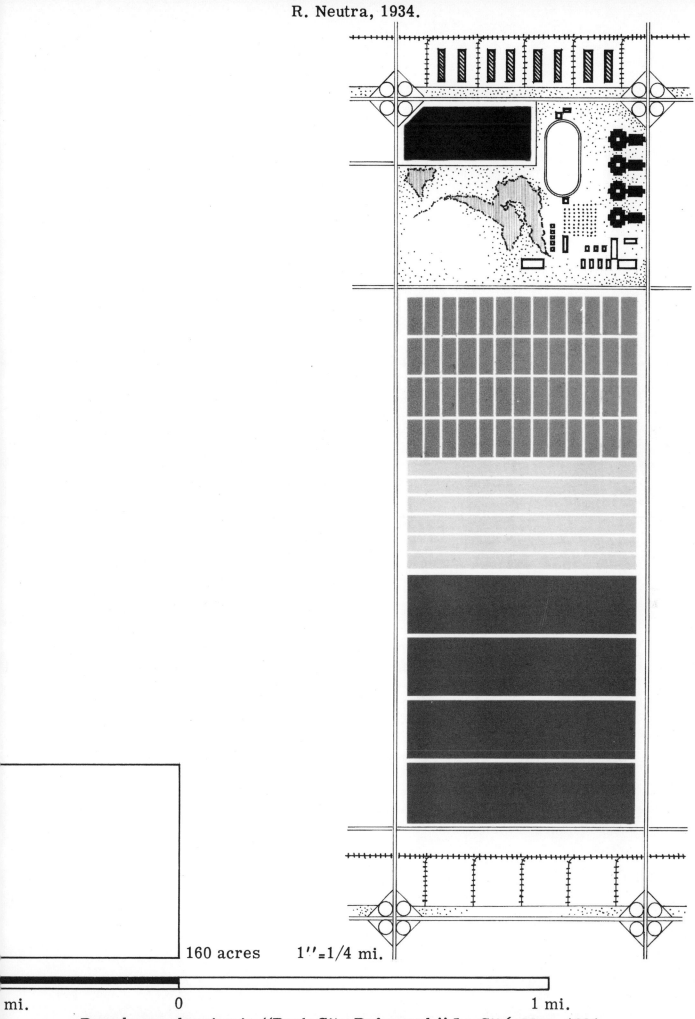

160 acres   1''=1/4 mi.

mi.   0   1 mi.

Based upon drawing in ''Rush City Reformed,'' La Cité, May, 1934.

that modern urban society should not be exclusively citified. Rather, an urban-rural synthesis should prevail.

b. Form: Rectangular neighborhood units combine to give the entire city (outside the high-intensity central business district) a linear form. Within the unit, land uses and types of housing are distributed in rigidly defined bands.

c. Circulation: The superhighways form a major rectangular grid within which the neighborhood units lie. Interior circulation also apparently shows rigid adherence to a rectangular scheme.

d. Population: Two hundred and twenty thousand adults, with an undetermined number of children, constitute a basic unit. Selection of this figure is not substantiated, but Neutra feels it is reasonable in view of such given factors as man's physical characteristics, the nature of childhood, and family size.

e. Density: The approach to density is by way of architecture. The aim is to conserve space while providing each family with some open land. Depending on the number of children, the resultant over-all residential area density is between twenty-five to perhaps thirty-five people per acre. The four housing types range from fourteen to about two hundred people per acre, depending on the household composition.

f. Consideration of future growth: There is no description of the dynamics by which such a city could grow, except one entire unit at a time. There is a hint of change in the use of prefabricated transportable buildings and in the suggestion that, with varying population structures, the proportion of land devoted to each housing type may be modified.

4. Evaluation

There is a basic inconsistency about a work which advertises itself as a utopian experiment and yet which relies heavily on data culled from the existing unreconstructed society. Such continuity in either income distribution or family structure can hardly be expected. So far as the physical elements of the plan are concerned, some questions may be raised regarding the desirability of separating household types as is here proposed. Such separation may well cause social disruption and personal inconvenience; it is a relatively inflexible environment probably too costly for any economies it may have to offer. The rigid segregation of circulation routes so that most, if not all, vehicular traffic is required to use the superhighways may well overload these facilities, though space for streets and movements within residential areas would be markedly reduced. The sharp isolation

[70]

of uses within a large area, paradoxically, it seems would make for even greater reliance on cars than is evident in today's society.

Rush City was the first major effort which directed itself to the different housing and environmental requirements of the various segments of the population. It deserves attention for this reason, even though in the development of the idea, certain difficulties arose; some of these have been noted above.

Bibliography

NEUTRA, RICHARD J. *Wie Baut Amerika?* Stuttgart, Hoffman, 1927.
———. "Rush City Reformed," *La Cité,* XII (May, 1934), pp. 71–82.
———. *Survival through Design.* New York: Oxford University Press, 1954. Especially, chap. 46, pp. 336–380.
BOESIGER, W. *Richard Neutra, Buildings and Projects.* Zurich: Girsberger, 1951.

F. L. WRIGHT, BROADACRE CITY, 1932

1. Context of Proposal

Broadacre City is the iconoclast architect's view of a reconstructed USA. It suggests an idealized version of a prairie town. First conceived during the 1920's, it was further developed in the decade before World War II. There is little concern shown for the work of planners or recognition of other Ideal Communities as prototypes. The scheme leans heavily on an agrarian basis for democracy and on Henry George's attack on unearned increment as the curse of modern society. This creative work is at least partly a framework for the study and display of the architectural solutions to a range of housing and other structural problems, but its major significance is as an expression of Wright's Midwest agrarian roots and his lifelong interest in the interrelation of soil, building, and people.

2. Summary of Proposal

One acre of land is each family's minimum "heritage." Low-density residential areas are grouped in close relation to agricultural uses. So-called urban functions are decentralized. Factories, bureaucratic operations, and marketing centers are scattered among the residential areas but placed in close relation to major transportation routes. They are much reduced in size, number, and scope. Superhighways are the all-important linkages.

F. L. Wright, 1932.

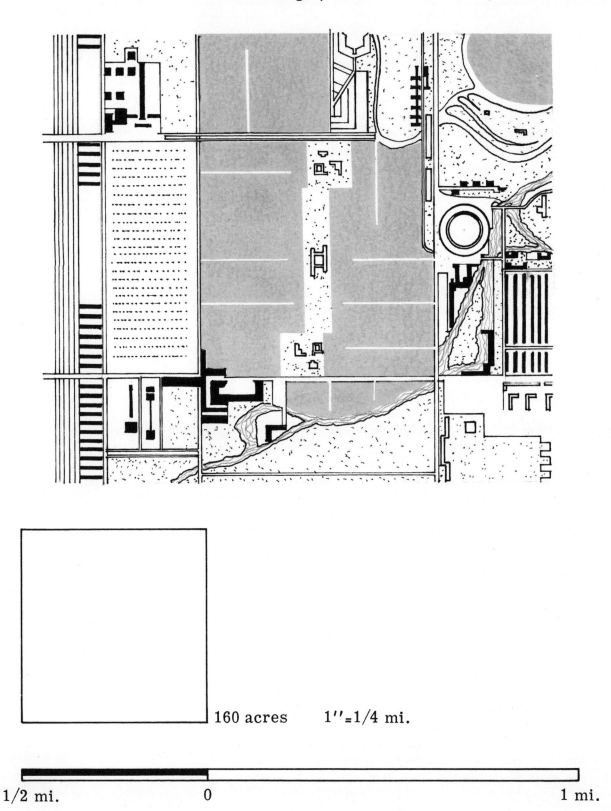

160 acres   1″=1/4 mi.

1/2 mi.   0   1 mi.

Based upon drawing in Taliesin Fellowship Publication, October, 1940.

3. Content Analysis

a. Assumptions: Land ownership and land cultivation are the bases of the good life. Wright takes direct issue with the values he ascribes to the contemporary urban environment: experiences there are largely vicarious; all interactions are characterized by a rent concept; the pace is too rapid; and bureaucracy, lack of culture, and the herd instinct are dominant. Broadacre City is to foster rugged individualism and creativity in a milieu of automotive Jeffersonianism. America, the great "Usonian" experiment, once more will be on the road to the destiny from which she was tragically sidetracked. But only a partial return to the past can take place, for the Industrial Revolution, in addition to debilitating urbanization, also provides great liberating tools. Decentralization can make sense in Broadacre City, what with electricity, the car, mass produced household artifacts, and new building materials.

b. Form: Similar uses of land are grouped together in large sections. Awareness of natural features plays an important role, particularly in the essentially flat environment selected for the model area. Public and semi-public facilities are deployed near highway intersections. Apart from these considerations, no guides to form or to land-use distribution are offered.

c. Circulation: Superhighways are seen to be indispensable national, regional, and even local links. They are prerequisites to the dispersed society and economy. The plan shows a major rectangular grid. The highways often serve to separate land uses. This may partly be due to the location on highways of commercial and other nonresidential uses. Although the proposals for grade separations at intersections were advanced for the time of their design, they are inadequate by modern standards.

d. Population: Consideration of optimum population is not given, for, short of breaks caused by major geographic barriers, there really does not exist a unit whose size could be measured. There is no implication that the families of the fifteen to forty children attending the same school in any sense constitute a community.

e. Density: One acre is provided each childless couple. This is the highest density. A typical 4-square-mile section would accommodate 1,400 families; the over-all density is nearly 2 acres per family. About one-third of the area, however, is devoted to uses not directly associated with the home: factories, highways, institutions, etc.

f. Consideration of future growth: Broadacre City is seen as a substitute for the present environment—which, in any case, is doomed. It would presumably be built, section by section, on relatively open rural land. By virtue of the low intensity of final development, changes in the use of areas or of structures could easily be accommodated, save perhaps for the heavy investment in highways. No explicit consideration, however, is given to this problem.

4. Evaluation

The main criticism is not directed at the frankly utopian nature of this work. It is that it couples its didactic spirit with a relatively limited range of living styles: its Leveller nature. On the other hand, one can question, in terms of the democratic considerations involved, whether it is desirable to group similar housing types so rigidly by income, particularly when this arrangement is accompanied by such small schools as are suggested. One might add, however, that the basic structure of the plan would not be much affected by a modification to encourage mixture of housing types.

The circulation scheme presents several problems. The distribution of activities places all in an extreme dependence on motor vehicles. In fact, there is a greater reliance on cars in Broadacre City than there is in today's environment. The consequences of a gasoline shortage would be severe; the investment that would be rendered useless by further technological advances would be immense. Archibald MacLeish's comment on the Fall of the City, to the effect that "the City of Masterless Men has found a Master," seems singularly apropos here: time and distances are overcome, but only at the price of yet further conquest by the master-car. "You'd say it was they were the conquerors; they that had conquered." One also is left wondering whether there is not something of the much-criticized herd instinct in this mass use of cars. The United States built up by Broadacre City standards would have some 1 million miles of superhighways. This proposed highway system implies the existence of a society which is perhaps more wealthy than that envisaged by Wright, and one that is certainly more organized and group conscious than that pictured in Broadacre City. One further point: the type of highway envisaged would be warranted only if there were in the vicinity of perhaps 50,000 vehicular users daily. This is quite inconsistent with the proposed levels of density, either daytime or nighttime.

The cavalier disregard of the advantages of agglomeration also must be questioned. One suspects that, in actuality, there would arise more and stronger foci than are shown. In brief, the scheme looks more like a slice of Midwestern exurbia than the prototype quarter section designed to cover a rebuilt United States.

Broadacre City's interest lies first, so far as this survey is concerned, in the relatively straightforward link between clearly stated assumptions and the physical form. Secondly, in its discussion of a planned-for life style, this proposal is more comprehensive than are most others. It is suggestive of the kinds of considerations which are involved in designing an Ideal Community. The design itself foreshadows a number of polynucleated schemes adapted to the automotive age.

Bibliography

WRIGHT, FRANK LLOYD. *Modern Architecture*. Princeton: Princeton University Press, 1931. *See* especially, chap. 6.
———. *The Disappearing City*. New York: Payson, 1932.
"Broadacre City, a New Community Plan," *Architectural Record*, LXXVII (April, 1935), 243–254.
"Broadacre City, Frank Lloyd Wright, Architect," *American Architect*, CXLVI (May, 1935), 55–62.
WRIGHT, FRANK LLOYD. *An Organic Architecture: The Architecture of Democracy*. London: Lund, Humphries, 1939.
———. "Broadacre City Issue," *Taliesin Fellowship Publication*, I, No. 1 (October, 1940).
———. *When Democracy Builds*. Chicago: University of Chicago Press, 1945.
———. *The Living City*. New York: Horizon Press, 1958.

W. GROPIUS AND M. WAGNER, A PROGRAM FOR CITY RECONSTRUCTION, 1943

1. Context of Proposal

These are a series of proposals growing out of classroom planning problems and solutions formulated during World War II. The work reflects concerns with both the major periods between the two world wars: boom associated with real estate speculation and the collapse with its contingent unemployment. It also tries to anticipate postwar housing needs and traffic congestion The authors bring American and European experience to bear on the problems and pay the greatest attention to housing and architectural aspects. The aim of this work is to bring to a wider audience what the authors feel are new techniques that can be employed in decongesting cities.

2. Summary of Proposal

A bold rebuilding of our depreciated cities is needed. This is made possible through the utilization of a government development corporation with sufficient funds to develop the large areas of vacant land which are the

W. Gropius and M. Wagner, 1943.

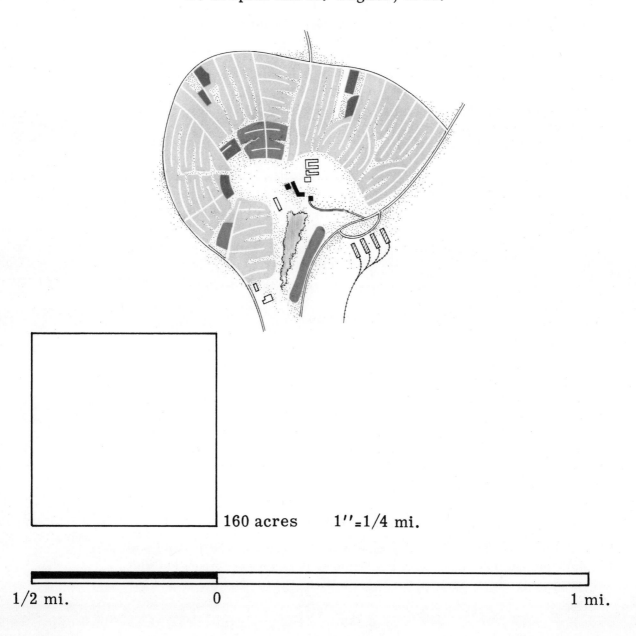

160 acres   1''=1/4 mi.

1/2 mi.   0   1 mi.

Based upon drawing in ''A Program for City Reconstruction,'' Architectural Forum, July, 1943.

heritage of premature subdivision. The corporation will also have power to supervise enforced reconstruction of all capital investments as these depreciate. Land ownership, following German examples, is in municipal hands. Since housing must be located close to job opportunities, the people should be moved to small suburban communities of about one-quarter to three-quarters of a square mile. Where possible, these communities should be closely tied to superhighways and should be composed of a variety of housing types.

3. Content Analysis

a. Assumptions: Man's environment must be at a human scale if it is to contribute at all to his well-being. Furthermore, modern man needs to live in an environment which bring him into touch with the rural virtues. In the urban-rural synthesis which is proposed here, he finds the contrasts required both for recreation and as stimulus. One can detect an aversion to some of the consequences of contemporary existence, as in the wish to reduce reliance on cars.

b. Form: The new town is in the shape of a crescent around a community center. Such a community center, resembling London's Peckham Health Center, will be the social focus which is so essential to a good neighborhood life. The environs of the new-town units are largely farms and woodland to provide sustenance during depression periods. Each town is to be clearly separated from other nuclei. Its size is limited by its pedestrian scale to about one-half to one mile in diameter.

c. Circulation: The road network is designed to permit pedestrian access throughout without the necessity of crossing vehicular paths. Aggregate street length is to be minimized.

d. Population: The optimum population is stated to be about five thousand people. This is based rather generally on the size of a psychological contact group: for example, reference is made to the observable success of the New England town meeting.

e. Density: The density level is apparently derived by reconciling the area within a fifteen-minute walking radius with the desired population. The scheme shows over-all gross densities of four to ten dwelling units per acre.

f. Consideration of future growth: New towns, apparently, are to be built in one operation. There is no consideration given to whether further change can be accommodated in the more remote future. In already developed areas, a government agency, through its power to acquire land, will develop vacant tracts and, directly or indirectly, rehabilitate existing structures.

4. Evaluation

This project is similar to others, such as Stein's Greenbelt design, particularly in its form concept. However, it calls forth the question: can controls as rigid as those envisaged here ever be instituted except under the most unusual circumstances? With respect to the site plan, there are grounds to question the desirability of cul-de-sacs in excess of a fourth of a mile in length. It is not clear where there is a place for facilities with a clientele and service area exceeding those of the community: high schools, department stores, etc., which presumably are set to serve the Precincts, or groups of about ten communities. Finally, though the choice of 5,000 people is a plausible one, its unique desirability is far from established by this essay.

As an example of "open-ended" thinking directed to the opportunities presented by the postwar period, this has considerable value. Coming as it did from a major architect, it probably had considerable impact on minds not previously brought into contact with many of the ideas current for two decades in planning circles.

Bibliography

GROPIUS, WALTER, and WAGNER, MARTIN. "A Program for City Reconstruction," *Architectural Forum*, LXXIX (July, 1943), 75–80.

GROPIUS, WALTER. *Rebuilding Our Communities*. Chicago: Theobald, 1945.

H. HERREY, C. PERTZOFF, AND E. M. HERREY, AN ORGANIC THEORY OF CITY PLANNING, 1944

1. Context of Proposal

This is a joint effort, reflecting both European and American backgrounds and the skills of an architect, an engineer, and of a physicist concerned with applying her discipline to traffic questions. Prepared during World War II, the main focus is on the anticipation of future growth and renewal needs. The scheme shares much with other neighborhood-type proposals, such as Stein's and Gropius's, although no reference is made to work done by others. The authors undertook what they felt was a unique, interdisciplinary attempt to derive basic principles. It appeared in the issue of an architectural magazine devoted to portraying paths to the postwar world.

2. Summary of Proposal

The provision of a substantial number of community facilities is necessary to counteract the disintegrative forces of modern society. These, dis-

H. Herrey, C. Pertzoff, and E. M. Herrey, 1944.

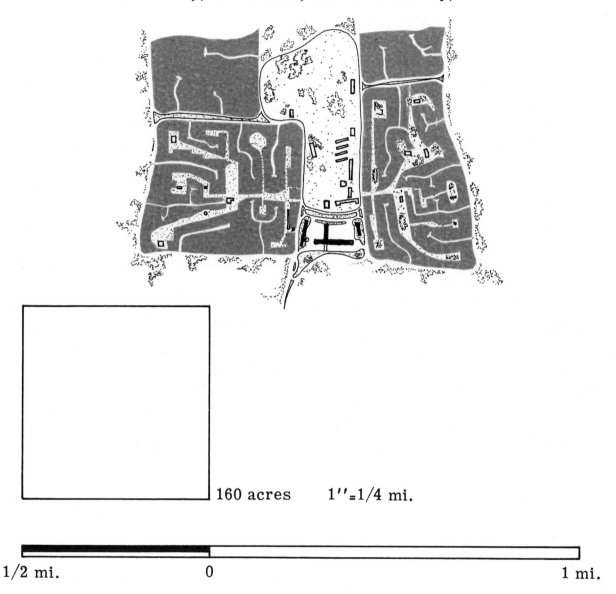

160 acres   1''=1/4 mi.

1/2 mi.   0   1 mi.

Based upon drawing in "An Organic Theory of City Planning," Architectural Forum, April, 1944.

tributed in residential areas, are spatially linked by a system of pedestrian paths. The walkway network and attached green spaces provide an interior skeleton for residential areas. Vehicular ways, which do not cross the pedestrian paths, separate the neighborhoods from each other. The design for the entire ideal town shows the central area devoted to public open space and communal institutions. The large-scale proposal thus has a basic resemblance to the neighborhood plan which, however, is presented in greater detail.

3. Content Analysis

a. Assumptions: The major difficulties of the contemporary urban scene are those arising from the lack of cohesiveness in community life. Nowhere is this shown more dramatically than in the extreme reliance on the automobile. The good life depends on the citizen's freedom to hold a variety of roles in numerous social groups. The ease and success with which this can be done hinges on physical planning considerations, such as the accessibility and size of communal facilities. It depends, furthermore, on the citizen's ability to identify, and identify with, a unit of the environment scaled to his size. The authors also state that the ideal environment functions as a unit: in their terms, it is "organic." Ease and safety of circulation are the most important physical planning problems treated in this work.

b. Form: The form of the residential units is determined by a spine of public open space, in which public facilities are located, and by the surrounding vehicular ways. The ideal city is doughnut-shaped, a chain of residential units. In this manner, the vital "social spaces" can be centrally located. Work areas are found on the periphery and receive peripheral attention.

c. Circulation: The major aims are to keep pedestrian and vehicular ways apart and to align the walkway-public-space system so as to bring commercial and public facilities within about ten minutes' walk of each home. Throughout the scheme the boundary function of roadways is emphasized. The design goes to considerable lengths, both literally and figuratively, to avoid roadway intersections.

d. Population: The residential unit totals 500 to 2,000 families (this is based on an "analysis of social activities and functions," whose source is not identified); the specific size depends on housing types and the ten-minute walking-distance criterion. The ideal-city example is designed for a population of 100,000 but no background information in support of this figure is given.

e. Density: Apparently the authors believe a wide range of residential

[80]

densities would be appropriate: the design shows from three to twelve families per residential-area acre.

f. Consideration of future growth: This proposal is offered as most appropriate to new residential areas. It could be adapted, however, to existing cities through judicious street closings. No consideration appears to have been given to possibilities of growth or change after the plan's execution.

4. Evaluation

While this proposal would, with little doubt, serve to facilitate social "linkages," it is interesting that the published setting of the Ideal Community is so suburban in tone. Work and extraterritorial interactions are not analyzed in any detail. The elaborate circulation pattern is designed apparently to maximize safety. Much of the resulting physical plan is determined by this traffic system. But, quite unintentionally, it demonstrates very neatly the difficulties encountered in maximizing one aspect of an ideal to the exclusion of others. The resulting pattern is exceedingly complex and prone to minimize other desiderata, such as street lengths or convenience. It would have been more appropriate to suggest standards; for example, identifying those points at which street crossings would be permitted, rather than reducing these to zero at great cost. Finally, this proposal is a good example of the selection of an appropriate but hardly necessary form to meet the requirements of the case, as stated. A linear city would satisfy the aims as well as would a doughnut-shaped one, quite conceivably with less extravagant use of public open space.

This proposal has considerable value as a well-thought-out example of the safe, "walking" neighborhood, but its very clarity serves to highlight some of the problems encountered in planning with such an end in mind.

Bibliography

HERREY, H., PERTZOFF, C., and HERREY, E. M. "An Organic Theory of City Planning," *Architectural Forum,* LXXX (April, 1944), pp. 133–140.

J. L. SERT, HUMAN SCALE IN CITY PLANNING, 1944

1. Context of Proposal

This Ideal Community has been developed by a European-trained architect-planner at work in the Western Hemisphere. It was presented to a relatively large public at the time the first post-World War II plans were

J. L. Sert, 1944.

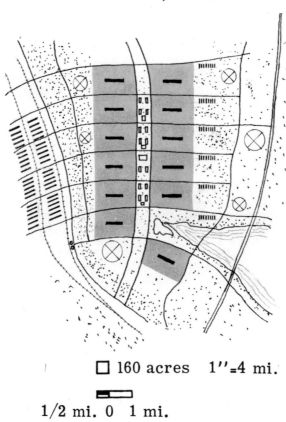

☐ 160 acres   1''=4 mi.

1/2 mi. 0   1 mi.

Based upon drawing in ''Human Scale in City Planning,'' <u>New Architecture and</u>
<u>City Planning.</u>

appearing. In the background there is full cognizance of the planning works of the previous decades; Sert himself contributed to the planning deliberations of the CIAM (The International Congress of Modern Architects). Familiarity is shown with the neighborhood concept. This particular proposal was presented as a symposium contribution. The over-all theme was the establishment of criteria and the formulation of an approach to all forms of postwar "three dimensional organization."

2. Summary of Proposal

A hierarchy of units, each based on social groups of residents, determines the basic characteristics of the city. So far as its form outline is concerned, this proposal falls in the linear-city group. This is particularly true with respect to the way in which growth potential is handled.

3. Content Analysis

a. Assumptions: Sert maintains that a direct causal chain leads from an organized physical environment to an adequate social structure and then to the individual's good life. The basis of this environment should be first, the controlled sizes of its constituent units, and, second, the creation of communities that are organic. That is, each unit should be a microcosm of selected urban functions available also at a larger scale. A hierarchy of facilities, appropriate to the resources of each level, should be provided. Around these, community life can grow. The author also speaks of the need to plan for accessibility to the revitalizing countryside, to segregate land uses rigidly, and to design at the human, walking scale rather than at that of the vehicle. Out of a general opposition to suburban sprawl, but also to conserve space, Sert concludes that the best housing type is that which permits high immediate density in open surroundings. This is the country-set apartment house.

b. Form: About eight neighborhoods are located around a "township" center; a number of such groupings in turn are ranged along a major civic center which runs the length of the entire city. This portion of the metropolis is separated by greenbelts from the major transportation routes and the main industrial belt. It is essentially a linear city, where growth in any one function can be paralleled by accretion to all functions and yet where growth itself, in the immediate vicinity of the resident individual, would be subjected to some form of control.

c. Circulation: An emphasis on walking sets the circulation scale. Automobiles apparently are to be kept from interfering with pedestrian ways.

[83]

A rectangular grid of highways gives form to the city. Regional traffic flows along the major routes separating industry from the residential areas, bypassing the settled portions of the city.

d. Population: The optimum size of units is a function of a service area concept. Thus, on the basis of calculations which determine the clientele needed to support one elementary school, the neighborhoods are to have five to ten thousand inhabitants. The selection of such criteria is admittedly eclectic.

e. Density: Average densities are derived from combining population and walking-distance considerations. Neighborhood densities on the order of ten people per acre are calculated, though the map presented in the book suggests densities more on the order of one hundred people per acre, gross.

f. Consideration of future growth: While much concern is voiced for the inadequacy of today's city, this is in essence a "new city" with no transitional proposals submitted. Growth in the future can be accommodated by adding new units, but apparently stability of use, size, and function are to be maintained in already built quarters. These units are definitely to be limited in size even if the totality is not.

4. Evaluation

As are many of the Ideal Community proposals, this one is subject to the criticism that the general goals this environment is to serve are not adequately linked, conceptually, with the form of the city. A more specific difficulty lies with the design itself, which is exceedingly open outside the residential neighborhoods. In view of the avowed dislike of vehicular travel, this would, in execution, give rise to numerous problems.

This scheme is of interest first, to the extent that it shows an elaboration of the linear city in a plausible direction. Furthermore, it voices, perhaps more clearly than do other proposals, the feelings and rationale of the socially oriented architect. By indirection, it also suggests the limitations of such an approach.

Bibliography

SERT, JOSÉ LUIS. "Human Scale in City Planning." In PAUL ZUCKER (ed.), *New Architecture and City Planning.* New York: Philosopher's Library, 1944.

———. *Can Our Cities Survive?* Cambridge: Harvard University Press, 1942. *See,* particularly, the appended "Chart of Athens," of the International Congress for Modern Architecture (CIAM).

LE CORBUSIER (ASCORAL), LES TROIS ÉTABLISSEMENTS HUMAINS, 1945

1. Context of Proposal

Le Corbusier's growing interest in urbanism, coupled with an intent to solve the problems made manifest by the German occupation of France, produces a comprehensive and flexible planning scheme for a variety of urban conditions. One notes a reliance on his ideas and plans formulated during the previous quarter century, as in the architectural base and in proposals for the large center cities. This particular scheme is one of a series of efforts by a group (ASCORAL), under Le Corbusier's leadership, designed to bring to a large audience a guide and vision for postwar reconstruction.

2. Summary of Proposal

Each of the basic socioeconomic processes ("establishments") has a characteristic urban form. Agriculture is carried on in communal villages, which are only superficially described. Industry is dispersed along a network of transportation routes in green-set towns, separated from each other by a few miles of open land. Exchange is conducted in urban centers at the crossroads of the linear function. Detailed analysis covers only the linear towns.

3. Content Analysis

a. Assumptions: The ethos of the industrial environment suggests an ideal company town: healthy people, open development, close-knit society. Admittedly this is deduced rather than explicitly stated, for there is an avowed reluctance to spell out details. In general, the same points which can be made with respect to Le Corbusier's City of Tomorrow also hold here: there is the same desire for order, the dislike of suburbia, the overbearing emphasis on transportation, and the architectural approach to the residential environment.

b. Form: In the interest of orderliness, the plan is based on strict separation of individual towns, and within these, of the various "human functions": work, residence, recreation, and motion. The danger of isolation is somewhat mitigated by planning at the "pedestrian scale" within the towns and by the provision of ample circulation facilities between them.

c. Circulation: Ease of intertown circulation is the *raison d'être* of the linear form. No points of major concentration exist, save at the intersection of linear towns; at these points the central commercial cities are located.

[85]

Le Corbusier (ASCORAL), 1945.

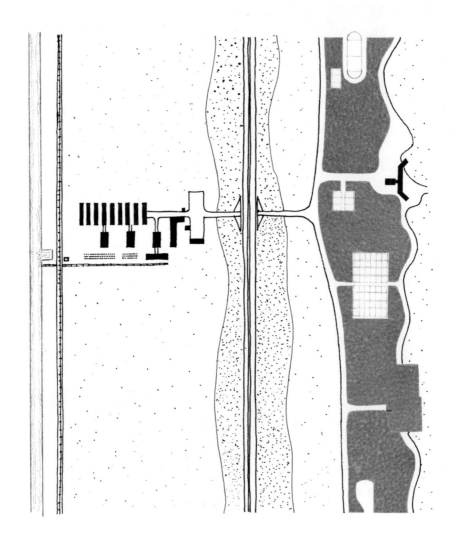

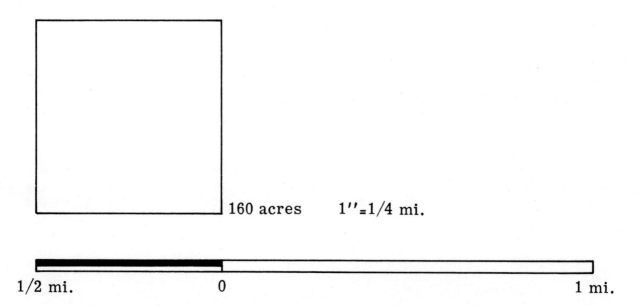

160 acres   1″=1/4 mi.

1/2 mi.   0   1 mi.

Based upon drawing in <u>Les Trois Établissements Humains.</u>

The various vehicular and pedestrian trafficways are kept apart, right to the individual structure. The separating function of trafficways is not overlooked.

d. Population: Each town unit should have 10,000 to 20,000 inhabitants. This standard is not elaborated.

e. Density: With the aim of bringing the real country close to the town and limiting the spread of the city, residential densities are kept as high as 170 people per gross residential acre. The architectural solutions emphasize low ground coverage.

f. Consideration of future growth: While this scheme is seen as a replacement of the existing order, no consideration is given to the dynamics of change, relationship to the present state of events, or to conditions and modifications subsequent to the design stage.

4. Evaluation

There is keen insight into the variety of urban experiences and activities. Why this should involve rigid separation of the various functions, such as production and commerce, is not clearly stated. There is ground, furthermore, to question whether the extensive circulation facilities between towns may not serve to destroy their walking- or bicycle-scale isolation. The temptation to commute and to widen employment choice may prove to be irresistible. The decision to ignore details raises many questions: how to justify a proposal which shows perhaps 50 per cent of developed land area as industrial; how to compensate for the absence of many financial, institutional, and social considerations; and so forth.

The major contribution of this approach lies in its attempt to distinguish limits of applicability. Not one but three basic forms are presented. The linear discussed here, the commercial center, and the rural small town. In a rather sophisticated manner, these are related to each other. But the scheme remains much of an architectural composition, if only because imaginative treatment is largely limited to the buildings and their placement, while societal forms and interaction are described largely as they exist today.

Bibliography

LE CORBUSIER (C. É. Jeanneret-Gris), ed. *Les Trois Établissements Humains* [Sections 5a and 5b, of ASCORAL]. Paris: De Noel, 1945.
———. *Oeuvre Complète*. Vol. IV. Zurich, Girsberger, 1947.

[87]

L. WOLFE, THE REILLY PLAN, 1945

1. Context of Proposal

This book is a joint undertaking of a psychologist and an architect-planner. It grew out of a planning consultation critique of a proposal for an English city's postwar, satellite suburb as drawn up by the local town engineer. Public discussion around the consequent issue attracted the attention of Wolfe, the psychologist. There is much similarity to other works on neighborhood planning, but there is no direct reference to these. This Ideal Community possesses a stronger social orientation than do others. The aim of this book seems to be to provide a planning framework for postwar building and rebuilding in England and to criticize government policy for excessively weak standards and goals in housing and planning.

2. Summary of Proposal

The area's foci are semipublic "greens" around which are built thirty to sixty dwelling units. Each constitutes a "Reilly Unit." Three or four such Units share a community center and other facilities. A much larger grouping of these Units is provided with schools, etc. A highly cooperative way of life is envisaged. Household work would be reduced to a minimum through use of communal nurseries, kitchens, and other domestic services. Vehicular traffic is restricted to the outside of the Reilly Units.

3. Content Analysis

a. Assumptions: In view of the patent inadequacies of man's current existence, a new social environment must be built up. It will be characterized by cooperation and a high degree of interfamily interaction, the full use of communal facilities, and local control over the environment. It will eliminate many wasteful activities, household and otherwise, in which people indulge today. This new way of life will be accepted by force of its reasonableness; it serves the rational self-interest of all. In many ways, the preindustrial village is seen as a satisfactory prototype. The plan shows also a wish for physical isolation from the surrounding industrial society and its ills.

b. Form: The basic Unit is a group of houses placed around a more or less circular public open space. These "greens" are designed in conscious imitation of traditional English villages. Shopping, civic, and apartment areas are provided centrally. Work opportunities as a whole lie outside. The

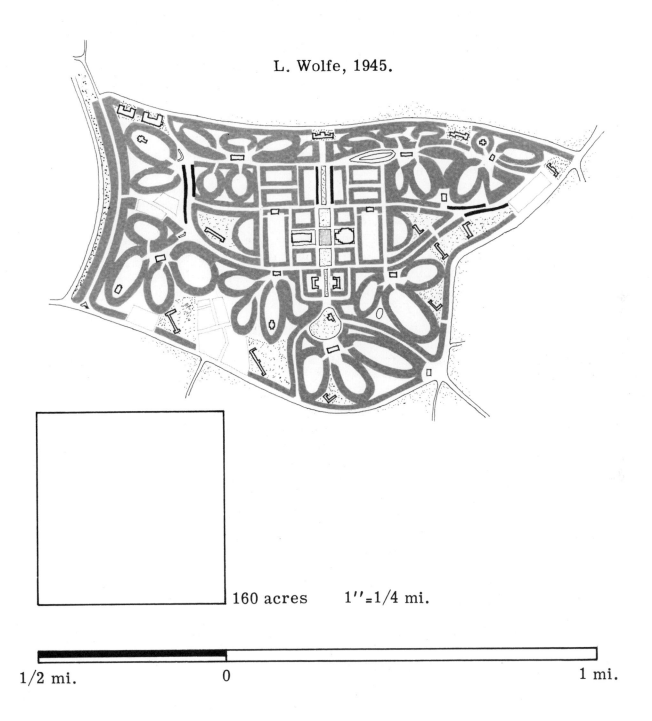

L. Wolfe, 1945.

160 acres   1''=1/4 mi.

1/2 mi.   0   1 mi.

Based upon drawing in The Reilly Plan.

entire area is bounded by standard row houses for people in a transitory stage of education and preference who eventually will move into the Units.

c. Circulation: An exclusively pedestrian residential environment is designed, with provision of a footpath network throughout. Vehicular circulation and garages are limited to the periphery.

d. Population: The Unit's size is essentially established on the basis of the assertion that a face to face group cannot exceed thirty to sixty families. Evidence in support of this is found in the typical size of the traditional English village. Population limits of other elements in the structural hierarchy are set by reference to clientele levels of communal facilities. Presumably because this Ideal Community is seen as part of a larger whole, no optimum town size is suggested.

e. Density: The example shown is at a gross residential density of ten dwelling units per acre; however, an undetermined number of apartments raises this figure somewhat.

f. Consideration of future growth: The physical environment is seen as essentially static and perforce built up at one time. So far as individual households are concerned, there is a variety of dwelling types and facilities to allow for internal mobility as the occupants' needs change.

4. Evaluation

Criticism must focus on the intrusion of the author's values on the plan. These are presented quite explicitly, but the issue is never squarely met. So much depends on the residents' acceptance of this collective and integrated way of life, yet their willingness to live so cannot be presumed. While this life style is quite consistent with the physical plan, it remains to be seen whether the improved physical environment itself would contribute materially, as is the author's contention, to the realization of the ideal. Much that is asserted remains in need of verification: the appropriate size of activity groups, the willingness to rely on communal facilities outside the house, etc. The author's nerve does seem to fail where, for unexplained reasons, as much as 40 per cent of the houses do not form part of the Units or "greens" system. There is no discussion of relations to the outside world, save to speak of the men working outside and of the new "city wall," which is in the form of attached houses bordering the community (and forming no part of the "greens"). There remain, finally, some questions as to whether selective factors would not arise in attracting residents, and let it be added, possibly to the detriment of the rest of society.

This work has much value in its pointing out, in far greater detail than is noted in other schemes, the environment of a highly collective community.

It pictures one extreme of the continuum along which the various neighborhood proposals lie.

Bibliography

Wolfe, Lawrence. *The Reilly Plan*. London: Nicholson and Watson, 1945.

L. Justement, new cities for old, 1946

1. Context of Proposal

This is the work of an architect long active in large-scale private- and public-housing development. It is written in recognition of the scope and necessity of postwar urban renewal requirements. The model is applied to the author's Washington, D. C. It shows much concern with the misapplication of the nation's resources which he found to be so characteristic of the previous decades. Although there is repeated reference to economic and architectural matters, the book turns only superficially to other works in planning, particularly those dealing with social aspects. It appears to have been written largely to gather support for the view that national housing policy should shift in emphasis from spot redevelopment to a basic renewal program consistent with a long-run picture of each metropolitan area.

2. Summary of Proposal

Those areas which most directly contribute to a city's economic base, together with supporting facilities, should be deployed along a major ring road a number of miles from the center of the metropolis. Partly as a concession to existing conditions, those activities which seem to require central location should be concentrated around an inner ring. The plan's effectuation is predicated on eventual municipal land ownership.

3. Content Analysis

a. Assumptions: A plan must allow for inevitable growth and decay. It must also permit swift interaccessibility; sheer proximity is not sufficient in this day and age. The extent of physical change envisaged is justified when one realizes the tremendous waste involved in the failure to utilize fully a nation's resources. The plan is consistent with the strongly held belief that the economic health of the United States depends on channeling savings into public and private construction venture capital.

[91]

L. Justement, 1946.

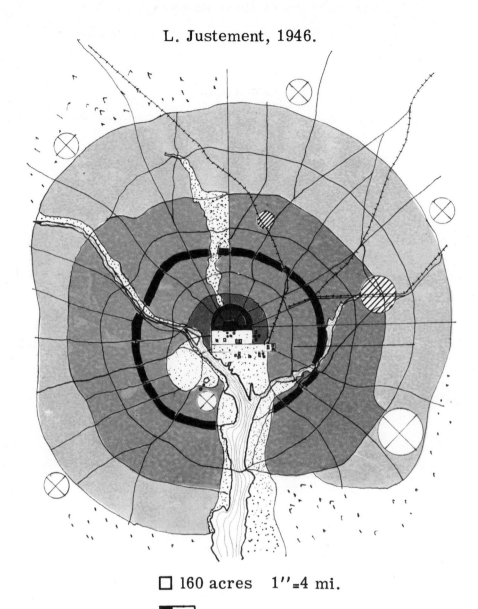

□ 160 acres   1″=4 mi.

1/2 mi. 0 1 mi.

Based upon drawing in New Cities for Old.

b. Form: The ideal city is built on a plan which is a modification of the ring theory. The basic form is given by the concentration of activity along the ring highway some 4 miles from the town center. Space for expansion of the central district is provided by an internal greenbelt, which becomes feasible as some downtown functions move to the outer ring. Densities of residential areas in general fall off from the core of the city; the high activity ring rests about midway in the range.

c. Circulation: The radial-and-ring highway system is designed with a view to the provision of rapid intercommunication, particularly along the major activity belt. The internal street system is not shown, but it is presumed that no basic innovations are anticipated here.

d. Population: The city's population is not considered to be an independent factor; it reflects the density and final land-use determinations.

e. Density: In general, density decreases outward from one hundred people per gross acre near the center of the city, to about thirty-five at the activity ring, to about ten in the suburbs. The relative concentration along the ring permits between $\frac{1}{2}$ to 1 million people to live where the job holders can walk to their jobs, assuming that employees live near the ring and relatively nearby laterally.

f. Consideration of future growth: The author specifically attempts to have his plan permit a gradual shift from the present pattern to that of the future, with forced amortization of all structures as one of the proposed tools. It is not clear whether the "final" plan, too, can pass on to still other, as yet undefined, forms.

4. Evaluation

It is not clear why this particular scheme was selected to exemplify his conclusions regarding the economy and the nature of the city. However, it is in general a plausible if not necessary organization. Neither is the choice of a band of uniform density self-evident. On the contrary, it is possible that concentration pressures would arise. For example, areas of greater intensity would very likely develop near the intersection of the ring with major radial highways. It is also not shown that such a system would work with an industrial economic base. With such a base, other circulation facilities and larger greenbelts along the outer ring would probably become essential, with a consequent greater spread of development.

This work is significant in its attempt to put city regeneration on a sound economic basis, although the absence of social considerations is unfortunate. As a plan which is specifically dedicated to the question of change and the time factor, this is a most welcome addition to the literature of the field.

Bibliography

JUSTEMENT, LOUIS. *New Cities for Old.* New York: McGraw-Hill, 1946.

S. E. SANDERS AND A. J. RABUCK, NEW CITY PATTERNS, 1946

1. Context of Proposal

Two site planners have designed a metropolis showing a strongly articulated neighborhood basis. Depression conditions, wartime growth experience, and postwar hopes are uppermost in their minds. The authors had
close contact with Federal government building programs and were particularly familiar with the Washington and Baltimore metropolitan areas.
Much reliance is placed on master plans from the United States and from
abroad. Sanders and Rabuck have a particular affinity for advocates of
density controls. Economic justification is sought for the proposal; secondary consideration is given other matters, such as legal institutions. The book
appears to have been written as a stimulus to postwar city rebuilding and
as an economic justification of the bold action deemed necessary. It is
directed at a rather broad readership.

2. Summary of Proposal

Sectors of medium- and low-intensity development radiate from the city's
center, which is composed of a business core and surrounding high-density
residential neighborhoods. There is interpenetration of open land at all
scales. Commercial and public facilities are distributed on a hierarchical
pattern. Control of form, of growth, and of densities appear to be the main
recurrent themes.

3. Content Analysis

a. Assumptions: It is assumed that there exists a need to control blight
and high-density living, as these are responsible for the social and economic
disintegration of our urban areas and of their residents, too. This control,
it is held, is largely a matter of reordering land uses and rebuilding at lower
densities. New conditions of living must take place in a new physical environment, in the "new city pattern." The good life will most likely be
found in relatively isolated neighborhoods which resemble small towns. This
would encourage the development of a more cohesive and less mobile society.
The authors state that this really would be the environment most desired
by the majority of the people.

[94]

S. E. Sanders and A. J. Rabuck, 1946.

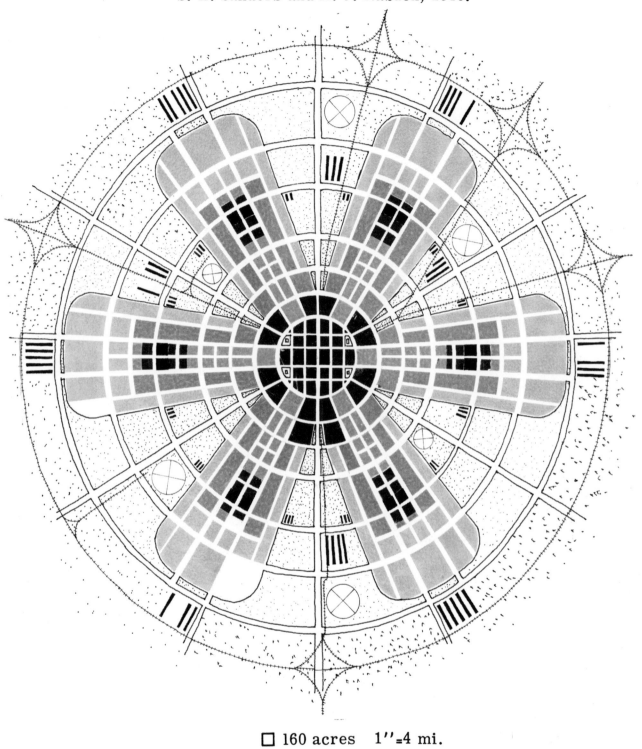

☐ 160 acres   1''=4 mi.

1/2 mi. 0 1 mi.

Based upon drawing in New City Patterns.

b. Form: The city center is composed of a commercial core with some in-town, high-density residential areas. Half a dozen essentially similar spokes radiate from the center, each in some respects resembling a linear city with somewhat heightened intensity of activity near the center. Neighborhood units dominate the pattern of all residential areas. The sectors are separated by wedges of open land which also house institutions, some recreation areas, and circulation facilities. The development limit of the metropolitan area is clearly indicated by a major transportation belt, along which lie the heavy industries.

c. Circulation: A ring-and-radial pattern at the city level gives form to the rectangular neighborhoods. These limited-access highways bear the bulk of vehicular traffic flow. There is an emphasis on freedom from traffic within the neighborhood, but, in consequence, major facilities of heroic proportions are required on the periphery.

d. Population: Population levels are dependent on neighborhood density standards plus consideration of appropriate walking distance to school and of factors in operation of schools. Neighborhoods of 3,000 to 10,000 people are envisaged. No specific size standard is explicitly set for the multimillion aggregate.

e. Density: The optimum urban density is declared to be less than thirty families per net residential acre, but the range may include housing from five to sixty per acre. Observation of existing housing densities both in the United States and abroad led to this conclusion. For democracy's sake, a diversity of housing types is sought for each neighborhood.

f. Consideration of future growth: Although the text speaks of neighborhood-by-neighborhood replacement of the old by the new, apparently no consideration was given to change at a smaller scale. No thought is given to continued growth or internal change when the model size and form is reached, although the green wedges might be utilized as land reserves for institutions and other specific purposes.

4. Evaluation

One of the plan's consequences is that the city, with its circulation girdle, is rigidly set in size unless densities were to change within residential areas or incursions into the green wedges were to occur. Neither of these contingencies would suit the authors. Unfortunately, no over-all population figure nor criteria for establishing optimum size are presented. The justification for low densities and for the desirability of neighborhoods themselves are given ex cathedra and with little substantiation beyond contrast with today's poor environment. Neighborhood size, too, is left somewhat in the air. The authors concede that given more than one school, neighborhood population could vary; such would of necessity be higher-density neighborhoods. But the authors do not seem to recognize that, in so doing, they eliminate the only quantifiable criterion which they employ to limit the unit's size. It appears, too, that the authors underestimate both the effort involved in obtaining open space so close to the city's heart and the power of metropolitan growth potential.

This proposal is quite consistent with numerous others which may lack the scope of this over-all plan. On the other hand, in some ways it almost serves as a caricature of planning thought, as where it presents neighborhoods walled in by four limited-access speedways.

Bibliography

SANDERS, SPENCER E., AND RABUCK, ARTHUR J. *New City Patterns*. New York: Reinhold, 1946.

P. GOODMAN AND P. GOODMAN, COMMUNITAS, 1947

1. Context of Proposal

Architectural, sociological, and humanist talents are joined here in an experiment in utopian thought. The Goodman brothers are concerned with the lack of "true imagination" in policy making for postwar America. They question what they feel is a fatal reliance on depression-time scarcity concepts. Instead, a mentality keyed to optimism and potential surplus should reign supreme. The authors have considerable familiarity with most planning literature. They also show great interest in the line of thought, exemplified by Ralph Borsodi and F. L. Wright, which holds a belief in the possibility of sophisticated rural life as a font of creativity and of demographic regeneration.

2. Summary of Proposal

Three proposals are presented, and each is summarized below. These differ from one another in terms of their approach to the economy of surplus with which we are now faced. More generally, the Goodmans are concerned with the relationship between underlying values and the content of the plans. The physical form of each scheme is a relatively massed, contiguous area of urban and semiurban development; but, aside from this, the proposals vary. How uniquely appropriate each of the plans is to the problems it is designed to resolve is something of a moot point.

[97]

3. Content Analysis

The Goodmans maintain that a plan, in general, should serve two purposes. It should be a guide to policy makers charged with bridging the gap between the potential of high production and low actual productivity. It should also analyze optimum relationships among technology, standards of living, and levels of political authority. These are appropriate foci for planning endeavors because of the deep tie between morality, way of life, and man's relation to man qua consumer or producer. Most significantly, they feel that our surplus-producing technologies provide the leeway within which a variety of plans should be proposed and can be effectuated. It is not hard to see why the authors believe most plans prepared to this point pay but scant attention to basic issues. Specific values to which the authors themselves adhere include the following: Today's standard of living is false; it is based on excessively complex production and consumption practices. It must be replaced by a morally richer yet simpler existence. The essential modern problems are the need to foster a selective use of the ranges of machine technology, the use of the potentially available surplus, and the nature and extent of the gap between ends and means. One also senses the wish that it were possible to design a relatively isolated and schematically consistent environment, for little consideration is given to ties with the outside world or, for that matter, to the impact of the models on other areas.

Paradigm I

A. Assumptions

This plan is a design for an environment promoting the most efficient consumption possible. The capacity to produce is fully utilized. The social mechanisms on which the scheme rests are imitation and emulation.

B. Summary of proposal

The city is composed of a highly concentrated distribution center, surrounded by institutions and neighborhood-organized residential areas. In the outskirts, rural areas provide a much-needed contrast to the highly urbanized environment in which people live and consume.

C. Content analysis

a. Form: Use areas are rather rigidly divided with reference to their place in the scheme of production or consumption activities. They are dis-

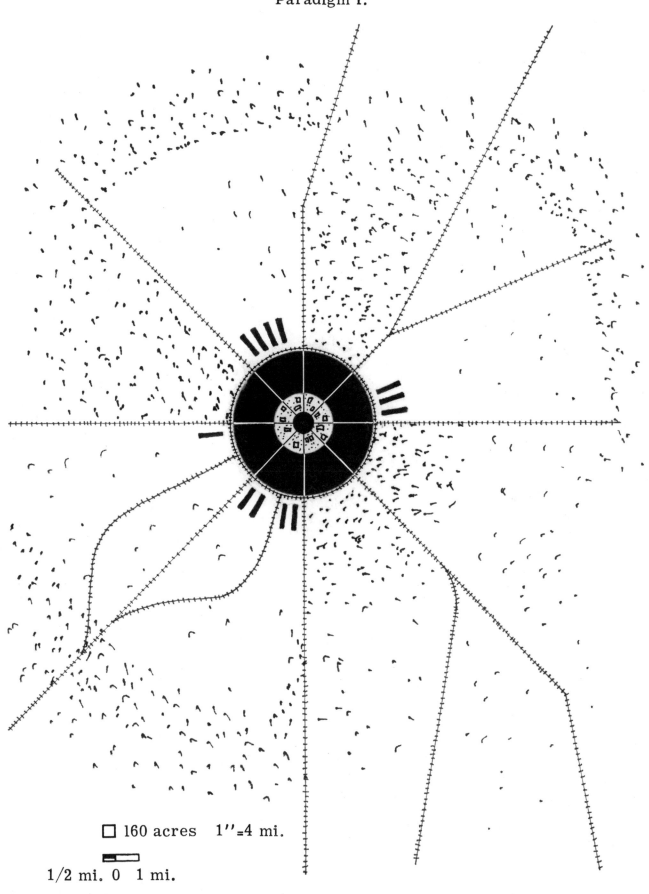

P. Goodman and P. Goodman, 1947.
Paradigm I.

☐ 160 acres   1''=4 mi.

1/2 mi. 0 1 mi.

Based upon drawing in <u>Communitas</u>.

tributed in a ring around the all-important focus of consumption, the central business district.

b. Circulation: A radial road system converges on a vast garage and a circulation system within the gargantuan commercial building that constitutes the city core.

c. Population: The population of the metropolis is held to 6 or 8 million people. It is patterned on the obvious success of New York as a market. Residential areas are broken up into units of 4,000 inhabitants. The authors maintain that neighborhoods of such a size will serve best to stimulate communication and, hence, emulation and consumption.

d. Density: Given the over-all population and the size of the area as drawn by the authors, density can be calculated at about three hundred and fifty people per gross residential acre.

e. Consideration of future growth: No specific consideration is given this factor. However, the design is, almost, a *reductio ad absurdum* of certain structural and centralizing tendencies evident in our own urban culture. It might conceivably evolve by operation of existing forces. Should change at a future time be desired, away from the model as shown, one might argue that the consequent waste and rebuilding would be consistent with the ethos of relative impermanence which is suggested here.

D. Evaluation

It is not clear from the societal considerations why basic land-use areas should be separated so rigidly from each other, or, for that matter, why the ring form was selected. Neither conclusion follows from the assumptions and may in fact result in an undesirable inflexibility. For example, given the economy portrayed here, the powers that be would most certainly have to reckon with the possibility of growth. But none can be accommodated at crucial points. It is also obvious that a choice was made to pay only limited attention to traffic problems. How else account for the proposed convergence of all highways in the tight, central district, or the failure to design ring roads, or the absence of a suggestion of relatively intense development at points of access or intersections? Yet, unless specific assumptions were made to the contrary, it would appear that a consumption economy on the American pattern would include the car and that car-based activities would rank high on individuals' preference scales. Finally, no consideration is given to the region related to the city. In fact, the plan's explicit intent to minimize the proportion of nonmanufacturing workers in the labor force may hide the wish to disassociate the metropolis from its hinterland, for the service and trade part of the labor force is generally linked most directly to other areas. In fact, this nonmanufacturing sector gives many cities their economic justification.

Paradigm II

A. Assumptions

The environment of the "New Commune" gives man an opportunity to express once more what the authors hold to be those instincts for creativity and workmanship almost obliterated by contemporary capitalism. These basic drives can best be expressed through institutional and geographic propinquity of home and work. Life proceeds at a relaxed pace, and the short working day permits that active participation in all community affairs and political and economic decision making which gives real meaning to local self-government. In comparison with Paradigm I, this proposal envisages a lower level of production.

B. Summary of proposal

Some half-dozen coequal city cores, more than 10 miles apart, constitute an urban region with 2 million inhabitants. The geographical and societal center of each element city is a congeries of "squares" around which all urban processes, intentionally intermingled, take place. Closely related agricultural and semiurban activities are found in surrounding rings.

C. Content analysis

a. Form: Concentric belts of increasingly open agricultural areas surround an intensive urban node located near the intersection of regional highways. Land uses and activities of the central core include the full range of urban experience and reflect no easily discernible pattern save the wish to promote frequent and convenient interchange between people.

b. Circulation: The physical channels along which the desired interchange are to take place are not spelled out clearly. Major expressways link the region's various centers. A hexagonal spider web of city streets is placed rather independently of the main roads.

c. Population: Each of the cities of the metropolitan region has 200,000 urban and 100,000 semirural residents. The choice of population size is suggested as being plausible but is not developed nor supported by the text.

d. Density: The urban core, which includes most of the industrial and commercial uses as well as civic and institutional facilities and residential sections, is built up to approximately 180 people per gross acre. Since most children are domiciled and educated in the semirural areas, this brings the density of inlying districts to about seventy-five dwelling units per gross

P. Goodman and P. Goodman, 1947.

Paradigm **II.** The town and its environs.

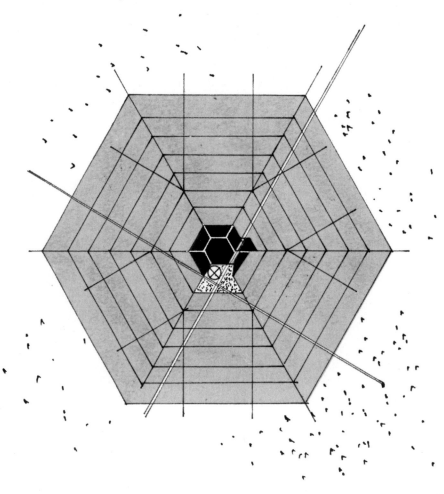

☐ 160 acres   1''=4 mi.

1/2 mi. 0 1 mi.

Based upon drawing in <u>Communitas.</u>

P. Goodman and P. Goodman, 1947.
Paradigm II. The new community center.

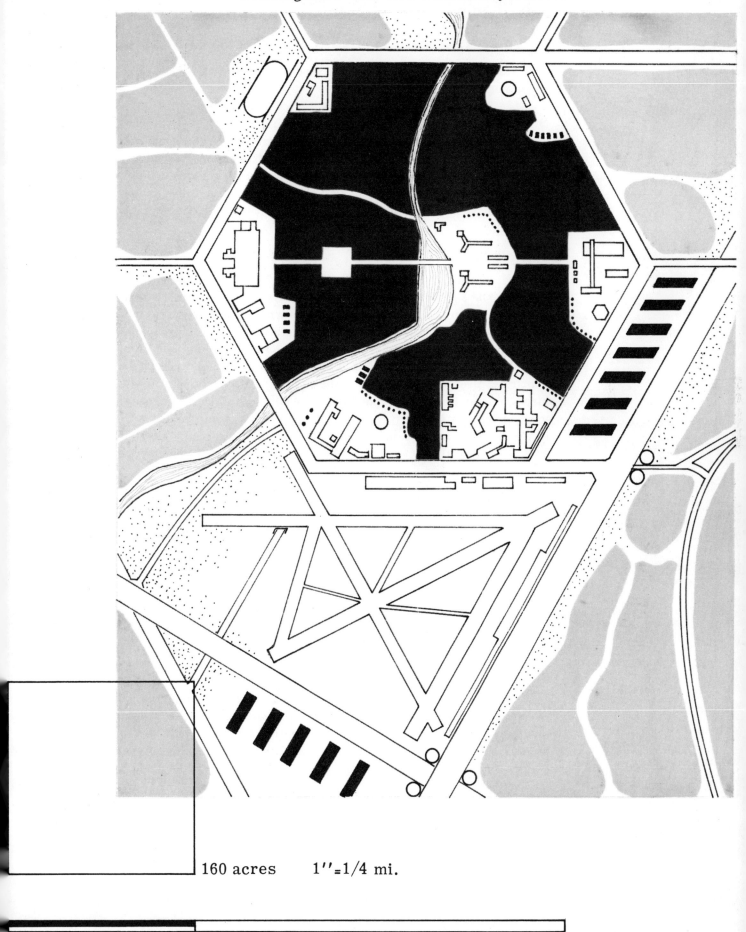

160 acres   1″=1/4 mi.

2 mi.   0   1 mi.

Based upon drawing in <u>Communitas</u>.

acre. Within the "squares," densities vary considerably; all kinds of housing accommodations must be provided.

e. Consideration of future growth: The New Commune is presented as a finished product, as are all three of the paradigms. It bears little relation to existing conditions, although the proposed intermixture of land uses does resemble the land-use pattern of existing city development. Change within the final scheme could apparently be accommodated quite easily, but growth beyond the planned stage would best take place were another similar unit built. Otherwise, the commune's equilibrium would be destroyed.

D. Evaluation

This is, in many ways, a particularly satisfying utopian scheme. Nevertheless, some significant areas of concern have been omitted. For example, it is evident that the authors are displeased with the automobile's impact on the contemporary metropolis; no consideration is given cars. Yet, in a scheme such as that portrayed here, vehicular movements would require careful and subtle consideration. This would be especially true in the core "squares," given the density level, the style of life, and the wish to promote interaction between people and places. Another problem revolves around the lack of demographic considerations in the planning of the central, relatively self-contained neighborhoods. As it is, the reader doesn't even have an idea of the techniques which might appropriately be employed in determining the size and composition of such areas. The over-all central-district density, when deduced from area and population data, is very high. The average ground area per household would be on the order of 250 square feet. Granted that ample public spaces will exist and that child-oriented open space will not be needed in quantity, this still is somewhat at odds with the picture painted elsewhere. It should be added, however, that the scheme would not suffer much were either the area or the population adjusted.

Paradigm III

A. Assumptions

This is the city of maximum security. Consequently, production is keyed to supply at the subsistence level. It also is designed to operate with a minimum of regulations. That is, those activities which are not directed to production to meet the subsistence level are removed from the orb of governmental regulations.

[104]

P. Goodman and P. Goodman, 1947.

Paradigm III.

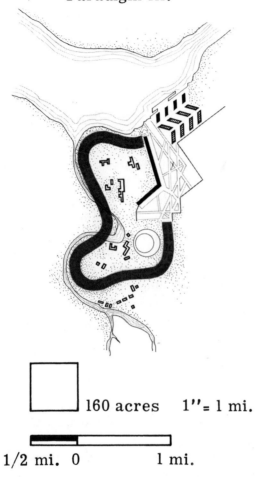

160 acres   1″= 1 mi.

1/2 mi. 0   1 mi.

Based upon drawing in <u>Communitas</u>.

B. Summary

This proposal is not developed as fully as are the others in its physical planning aspects. The authors hold that to achieve the stated goals, work and home should be placed in close proximity to each other. Facilities are planned to maximize return from the productive effort of the labor force. Several production centers for such an economy are sketched as examples. Their populations range from 5,000 to 75,000 inhabitants.

4. General Conclusions

The Goodman brothers go far in stating explicitly their values and assumptions. Gaps nevertheless do exist even in this work, and not all conclusions and proposals offered are uniquely consequent from the assumptions. This is particularly true so far as the form of the city is concerned.

The possible interrelationship between the three paradigms is a matter which the authors do not consider. A subsistence economy may well move towards a level of greater productivity. A high-production-oriented society could work toward attaining the more sophisticated, mature, or advanced level of existence pictured in Paradigm II. Yet it would seem that each of the models shown is fixed; each represents such a degree of investment that transition from one to the other would be inhibited or impossible, or would involve transition stages of low amenity, efficiency, or equity. Reference has already been made to the relatively isolated nature of the proposed cities. These considerations aside, this group of plans remains among the most significant contributions to the field's effort of ideal building.

Bibliography

GOODMAN, PAUL, and GOODMAN, PERCIVAL. *Communitas*. Chicago: University of Chicago, 1947. Second edition, revised, New York: Random House, 1960.

RIESMAN, DAVID. "Some Observations on Community Plans and Utopia," *Yale Law Journal*, LVII (December, 1947), 174–200. Also reprinted in DAVID RIESMAN. *Individualism Reconsidered*. Glencoe, Ill.: Free Press, 1954. Also, *ibid.*, New York: Doubleday, 1955.

A. KLEIN, MAN AND TOWN, 1947

1. Context of Proposal

An architect-planner, with a European and American background, designs a new town for Israel, a new country. The plan reflects a specific

A. Klein, 1947.

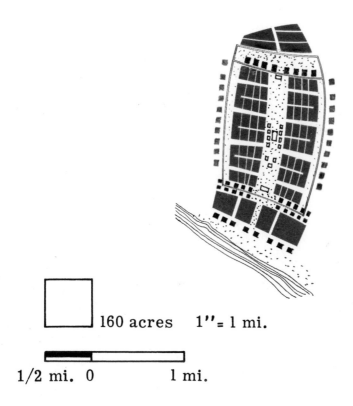

◻ 160 acres   1″= 1 mi.

▮▯ 1/2 mi. 0   1 mi.

Based upon drawing in "Man and Town," Technion Yearbook, September, 1947.

locality as well as, more generally, the Middle Eastern environment, but there is the intention to plan for a universally optimum environment. Though no direct reference is made, familiarity with the works published under the auspices of the CIAM, Hilberseimer, and other planners is shown. This prototype design apparently was prepared to give new-town building in Israel a stimulus. Its publication in *Technion Yearbook* suggests it was also intended to appeal to those with a more general interest in Israel.

2. Summary of Proposal

The ideal city must be one of predetermined and fixed size. Production and distribution areas are on the periphery and must be separated from residential districts. Vehicular and pedestrian circulation routes nowhere interfere with each other. Residential areas are designed basically in terms of accessibility to community facilities.

3. Content Analysis

a. Assumptions: The document shows the author's displeasure with machine-centered living. The plan presumes little reliance on cars. It is desirable to minimize motion and to segregate by type whatever traffic there is. Just as circulation is strictly organized, city size, land use, and other aspects of the urban scene are also subject to apparently rigid control. The ideal city itself is to house closely knit and cooperating groups of residents living in highly interacting communities.

b. Form: A concentric form is felt to be most desirable, since it sets limits to the size of the city, can provide clear boundaries, and is consistent with a circulation system which minimizes both traffic in the residential interior and walking distances. It also encourages location on the periphery of uses which have frequent contact with the outside. Internal organization of residential areas is of the neighborhood type, with nursery schools and small shops within three minutes of the home. Eight such units are grouped together. In this manner, schools and larger shops lie within ten minutes' walk of each dwelling unit. Houses are, largely, served with pedestrian walks.

c. Circulation: Inasmuch as vehicular and pedestrian traffic have different requirements, walkways and roads are designed to be separate. If kept apart, Klein maintains, they can also be reduced in length and in cost. Distribution of communal facilities reflects standards for maximum distance from homes measured along the pedestrian walkway system.

d. Population: The population level which is selected shows, on one hand, the intent to prevent typical suburban sprawl and, on the other, the wish to recognize levels of efficiency as indicated by fiscal and administrative studies. The latter, unfortunately, are not identified in the publication. With these criteria in mind, desirable town size is established to be in the 50,000 to 100,000 population range.

e. Density: Density is derived from geographic size and population. It is not an independent consideration. The gross density of the residential area is about ninety persons per acre. This figure includes, however, institutional, civic, open, and some commercial areas.

f. Consideration of future growth: It is assumed that the town will be developed as one unit, although reference is made to the possibility that "organic" neighborhoods will be built one at a time. When population passes the set size, it is time to construct another town. There is no provision for, nor consideration of, the possibility of change in the future.

4. Evaluation

Civic and institutional structures are centrally located. This would seem to be inconsistent with Klein's wish to relate such uses to peripheral precincts. Given the wish to maintain an internally traffic-free town, yet one which is a regional center, location of commercial and industrial areas on the outside seems reasonable. One undesirable consequence is that residential areas are effectively blocked from surrounding open land. In Israel, this may not be a serious consideration. There are some grounds to question the efficiency of the system. The system of internal circulation presumably suits the resident but may prove hampering to visitors' movements to the interior or between commercial locations. Ringing the city with commercial uses may be a high price to pay for internal freedom from traffic. The circulation scheme follows quite clearly from the basic assumptions. There is, however, little in the plan which shows how the town will promote, better than would any other contemporary scheme, the growth of a cooperative community and other posited aspects of the good life. Finally, the scheme ignores evidence which points to the futility of rigid population controls and to the desirability of at least accommodating if not planning for future change.

This scheme shows further development of the traffic-free or traffic-control approach suggested by Stein and others. It points to the need for further verification of some of the assertions regarding the desirability of a pedestrian way of life and of some of the consequences which might result.

Bibliography

KLEIN, ALEXANDER. "Man and Town," *Technion Yearbook,* VI (Sept., 1947), 72–90.

IV

The Physical Planning Content of Ideal Communities

IN THIS CHAPTER we continue with the second part of the analysis of Ideal Communities. Earlier (in Chapter II) we sought to come to some conclusions as to the methodological variety and types of propositions which are involved in their development. On the following pages we shall present the substantive content of planning propositions set forth by means of such schemes.

Rather than analyze all aspects of Ideal Communities, we have narrowed down the study of substance to those dealing with land use and other physical elements of the urban environment. Physical considerations, however, vary in meaning depending on the character of the total urban environment involved. Consequently we shall also try to come to some conclusions as to the over-all pictures of the urban ideal. The identification of this life style is in itself a crucial part of an intelligent critique of an Ideal Community, particularly since the initial selection and development of many of the physical propositions result from societal ideals rather than being independently derived from the physical criteria.

A further self-imposed limitation of this review should be made explicit. The summaries of Ideal Communities presented in the previous chapter, and their analysis here, emphasize propositions of the "middle range" (Merton, 1957, pp. 6–10). These are propositions of a general applicability (but not an applicability without specified limits) which can be so designed as to be susceptible to empirical verification.[1] This middle range excludes

---

[1] Implicit goals may have to be specified or elaborated before the verifications of the propositions can be undertaken. Thus, a scheme may indicate a net residential-area density of X families per acre. Unless it is clear what the implications of this standard are, however, such as ability to walk in Y minutes to a school of adequate size, consistent with such and such economic use of land and utilities, the X families per acre remains a relatively uninteresting statement. Not only should there be analysis of the proposition; at a certain stage, the aims or the assumptions are appropriately questioned. Thus, in

on one hand the all-embracing principles attempting to provide frameworks for the derivation of guides to action. Such would be the dictum that the city's physical structure must reflect the fact that it is the product of man's will. On the other hand, excessively specific propositions must be discounted in this analysis for their failure to provide a decision-making framework and for their inapplicability in a sufficiently wide range of circumstances. Street-width standards would fall in this category.[2] Theories of the middle range are broad enough to permit gradual consolidation into expanding sets of generalization.

Propositions in four substantive areas were subject to detailed scrutiny in the previous chapter:

1. The form of the total urban area; the relationship of the developed area to its surroundings; relation of the entire urban area to its subparts; basic land-use considerations.

2. The circulation pattern; function of circulation; its importance relative to other considerations, particularly to land use.

3. Establishment of optimum population for the city or the neighborhood unit; the alternatives of planning for a specified size or for flexibility.

4. Consideration of optimum density for the city or for the neighborhood unit; again, alternatives of planning for a specific density or for flexibility.

These concern matters which are part of every urban area. Therefore, we are dealing with what amount to lowest common denominators for the description of the schemes. They may thus facilitate comparison not only between proposals referring to different types or sizes of urban places, they are also the link between the schemes originating in a variety of nations and periods. They further show that degree of interdependence which permits checking for internal consistency and reasonableness of the individual Ideal Community.

Form of the Urban Environment

The determining quality of the physical environment

There is general agreement that in Ideal Communities the city's social and economic life reflects the urban area's physical arrangements. When

---

the example cited, it is proper to ask: "Why a walking scale?" "What is the reasonable size of the school?"—not only in terms of the specifics of the situation (is the walking distance of Y minutes reasonable?) but also whether certain alternatives to walking should be considered within the larger framework of the scheme, and so forth. This is the link to propositions that are not of a middle range.

[2] This very rough breakdown highlights one of planning's fundamental needs: the development of methods which reduce broad ends to operational principles. The study of Ideal Communities offers an opportunity to study processes by which the general is made more specific.

[111]

linked with a reformist point of view, such a deterministic approach is often tied to the belief that individual and social ills arise from a malfunctioning or impoverished environment. Conversely it is generally held that reconstruction of society can only proceed on the basis of rebuilt homes, neighborhoods, and cities.[3] The certainty with which such a viewpoint could be held has been questioned in recent years. Analysis of evidence culled from improved areas (such as subsidized housing projects for low-income families) has led to serious doubts, though not in the Ideal Community literature. Even among the most recent of such designs one detects the confidence that the stage sets the play, that the most reasonable and efficient road to the better life is by means of reconstruction of the environment. This confidence is at least partly a reflection of the interests and skills possessed by planners, especially by those who design Ideal Communities.

The critical nature of the physical arrangements is seen to affect all levels of the environment. The satisfying interfamily life around the cul-de-sac blends into superblock and neighborhood feelings of community, creativity, and control of affairs. At the city scale, harmonious land-use arrangements promote an efficient economy. They also contribute to that kind of a feeling of well-being and satisfaction with one's surroundings which in former ages, supposedly, characterized the citizen's relation to his urban environment and which arose from his ability to identify and orient himself in, and with, the city.

The Neighborhood Unit is one specific example of this approach. The neighborhood concept has had profound effect on the way planners, as well as their clients, look at cities. It arises out of a concern with the defects of residential areas. The ascribed shortcomings include the failure of citizens to involve themselves in civic affairs, the consequent inadequacies of government, the hazards and inconvenience of traffic, the absence of amenities, and the actual existence of antisocial behavior. According to proponents of the neighborhood approach, such ills stem from poor arrangement of land use, circulation, and facilities. Placing these in a more efficient and ordered manner creates strategic savings. But, more important, new patterns of human relationships are established. Use of a newly provided community center or common enjoyment of green areas can convert the drab vicinity into a neighborhood, i.e., a better place in which to live. Perry (1929) in the 'twenties and Stein (1951), particularly in subsequent decades, have been vocal proponents of this approach, but one can find as far back as in Howard's writings (1898) certain important elements of such a viewpoint.

Unfortunately, implicit faith in the existence of a causal relation between

[3] *New City Patterns,* by Sanders and Rabuck (1946), is only one of several works where this concept is explicitly stated.

the physical environment and individual and group behavior has led most writers to overlook a host of problems. Even were the basic hypothesis verified, other difficulties would remain. Among these are the operational questions: what means can exist for manipulating the social relations by way of changes in the physical environment? Furthermore, the value questions are put into yet sharper focus: What, indeed, are the good social relations or personality traits within the range that can be affected by change? There is implicit here a willingness to determine these life-style choices, not only a willingness on the part of the planner to identify them. This applies as much to the conservative, who most generally seeks to apply to one group of people what he feels they lack (that is, the way of living of another group), as to the more reconstructionist planner, who would seek to build a new social environment for the total population.

The general form of the community

There is a wide range of proposals regarding the form of the Ideal Community and its constituent parts. These are rarely preconceived notions as such: no writer begins his work with a statement that a city ought to be ring-shaped or should have a linear basis. There is considerable effort expended to have the form of the community reflect circulation, land use, etc., lest these be inconsistent with each other. Consideration is also given to values such as the optimum adaptation to an industrial age or reduction in the use of land for nonagricultural purposes.

The "form" that is under consideration here does not, by any means, reach the fundamental spatial characteristics that make up the basis for an analytical system. Authors of Ideal Communities themselves have skirted some very basic considerations, such as the intensity and heterogeneity of activities in the space. The works express concern with only a limited range of adapted spaces and are confined to those problems observed in contemporary, Western urban environments. (It should be repeated that it was partly this consideration which led us in the first place to choose the examples selected for this study.) Furthermore, the authors as a group have not applied nor possessed the most rigorous analytical techniques. For an introduction to the type of theory that may prove to be much more basic and general, the reader is referred to the article on "The Theory of Urban Form" by Lynch and Rodwin (1958).[4]

The form proposals can be categorized in several ways: Table 2 suggests

[4] The kind of form considerations which are discussed here correspond to Lynch and Rodwin's "catchall" category: "(6) generalized spatial distribution" (p. 206), although at other points attention is given in this study to such aspects of their system as are labeled "Quantity," "Density," "Grain," and "Focal Organization."

Table 2. Basic Form Characteristics of Ideal Communities

	Example	Sketch
I. THE METROPOLIS		
A. URBANIZED AREA ORGANIZED ON BASIS OF CONTIGUITY		
1. Concentric	Justement	
2. Segmented		
Sector	Edwards	
Star	Comey	
3. Linear		
Linear city	Soria y Mata	
Multi-land use	Sert	
B. DEVELOPMENT ON BASIS OF NON-CONTIGUITY OF URBANIZED AREA		
1. Satellite proposals	Howard	
2. Polynucleated	Gloeden	
3. Low density regional	Wright	
4. Contemporary linear	Le Corbusier (ASCORAL)	
II. THE NEIGHBORHOOD UNIT		
1. Open space centered	Herrey	
2. Facility centered	Gropius and Wagner	
3. Facilities distributed	Perry	

one way of so doing. Although all conceivable possibilities do not fall in these categories, this classification includes the major forms noted in the survey of Ideal Communities.[5]

[5] Insofar as this outline is essentially two dimensional, it fails to note three-dimensional schemes such as Mazet and Chauvin's proposal (1951) for an immense cone to house all urban activities. Neither is the outline suited to the notion that form may be dynamic and change over time. Certain unusual two-dimensional forms, though not noted in the literature, are also possible. Elaborations of these categories also can be made when form types are combined. In fact, many of the proposals studied do incorporate more than one basic type.

What generalizations can be made regarding these designs? One caveat should be voiced. While it is often implied that "pure" urban forms are presented, many actually are amalgams. Thus, a design for a sector city may, in fact, show a concentric element in the heavily articulated center. The design offered by Sanders and Rabuck (1946), for example, shows a circulation system surrounding raylike residential sectors and focuses on a high-density residential and business center. Or a linear city may have points of relatively high intensity, as does Miljutin's Stalingrad proposal. Under these circumstances it becomes hard to differentiate, in some respects, a linear scheme from a sector-with-core design. The writer may also concern himself with several levels of urban development. As Mumford (1945) and Purdom (1949) have pointed out, Howard's contribution lay not only in his ability to design one new town (which in Table 2 would fall in the concentric category), but, in addition, he had the foresight to think in neighborhood terms. The "ward" he proposed anticipated Perry's Neighborhood Unit formulation by about three decades. At the same time, Howard had a sufficiently clear picture of metropolitan growth patterns to present his public with a scheme for a complex group of dominant and satellite towns —his "social cities."

Contiguous urban development. The massed city, contiguously built up, has several advantages whatever its specific form: sector, starlike, or concentric. On a regional or nationwide basis, a massed concentration can be economic in the saving of real open or agriculturally used land. This line of argument further holds that while the individual city dweller may, under these circumstances, have less direct access to the country than does his small-town cousin, the agricultural, open, or forest land can only preserve its character if kept free from periodically interspersed satellite towns. The validity of this reasoning, of course, rests on the uses and purposes to which nonurban areas are put and how these are evaluated.

The massed city is also regarded as economic in the use of transportation facilities. This is particularly significant if the main function or advantage of a city is seen to be the existence of a variety of job opportunities for each job seeker or, conversely, the availability of a large labor pool for each employer. There are other advantages arising from massed development— economists refer to these as agglomerative factors. But, to the degree that transportation is not considered as a scarce resource and to the extent that congestion, inflexibility, and other deglomerative factors enter as planning considerations, disadvantages of the massed city become dominant.

A city designed on the ring pattern suffers from relative inflexibility, particularly in its inner precincts. The rigidity of the form can be somewhat relaxed by provision of green spaces between the main rings on the order of internal greenbelts. But this serves, unfortunately, to expand the geographic size of the city beyond functional requirements in intervening years. A more serious drawback would be the decline in the amount of green space available precisely as built-up areas expand.[6] But a more practical consideration enters. Each of the schemes presented is based not only on the desirability of a city planned with a predetermined size in mind, but there is also an assumption that such controls are possible. Evidence, unfortunately, points in the opposite direction and leads one to question any scheme, such as that for a ring form, which does not allow for expansion of significant parts of the urban area.

The wedge- or star-shaped city can provide what the concentric city generally cannot: open areas close to the core distributed on a systematic basis.[7] The open interstices are also available for the location of major circulation routes, so that, compared to a ring city, these interfere less with urban activities. The green wedges also provide sites for institutions, recreation, and other facilities close to the center, but in the low-intensity surroundings they require. Furthermore, not only is the city opened up; the wedge form is more flexible. To a certain degree, lateral expansion into the adjoining shafts is feasible. Particularly at the outer extremities, the green sectors do not have to maintain a constant proportion of the circumference.[8] Growth also can occur along sectors, especially if these are functionally differentiated. The area that is intensively developed can be limited by planned factors, such as a ring railroad[9] as well as by natural features. However, when this expedient is incorporated in a sector design, so are some of the inadequacies of the ring system. One disadvantage of sector designs as presented in the Ideal Community literature is that, for a given population, they do not seem to house all activities with as much economy as do other schemes. This may be due, however, to a lack of sophistication in calculating basic land-use requirements.[10]

The first linear-city proposals rested their case on their contribution to efficient transportation and the uncongested nature of development. The expansion possibilities of the basic linear form still holds an attraction for many planners. Likewise, one suspects, planners find appealing its resem-

[6] Of course, this assumes that growth occurs through geographic expansion. That this need not be so has been pointed out by Lynch (1958). Referring also to other disciplines, he shows how growth can take other forms.

[7] Herrey's proposal (1944) for a doughnut-shaped city may be taken as an exception. The possibility that central locations be kept vacant has also, on a smaller scale, attracted others: *note* Ferriss's (1929) magnificent central park.

[8] Blumenfeld's proposal (1949) specifically calls for green sectors of given width with a growing proportion of the circumference devoted to development.

[9] Such a constraint is found in Sanders and Rabuck's scheme (1946).

[10] In this connection, note the large proportion of land devoted to nonresidential uses in Edwards's (1933) scheme.

blance to the growth pattern resulting from uncontrolled yet vigorous forces shaping the contemporary urban environment. In more recent decades, the linear form, particularly as adapted to a metropolitan scale, has provided some of the most convincing examples of Ideal Communities. These appear to develop an efficient transportation system, although some of the inherent difficulties have already been noted above (Chapter II). The main secondary advantages concern land use and activities: those which benefit from proximity can be next to each other over considerable distances, while, similarly, areas not suited to one another can be totally separated by other linear factors. They have lost favor as it became evident that, in fact, life on the Main Street was neither desirable nor consistent with efficient circulation. The absence of a notable center has also given rise to criticism. Further problems are the inconsistency between design for a walking existence and the almost seductive proximity to efficient transportation routes, the problem of foci for major facilities, and the possibly undesirable parochialism with which life in the individual communities may become tainted.

Noncontiguous urban development. Many satellite and independent small-town proposals often suffer from the failure to express clearly relationships with a larger entity. The basic questions center on their relative independence or completeness of services and functions and their place in the regional and national economy. Up to a point, such towns can be regarded as self-sufficient, but for certain services they would have to rely on a central city and on each other. While early designs show an expectation that such towns could survive in almost any location within the nation, given modern transportation, power, and communication methods, more recent proposals of this type indicate there is awareness of industrial location factors, cost of travel, and other considerations of linkage between the town and the central city or other reference points.

Granted the premises that the small, green-set town is an improvement upon the overcrowded city, that plausible arguments can be made for an enriching town-country synthesis, and that better living conditions result when work and home are located close to each other, shortcomings in small-town plans may still be noted. The distribution of industry and residence may, for example, limit the choice of jobs available to any one worker. These schemes are also subject to the criticism that the true countryside is despoiled by the presence of towns some distance from the central city.

The polynucleated metropolis composed of cells of about equal size rests on the belief that an efficient specialization of functions is feasible. There is question whether this is a reasonable expectation beyond certain particular districts, such as a university center. It seems likely that characteristic societal problems might arise. There is a risk of parochialism where the bulk of local activity has but one focus. Again, there arises the possibility of reduced job choice within convenient distance, particularly in a society where several members of a household may be engaged in diverse types of occupation. There is, furthermore, a need to plan the various cells to be in definite geographical relation to each other when these are characterized by different functions; this is rarely given adequate consideration. Finally, there may be a rather fundamental internal inconsistency in the quest for a relative independence of the unit while, at the same time, seeking to provide complex and extensive transportation networks.

A slightly different interpretation of the polynucleated ideal is offered by Gutkind in his search for a new "expanding environment" (1953). He anticipates and is thereby able to avoid some of the limitations just noted. The reconstruction of society must be based on decentralization to equally sized small units in a rural setting permitting the true urban-rural synthesis. Their equality, he writes, precludes the development of any hierarchy and thus this is not to be construed as a metropolitan scheme in the usual sense.

The most recent linear-city proposals (as exemplified by the Corbusier [ASCORAL] design, 1945) suffer from some of the defects noted in the discussion of the polynucleated metropolis. This linear-city scheme, however, stresses the essential similarity of cells rather than their functional differences. This approach seems to be equally extreme in its demands on a working economy.[11]

The low-density regional system remains to be discussed. The heavy reliance on vehicular transportation has been noted in the course of the critique of Wright's scheme (1945). Such a dependence, it was stated, is the inevitable consequence of this type of a proposal. Provided close attention is paid to its transportation network, a considerable range of local urban patterns can be accommodated when the population is organized on this basis.

The one design which falls most clearly in this category (Wright's) seems to make a virtue of its afocal internal structure. Commercial areas are removed from the civic centers; schools are distributed in another pattern; working districts in still another. This seems necessarily to follow. The provision of these several foci in any one place would create such a powerful attraction as to destroy the even, low-density tone of the Broadacre City type.

[11] It will be recalled that the linear city, in the ASCORAL proposal, is but one of three basic urban forms. At the major crossroads of the circulation systems, central cities of a higher order of diversity apparently serve numerous linear-city systems. Agricultural villages, the third urban type, fill the interstices between the linear city systems. *See* above, Chapter III.

The neighborhood unit. The neighborhood-unit approach, in general terms, reflects the desire to break down the city into manageable units. Perry's definition still holds as an explicit statement of the aims of neighborhood planning (Chapter III, above). In physical planning terms, this is quite justified, but in other connections there is much that lacks conclusive treatment. The very variety of concepts of the elements of the good life which are used as a justification for one or another neighborhood type tends to pose more questions than are answered. A particular danger would seem to lie in the attempt to delimit areas too sharply. The wish to draw precise boundaries results from the quite laudable intention to plan for the automotive age, protecting the resident-pedestrian in his world while providing for efficiency of circulation at all other levels. Whether urban life can or cannot be so clearly structured is another question.[12]

There is considerable doubt whether the various residents of a neighborhood, with differing ages, economic activities, and other characteristics, could be satisfactorily served by facilities available in any one neighborhood. For example, is a school—one school—an appropriate focus? Furthermore, there seems to be conflict between the homogeneous society that may be required to make a neighborhood operative in terms envisaged by adherents of the neighborhood unit and the heterogeneous neighborhoods which may be required in a democracy.

So far, much of the defense and criticism of the neighborhood concept has centered on the need for something called *neighborliness,* on the provision in the immediate environment of an expanding circle of security-giving acquaintances, and on a vision of the neighborhood as a vehicle for personality growth through activities conducted in groups having interests in common. This interest includes control of the neighborhood's destiny. The neighborhood, many of the writers feel, is a framework for social and geographic orientation in the large city. It excludes all that is superfluous, such as traffic in a pedestrian world and, perhaps unconsciously, strangers in a close-knit society. Administratively, we have here a convenient unit for the provision of community facilities. But each of these considerations has been subjected to rather damaging criticism: acquaintances based on proximity are superficial and may even preclude the real friendship that the Lonely Crowd or the Organization Men lack; the neighborhood is a failure in a larger context if it is not democratically heterogeneous or, if heterogeneous, if it fails to provide the environment for more extensive personal involvement with the neighbors. It has even been suggested (Mann, 1958) that all the neighborhood amounts to is an upper-class wish for the lowers

[12] *See* in particular the study by Foley (1950), which suggests that client, customer, and participation areas tend to overlap and vary.

to pal together and that it is an historically invalid picture of traditional urban life.[13] This is a sufficiently important area that perhaps some alternative justifications for organizing the city on a basis corresponding to, but different from, *the* neighborhood should be explored.

Other important questions arise, though so far as our knowledge goes these refer to physical planning questions only peripherally. How widespread in the first instance is the wish to "neighbor" and, even if it is universally held, how much is it really lacking in those drab areas of anonymity which are contrasted to the lively neighborhoods? Will the new neighborhood, in fact, provide these benefits to people who lacked them before? What happens to those who today are deprived when they are faced with the new possibilities? A number of recent works ask these questions. On the basis of observation and analysis of precisely such areas as neighborhood planners would seek to replace, Gans (1959) and Seeley (1959) point to the clearly evident social organizations of slums and the definite satisfactions they provide and functions they perform, stressing the undesirable consequences which sometimes arise when "bad" areas are threatened with extinction or with transformation into "good."

There remains, nevertheless, faith on the part of planners in the health and curing aspects of the neighborhood unit as a way of arranging the domestic quarters of the city. We may say this has been one of the articles of faith of a substantial portion of the planning profession, and it remains one of the basic shared elements of most Ideal Communities.[14]

Hierarchical structure

Certain characteristics of form are basic to all types of Ideal Communities. The first of these we shall discuss is the hierarchical nature of the reconstructed urban environment. It is generally agreed by authors of Ideal Communities that the urban environment serves its population most efficiently when it is composed of a series of building blocks such as neighborhoods or the units of a polynucleated city. When so designed, it is believed the city can best satisfy the needs of its residents to belong and be oriented.

[13] There exists now quite a substantial literature of criticism of the neighborhood theory. *See,* among others, Bauer (1945) and Isaacs (1948, 1949). These writers point to the danger of homogeneity which is a frequent concomitant of neighborhood designs, stress the difficulty in reconciling various service radii, and question whether anonymity, rather than sociability, is not one of the desired features of city life.

[14] Ferriss (1929) is the only major exception that comes to mind, and his failure to consider more than superficially the residential areas of the city is a major weakness in the scheme. Broadacre City (Wright, 1945), with its focusless character, largely lacks a neighborhood basis.

This view of the city carries with it an implicit belief that planning effort and implementation can proceed more effectively when the urban area is divided on a hierarchical basis. Among the many schemes which focus on this theme, those of Adams (1934) and of Sert (1944) may be offered as prime examples. Generally, each of the elements in the hierarchy, which is developed primarily in relation to its residential function, has a characteristic group of nonresidential uses associated with it. This may take the form of a parallel structure of educational, recreational, or commercial facilities. Thus, the typical Ideal Community would provide elementary schools at the level of the neighborhood, high schools in the major sections or "communities" of the city, and specialized schools and a municipal college to serve the entire urbanized area. This approach is one which often brings analogues from rural life onto the city scene, as does the closely allied neighborhood concept.[15]

The cities of today generally lack such a clearly differentiated structure, although roughly delineated, noncontiguous subareas can often be found throughout. Facilities usually have overlapping service areas. But one wonders whether the establishment of order and the introduction of a systematic arrangement of subareas would contribute much to a better environment, and, if better, "better" in what way? To a large extent, the proposed hierarchical arrangement of the city has an artificial ring to it. It runs counter to the fact that in our dynamic society there are always vestigial intermediate levels which are in the process of being abandoned and new ones which are being created. Such a physical arrangement would also serve to freeze relationships where, in general, flexibility should be sought. Certainly, boundaries and levels in so complex a matter as a city can not be prescribed and proscribed as neatly as in Sert's ideal city (1944) and in many other schemes, efficient and logical as it may seem to do so at the designing stage. Interestingly, one group of writings which lack a hierarchical basis of this kind, the early linear cities, make a virtue of the flexible arrangement possible in these schemes and point out how community facilities, stores, and transportation termini can be expected to arise in response to the real need. Something of a similar approach is evident in Wright's Broadacre City (1945), which, too, is grounded in a laissez-faire ethic. Such proposals, how-

---

[15] Some of the writings are quite ingenuous in their reliance on village or small-town prototypes. Specific references are made to their social closeness and richness, particularly in the historical past. Such an environment, to be duplicated in the modern metropolis, requires a conscious fragmentation of the urban mass. *See,* for example, Wolfe's presentation (1945) of such a scheme. In this design, the rural and hierarchical bases of the ideal urban life are clearly joined and explicitly presented. Although sharing the wish to synthesize urban and rural advantages, Gutkind (1953) specifically avoids a hierarchical structure as he seeks the establishment of units coequal in every respect.

ever, do ignore a number of other significant problems, such as the need to plan certain facilities sufficiently far in advance.[16]

Land use and its differentiation

Ideal Communities do not provide any unusual insights or employ novel techniques with respect to the relations of land uses to each other. Relationships are established as appropriate or inappropriate on the basis of what is presumed to be common knowledge or beliefs: e.g., that factories located in or near residential areas are inimical to safety, comfort, or the preservation of real estate values. They may also be analytically deduced from a vision of the good life or from broad concepts of economy, as, for example, in justifying the location of industrial and residential areas within walking distance of each other. The thought behind land-use arrangements of Ideal Communities resembles that on which zoning is based, though the proposals are formulated more rigidly, being conceived in a more rarefied atmosphere.

Almost all writers maintain that functional differentiation of areas has universal applicability. Although there is a recognition of the interaction and mutual dependence shown by various parts of the urban environment, it would appear that the authors were most concerned with the disorganization brought upon the city by the industrial revolution and consequent chaotic growth.

Here, as is the case whenever we are faced with consensus, there is significant disagreement when the proposition is further developed. For example, at which level is the desired segregation of land uses appropriate? (This is closely related to the concept of urban "grain" as developed by Lynch, 1954.) For some authors, it is the individual town units forming nuclei within a larger metropolis which should be so characterized. To other writers, the differentiation is more properly at the block level or at an even smaller scale.[17] The Corbusier (ASCORAL) scheme for a linear city (1945) and Edwards's New Town proposal (1933) take a position midway along this continuum. But at some point, homogeneity is stressed.

The one notable exception is the Goodmans' (1947) second paradigm. This design for a New Commune places a high value on the synthesis which arises from the intermixture of various uses. This enables each individual, in his most immediate environment, to participate in, or at least

[16] There is also the more specific question whether the early linear cities and, to some extent, Wright's proposal, result in dense enough settlement to support the traffic facility. Low density is, of course, a necessary condition for such flexibility in development as these proposals envisage.

[17] *See* Gloeden (1923) and Perry (1929) as examples of these contrasting views.

to observe, the full range of human experiences: creation, recreation, work, rest, family, society, the richness emanating from the close contact of youth with age. Jane Jacobs's last word in *Exploding Metropolis* (1958), by the Editors of *Fortune,* would also fall into this category by virtue of her belief that it is precisely the mixed land uses that give downtown its worth and vitality. But to most writers, sharing a quest for order, this would strike a disharmonious note akin to chaos and would not meet with approval.

Just as areas should be clearly differentiated in terms of their function, or land use, it is generally held desirable to separate them clearly one from another. This is another way of saying that both the core and the frontier or the fringe of an area should possess the same clear characteristic.[18]

Highways are the most often suggested land-use boundaries, as for example in Perry's Neighborhood Unit proposal (1929) or Sanders and Rabuck's metropolis (1946). Another type of boundary is formed by belts of recreational or institutional uses. This is most clearly seen in such poly-nucleated proposals as Gloeden's metropolis (1923) or Howard's Social Cities (1898) where the internal arrangement of the nuclei, too, shows conscious and liberal use of green space as dividing belts. It also characterizes the linear cities of more recent vintage, as in Sert's design with its generous provision of presumably public open space.

This, of course, is at least partly a matter of definition and of scale. Those institutional land uses which some authors consider most appropriately located between residential and industrial land uses could, by another interpretation, be viewed as modified forms of residential use on the fringe of a residential district. It depends on what precisely is meant by "residential." Similarly, a highway bordering a residential area could either be interpreted as a sharp break or boundary, or it could be placed along one continuum with the type of circulation facility found inside the residential area and serving it in the capacity of an interior, delivery channel. Again, this partly hinges on the definition and even on techniques of graphic presentation as much as it does on the author's explicitly stated ideas.

Neutra's ideas in this connection suggest a different approach. Referring to his planning experience, and particularly to decisions regarding the location of certain uses such as local shopping, he writes: "Neighborhood boundaries (can be) likened approximately to synapses between nerve cells, which are boundaries in a sense, but at the same time planes of contact, electro-

[18] An alternate plausible norm would provide that the core and the frontier should differ by virtue of their different positions in the structure. For example, the core could show the characteristic use with greater intensity, or the frontier areas could provide for specific transitional land uses. Thus, a design could incorporate provision for higher residential densities or for certain commercial establishments (as florist shops) in such frontier districts. The latter concept parallels zoning practice.

[123]

chemical transmission, and subtle but vital energy exchange" (1954, p. 341). In a similar vein, Mumford notes that boundaries of geographical regions are typically rich and creative areas of contact (1938, p. 385).

While most proposals stress the wish to differentiate areas, there is also concern with the need to relate bordering districts. Form proposals of the sector or concentric-belt variety generally take pains to show the reasonableness of placing certain uses near each other. Similarly, there also is concern that uses detrimental to each other should not be contiguous or that special accommodations should be made if propinquity is unavoidable. Usually, problems are seen in industry's relation to residential areas and to transportation facilities. For example, one observes in Le Corbusier's proposals (1924 and others) a stress on the need to separate all factories from residential and commercial uses, while Hilberseimer's scheme (1944) accommodates industrial areas only with considerable effort, since adaptation to smoke, which is seen as the prevalent nuisance, is a key factor influencing the organization of his ideal city. It is not surprising that such considerations play an important and almost universal role in the formulation of the physical aspects of Ideal Communities. Urban planning has a land-use basis and bias and planners have been most successful in developing techniques of control and effectuation, and of symbolism and communication, in this portion of the field.

Specialization of function

There are at least two ways to study the land-use relationships within the urbanized area. The first focuses on the characteristics of the hierarchical unit which compose the whole, and the second begins with a study of the land uses and their distribution. Let us consider the first of these alternatives. One can ask of a scheme whether each neighborhood in the city, or each town in the metropolis, is independent: that is, is it in itself a microcosm of most if not all services, activities, and opportunities offered in the totality? Or should specialization be the touchstone by which one measures the adequacy or the desirability of a subpart's relation to the whole? Should most of the daily needs be met within the bounds of the unit, or should the average citizen travel? Should land uses be relatively homogeneous within the unit, or should each unit show the full range of activities within its bounds? What, in other words, is felt to be the most desirable functional relationship between the parts of a whole? The Ideal Community plans include several approaches to this basic question. The housing areas of Neutra's Rush City (1934)[19] and Le Corbusier's Cité

[19] The decision to place Neutra at this end of the continuum is partly a matter of interpretation. If the neighborhood unit is conceived to be the total sector of Rush City, it becomes an example of a more diversified unit.

Contemporaine (1924) may be cited as examples of specialization, while the highly diversified environments proposed by the Goodman brothers (1947) in their second paradigm strike the opposite note.

There is, however, a second way of considering this problem: from the point of view of land use and the facilities provided in a city. The critic-user of a scheme can begin the analysis with a study of the distribution of the land uses, for the designs vary to the extent that a certain facility or land use is concentrated in one place or is partly or entirely distributed throughout the city or even among adjacent urbanized areas. This applies particularly to such uses as may define, give character to, or provide the economic or social base of an area. Industrial, commercial, recreational, and institutional uses are particularly important in this connection.

Contiguity and noncontiguity of developed areas

Table 2, above, breaks down metropolitan proposals in terms of the contiguity or noncontiguity of the constituent parts. This division serves to call attention to problems of transportation, availability of land, possibility of geographic expansion, and the nature of urban living. Consideration of the benefits of flexibility, semirural amenity, and freedom from nuisances would bring forth a design based on separated units. Adherents of contiguous development stress the economies of agglomeration and in the use of land and intangibles inherent in life in a truly urban environment.

While greenbelts are often set forth as the limits to contiguously developed Ideal Communities, they make their appearance with still greater frequency in the fragmented schemes. The predominant function of the greenbelt here would seem to be that of a separator, with other benefits a convenient but somewhat secondary bonus. At times, one is left with the impression that an author is rather dismayed by the size of the unplanned spaces between units of development, hence the almost frantic inclusion of "greenbelts." Be that as it may, the use of greenbelts is almost universally accepted in the Ideal Community literature, and their potential contribution to the area's welfare is highly praised.

A wide variety of these secondary uses are suggested as appropriate for inclusion in greenbelts. A few schemes, such as Edwards's proposal (1933), hold to their strictly recreational value. More generally, a tradition that the greenbelts be put to other and sometimes more intensive use is followed. The list of activities proposed in Howard's Garden City (1898) is almost as extensive as any since: agriculture, certain extractive operations, industries and services vested with a public interest or subject to public control, eleemosynary institutions, as well as regional parks. More recent

[125]

proposals stress the utility of such greenbelts for vehicular routes or transfer points; thus, airports, parkways, and freight yards find their way into such areas. Sanders and Rabuck (1946) particularly stress the use of greenbelts for such purposes in their ideal metropolis.

Urban form and considerations of growth

Growth and change have been frequently mentioned. The various forms differ, obviously, in the degree to which they can accommodate expansion or change qualitatively.[20] In general, a ring city is not conducive to growth by expansion nor is one where one crucial element serves to inhibit flexibility in another. Such would be a ring railroad around a sectored city or a central business district constricted by residential uses. Some of the linear and polynucleated proposals, the sectored city, and the low-density regional schemes are designed with expansion possibilities in mind. The matter of internal changes in structure or use is harder to categorize, partly because this kind of an approach is rarely attempted. When it is, it is thought of only as a step to reach the final stage as pictured in the scheme and not as a quality possessed by the ideal. Such is the tenor of Justement's (1946) proposal. Otherwise, change is viewed at best as a process of neighborhood by neighborhood replacement, as in the Sanders and Rabuck (1946) design, or as an element of growth where settlements of low intensity, such as agricultural areas, give way and are incorporated into urban developments.

One form feature which has significant theoretical interest, tying into several of the aspects already discussed, is that of rhythmic structure. Certain designs are drawn so as to allow almost infinite repetition of a basic constituent element. Repeatedly, one finds the neighborhood unit viewed in this manner. The linear city proposal of the ASCORAL group (1945), of Sert (1944), and of Hilberseimer (1944) permit accrual of units of a standard size seemingly without limit. Le Corbusier, commenting upon the first of these, referred to a belt of such transportation-based towns extending from Russia to the English Channel, as well as in several other directions. The polynucleated proposals, whether of the coequal-units variety (Gloeden, 1923) or the strong-focus type (Howard, 1898) also permit, indeed, encourage, growth by adding essentially equal units. The only limitation which is not clearly faced is the ceiling on the needed contingent expansion of center-city facilities at the nodes. By virtue of the suggested designs this expansion does not seem possible in some of the schemes.

The other type of growth is one, as in the sectored city, where expansion

[20] A variety of ways in which growth and change can take place is discussed by Lynch (1958).

[126]

takes place by contiguous accretion. In this instance, no repetitive pattern is discernible, for as each of the expanding elements grows by spreading into open areas next to those already developed, the structural relationships within the entire unit change. This approach can muster few adherents in view of the general opposition to urban sprawl.

Intensity of development

The over-all quality of looseness or tightness of development is related to several of the considerations just presented. Many discussions focus on the question of whether open or compact settlement is more conducive to the good life. This whole area deserves fuller treatment as part of a thorough analysis of values underlying the ideal environment. Because of the many direct consequences for physical planning, we must at least see what is implied by such goals.

Among the many forms that this argument takes is that between protagonists of apartment-house living and those who support a way of life based on the freestanding house. Even though provisions for gardening areas are often included in the higher-density apartment designs,[21] there is more awareness of and contact with nature in the freestanding house. The attached garden, particularly in several of the English Ideal Communities, becomes the *sine qua non* of decent living, providing private play space for children and outdoor sitting space for older persons. The opposing viewpoint attacks the meanness, the pettiness of the detached house existence and points to the very definite gains which come with denser settlement, including the interpersonal benefits of community living and the availability of a wider range of community facilities.

Some of the writers maintain that an alternative such as the garden city or garden suburb is to be preferred to city living; this was the contention of Howard (1898) and many of the writers who followed in his footsteps. Others hold that the intrusion of low-density housing between city and the "real" country minimizes the opportunities to utilize these rural areas. Pleasure-giving opportunities are reduced and removed further from clients, and scarce agricultural land is often wasted. This issue is sharply presented in the Corbusier (ASCORAL) proposal (1945). The problem was faced some thiry years ago by the planners in the Soviet Union, who started with decidedly different values. Their linear city was designed so as to underscore the political and social goals of an urban-rural synthesis, combining the virtues of both elements and creating a new, better society.[22]

[21] *See* Fritsch's design (1896), for example.
[22] On this subject, *see* Parkins (1953) and also a contemporary exposition of the Russian planner Miljutin's viewpoints (Kampffmeyer, 1932).

A third aspect of this question has received considerable attention over the years. On one hand, it has been maintained that low-density housing can give a fuller life to the individual family, through its use of the garden, the activities in a workshop, etc.[23] On the other hand, such a distribution of residences, when compared to densely settled urban areas, reduces the employment choices within a given distance open to the workers of the family. It also tends to reduce the number or increase the cost of community facilities, shops, and even the transportation routes which can be made conveniently and economically available to the families. The alternatives, as can be seen, reflect the different values the authors attach to home, consumption, production, and other spheres of contemporary society. Nevertheless, it is important to note that these values do not exist in isolation. Thus, the possibility for greater consumption may have profound effects on the ties between home and the family: the critic as well as the author must identify the predominant value.

There is some relation between the nationality of authors and the substance of the proposals dealing with questions of over-all compactness or openness. However, over the period under study, each region seems to show interest in the full range of possibilities. Thus, on the Continent (perhaps due to the heritage of medieval cities and early housing and planning developments related to Bismarckian Socialism) one tends to see the proposals for the highest densities. In England, the demands of what is perceived to be an acute land shortage conflict with the persistent interest on the part of reformers and planners to return the urban resident to his rightful place on the land. The typical English proposal is of the suburban, twelve dwellings to the acre variety, coupled with a statement that this plan, nevertheless, is sparing in its use of agricultural land. America, on one hand, has witnessed an emphasis on the open, almost agricultural and certainly car-oriented world of the Broadacre City variety, and on the other has seen writers stress the role of the skyscraper which suggests the dwelling as an element of mechanized construction. Among writings on this side of the Atlantic, Neutra's *Rush City Reformed* (1934) perhaps best of all exemplifies this last viewpoint.

CIRCULATION

Function of circulation layouts

A survey of Ideal Communities reveals extensive and long-term interest in matters of circulation. Considerable imagination has been applied to

[23] *See* Wright's Broadacre City writings (1945) for one lucid presentation of the desirability of low-density living.

problems of movement of goods and people. In one of the earliest works considered, Fritsch's *City of the Future* (1896), we find reference to two themes which have been incorporated in most plans submitted since then. The first is that, just as land use should be zoned, so should the characteristics of circulation ways reflect their use; the second is that routes have some functions which go beyond simply moving goods or people.

Circulation ways of different kinds are not alike in terms of safety and convenience, and there is variation in the type of route which most efficiently moves the specific goods or people it is designed to serve. Walkways and trafficways, it is uniformly held, must be kept apart, both en route as well as at intersections. This should be so not only on the grounds of safety but also because each serves a different clientele, has different construction needs, and should not be aligned along the same right of way. Both, in a sense, are thus liberated from each other to function better. In early schemes, there was a tendency to think in terms of two or even three levels vertically separated to serve pedestrians, cars, and freight-hauling vehicles. In more recent years, along the lines first explicitly suggested three decades ago by Stein (1951) but since then more generally accepted, the designs are more two dimensional, with an interlacing of the two systems.[24]

It is also generally acknowledged that a circulation way is more than a motion path. In some respects it joins what is on either side, as in the case of a shopping street with facing rows of commercial establishments. But, since an impediment to motion along the route would commonly occur in such cases, there is little favorable consideration given this treatment. Much more important is the contention that a highway or other circulation route serves to separate laterally while joining longitudinally. Most proposals implicitly show that a circulation way would serve to divide sideways in proportion to its linking function along its axis. In other words, there is a relation between the load a trafficway bears and its performance as a boundary. This would particularly apply to pedestrians in a vehicular world and is part and parcel of those proposals which have as their aim the separation of the city into distinct neighborhoods or other subareas. This proposition is quite reasonable, in that the more sizeable the area that is not served by a throughway, the larger and more important becomes the highway that does bypass it, and the greater its separating function would be. This is the acknowledged price (often counted as a virtue) of an area's liberation from interior traffic.

The two propositions (that circulation ways should be zoned and that they possess *raisons d'être* other than simple motion) are joined in one significant respect at the initial stage in the circulation hierarchy: the cul-de-sac. As

[24] The designs by Fritsch (1896) and Le Corbusier (1924) are in the first class. Herrey's plan (1944) is a good example of the more recent treatment of this problem.

Stein (1951) clearly pointed out, at this point, where the pedestrian becomes a driver the roadway serves once more as a unifying force.

Types of circulation layouts

The circulation layout of the Ideal Community is one of its most easily identifiable features. There is little doubt that the physical structure of the city, to no little extent, hinges on its circulation system. A rather limited number of network types have been proposed in the literature surveyed. In the following few pages we shall present these and draw some conclusions as to their relative merits and disadvantages. We shall also point to the relationship between the choice of circulation system and other elements of the plan.

Rectangular grid. The rectangular grid has been subjected to considerable attack, and few of the Ideal Communities show an inclination to use this simple form. The criticism is based largely on evidence culled from nineteenth-century America. There obviously had been a tendency to apply it rigidly with little regard either for natural features and orientation or for varying load demands. Some of the further shortcomings ascribed to the gridiron are lack of focus, essential planlessness, and dreariness. Critics further maintain that in use excessive subdivision results and, almost inevitably, a high proportion of land is devoted to the streets themselves.

The points to be made in favor of the rectangular grid can be summarized as follows: While such a system does result in longer distances between any two given points, a city is anything but a collection of random points. Rather, there exist a relatively small number of foci of high activity which need to be connected. If these do not already lie on a straightway of the grid, as is not unreasonable to expect, a major circulation facility may be designed to cut athwart the grid without too much damage. The rectangular pattern has the advantage of simplicity and clarity, particularly to strangers. Obvious aesthetic defects could be remedied while maintaining clarity, were the grid size to vary and were major axes to depart slightly from absolute rectilinearity. And if the rectangular grid has heretofore led to deficiently sized lots and too numerous intersections hampering traffic flow, there is no reason why fewer streets and superblocks should not set the pattern. Here, as elsewhere, it is important to isolate the crucial variables. Those elements alone which merit criticism should be abandoned; worthwhile features should be preserved.

Radial system. Where city structure is seen as concentric or sector-like, or as a combination of the two, the radial or spider-web system reflects the urban form—and vice versa. This system seems to permit the best internal interaccessibility, while at the same time, it can provide a way to bypass the core when necessary. Support is given the nodal points, although the schemes do not always show the same concern for ring roads.

Unfortunately, the design becomes unwieldy when more than one major focus exists or is planned. This system further lacks the flexibility of others if the focus of activity shifts or new centers arise. It can be constrictive of growth if linked to a ring distribution of land uses. When carried out on too small a scale, misshaped blocks and a confusing and congested traffic system are sure to result.

Hexagonal grid. The protagonists of a honeycombed or hexagonal grid assert that it is the safest and most efficient system for distributing people and goods. By reducing points of conflict at intersections, traffic can flow with greater ease and safety. The total length of linear-circulation factors in a given area is less than if other grid systems are used. The pattern seems well adapted to certain superblock designs and avoids the endless vistas so characteristic of the rectangular street scheme. Lastly, if planned on a larger scale, the hexagonal grid is ideally suited to link relatively coequal centers of a polynucleated city or points of strong attraction scattered more or less equally throughout a metropolitan area. When linked with a radial system, it is likewise suited as a framework for major circulation routes which seek to avoid more or less equally spaced developed portions of a metropolitan area.

If an urban area's circulation system were simply a series of links between many points of equal attraction, more or less equally spaced, then a hexagonal grid would indeed serve best. But strong foci do exist; with this in mind, certain shortcomings of the hexagonal grid become apparent. In time, either straight-line connecting roads are superimposed on the grid or a large proportion of the traffic must follow a route that is more circuitous than necessary. In the former case, one of the consequences would be oddly shaped blocks as well as intersections more complex than those rectangular ones that the design seeks to replace. Finally the hexagonal grid, because of the very neutrality of direction—a quality on which its protagonists seek to capitalize—can become confusing and lead to poor orientation.

Spine-and-rib layout. Spine-and-rib circulation systems are of two types. One provides the basis of the linear city, either the early or the more recent models. The other type is found in neighborhood or small-town designs where a major street surrounds the developed area and cul-de-sacs extend into the center. In this case, as well as in the linear city, all except strictly local traffic moves along the major spine (which is more or less straight in the first type, curved in the second). In such designs, the major roadway and other circulation routes can serve as boundaries, either between land uses or to distinguish one neighborhood or similar unit from another. The traffic function, too, can be clearly separated from other activities, with supposed gains in efficiency. Such a scheme can be designed to have fewer intersections and these to be relatively simple. The qualitative differences between the local streets and the spine road should contribute to good orientation, though this advantage would appear to apply more to the linear city.

The shortcomings of the spine-and-rib system center on the fact that this design puts all its eggs in one basket. Floods, accidents, or intentionally caused ruptures of the main circulation route during hostilities can disable the entire system. Congestion on the strategic main spine would have the same effect and is probably inevitable. At least, it is a contingency that not even a model of this type should ignore. A secondary problem associated with this circulation type has been discussed earlier: an unanticipated consequence may be an over-all increase in traffic, particularly if there are personal or public incentives to utilize the heavy investment in the major linear facility.[25]

On the neighborhood level, this circulation type may require substantially longer vehicular travel to connect any two points. This criticism may be countered by reference to pedestrian walkways, which are almost universally provided in such designs and which would serve to reduce much of the need for streets.

Loose circulation layout. A loose circulation pattern, generally organized with reference to topography or other features of the area (such as notable edifices), can often result in an appropriate design. Some of these proposals compared to other, more formal, schemes seem to show far better recognition of the aggregate movement needs of an area, particularly where the design also incorporates efforts at the separation of pedestrians from vehicular traffic.[26] A critique of these designs would stress that a loose form can become superficial, coy, meaningless in an area without significant topographic or other features. This particularly aggravates the second shortcoming which is frequently noted, that the very absence of pattern is a source of confusion. It is appropriate only when carried out in conjunction with a site plan which can easily be grasped and which provides for foci of activity or other elements of orientation.

[25] It may not be implausible to suggest that such an efficient transportation scheme could actually serve to stimulate movement among residents. This might well occur, particularly in the almost "company town" ethos of the Corbusier (ASCORAL) linear-city town unit (1945). The results may bring aggregate movement in excess of planners' estimates and may point out inherent limitations to concepts stressing spatial separation of constituent town units.

[26] These designs avoid, of course, many of the pitfalls facing those who are attracted by rigid, geometric schemes in the hope of creating a logical and simple environment.

Blending of circulation types. Few of the Ideal Communities hold to only one kind of circulation system. They generally show recognition of the need to use more than one approach to resolve complex urban problems. Thus, the interior arrangements of the large hexagonal blocks of Humbert's city (1944) resemble the cul-de-sacs of some spine-and-rib systems. To take another example, in Sanders and Rabuck's scheme (1946) the gridiron is the organizing principle at an intermediate scale within the residential sectors, while the metropolitan circulation system is a radial system. In this way, it is possible for an author to avoid some of the characteristic pitfalls inherent in any one particular design, while recognizing the different needs and problems of circulation at various scales.

Characteristics of circulation systems

Analysis of specific forms of circulation systems is only one of several ways of regarding movement within the Ideal Community. Perhaps the most basic of these is the degree to which the successful operation of the planned area depends on use of circulation facilities. One extreme may be set by a proposal such as the New Commune by the Goodmans (1947). Here the satisfactory, day-to-day existence is led within most circumscribed geographical bounds, almost without recourse to any vehicular transportation whatsoever. This is quite in contrast with Garnier's Cité Industrielle (1918), which requires considerable reliance on transportation in the conduct of most of the average citizen's activities.[27]

Another approach to the problem of circulation focuses on the identification of the clients for transportation services. The citizen in the Soviet linear-city proposal (Parkins, 1953), and to a still greater degree in the Corbusier (ASCORAL) linear city (1945), would exist in an essentially pedestrian world. The impressive circulation ways which provide the physical backbone and the conceptual rationale of the design are intended to serve movement of industrial raw materials and goods. The scheme envisages only occasional use of the transportation network by the average citizen.

Generally the neighborhood world is a pedestrian world. This is borne out by the frequent references to the "human scale," to walking radii, and to the benefits of walkways protected from traffic, in a green, parklike setting. At most, the neighborhood is visualized as a traffic terminus. The spirit of this existence is described lucidly, and with considerable force, in Stein's writings (1951). Many other writers echo his thoughts, with the possible exception of the commercial Valhalla that is Ferriss's Metropolis (1929).

---

[27] This is the consequence of designing purely residential, industrial, and other unmixed sections.

Proposals differ to the degree that vehicular incursions are permitted into the residential areas. One form this exclusiveness can take is the expulsion of vehicles from daily life. Such is the situation in the relatively sparse New Commune which the Goodmans (1947) have presented as their second paradigm. Or, if the residential area is composed of giant buildings, vehicles can similarly be held to be eliminated from neighborhood life. This is the picture in the inner precincts of the Cité Contemporaine designed by Le Corbusier (1924). A more usual ideal scheme strictly limits the vehicles to the periphery, which is consistent with the hypothesis that the neighborhood boundary road serves as a dividing force. Several such proposals show cul-de-sacs as terminal elements of the street network. Earlier schemes resolved the problem by varying internal street widths, designing circulation discontinuities, and otherwise discouraging traffic flow in residential areas. Perry (1929) shows considerable creativity in this respect. Especially in the first decades of this century, when cars were seen as less of a menace, street access was a *sine qua non* of the ideal home, and, if anything, a surfeit was provided.[28] Although written after others became aware of the problems accompanying widespread car ownership, Wright's scheme also relies heavily on automobiles and access.

It is at the next level, that of the town, that reliance on vehicular motion truly becomes an issue. In contrast to those Ideal Communities that see each subarea as a microcosm, those which are composed of specialized units or low-density proposals must pay for the greater specialization or space in one way or another. Low densities, generally, extract their toll in the form of greater reliance on use of vehicles.[29]

From the earliest models to the present there is recognition of the danger, inconvenience, and unpleasant effects brought on by certain types of traffic. Fritsch's (1896) concern in this respect led to his recommendation that freight traffic be confined to a subterranean street network. More recent writers tend to urge the separation of traffic in terms of its general destination and its effect on the areas through which it passes, in a manner not unlike the zoning concept of performance standards.[30] We see in most Ideal Com-

[28] We note a similar situation in the first linear cities, including transit-bound Roadtown (Chambless, 1910) where this is carried to excess. *See also* the several ideal designs shown in Triggs's summary of contemporary planning precepts (1909), such as the proposals by Müller and Lamb, early examples of the hexagonal grid. This grid has the virtue, they maintained, of promoting interaccessibility and of opening up tightly knit residential areas to traffic.

[29] A tight over-all pattern may reduce distances somewhat. However, let it be noted the result is a loss of open space. Compare Gloeden's (1923) thin greenbelts with Howard's (1898) ample ones.

[30] The earlier approach might be considered as a parallel to land-use zoning of the more conventional variety.

munities the general suggestion that categories of circulation ways be established, each with its design standards, characteristic flow pattern, and impact on abutting uses. There usually are pedestrian walkways, cul-de-sacs, local streets, major streets, and limited-access highways. Many other gradations are suggested in individual proposals, but some such hierarchy is involved in each of the more recent proposals.

Transit

One aspect of the circulation question which has received inadequate consideration in Ideal Community proposals is the relative importance assigned to public transportation compared to private vehicular traffic. Although most schemes have in mind a reduction of travel, particularly of commuting, and while a number express the hope that transit can better handle the reduced load, only a few Ideal Communities show an explicit concern for public transportation. Among those that do are Comey's Regional City (1923), the early linear-city schemes, and Le Corbusier's Cité Contemporaine (1924). Probably the more recent Ideal Communities fail to elaborate transit proposals because, today, no permanent fixed facilities need be installed. In all but the largest cities transit can be considered part of the expressway system. Furthermore, some of the authors show a commitment to the freedom and flexibility which the automobile provides. Wright (1945) and other American writers, some of whose proposals show a measure of fatalism in this regard, have authored Ideal Communities relying exclusively on highway-borne traffic.

Scale of circulation and form

The problem of scale is closely related to that of circulation. Will the citizen find the community's facilities and his workplace within walking distance, or must he rely on vehicles to reach them?

In those proposals which incorporate or show any awareness of the ideal of the neighborhood unit, permitting life at the walking scale is the major design criterion. This is also referred to as the "human scale" and often is couched in moralistic or ethical terms, as in the Goodmans' New Commune (1947), the Corbusier (ASCORAL) linear city (1945), and Herrey's neighborhood proposal (1944). While the elementary school, some shops, some facilities for recreation and access to the outer world are always included within the area encompassed by the walking radii, some writers feel other urban functions are more appropriately reached by vehicle. Thus, Herrey's scheme makes no provision for work in his pedestrian world, while the

Corbusier (ASCORAL) linear city emphasizes that its factories are within walking, or at most cycling, distance. And the New Commune seeks to offer the full life within a stone's throw, with periodic moves of residence as a source of stimulation and variety. As with many other proposals, the issue of maximum choice arises here. It is obvious that this cannot be attained within the area described by the walking radius. A similar disagreement exists among writers when thinking in terms of higher schools, shopping centers, administrative and cultural facilities, etc. The small town can, conceivably, provide these without recourse to car or transit. As Klein's New Town proposal (1947) shows, the size of the city may be tied precisely to this criterion. The polynucleated city may be so conceived as to offer within the confines of each satellite or unit all but the most specialized of activities, services, or facilities. When this consideration is linked to a pattern made neatly hierarchical (as in the case of Sert's design, 1944), the various modes of movement, the provision and distribution of such facilities, and the form and structure of the city all become closely interrelated. It is worthwhile to note that in those schemes where there is the least differentiation of circulation modes, there is also relatively little formal structural theory of the city concerning fixed neighborhoods or any other physical hierarchy. In such schemes, few formal principles are offered to guide the physical distribution of services or points of activity. The two schemes where this is particularly evident are, of course, Wright's totally automotive Broadacre City (1945) and the Goodmans' almost exclusively walking Commune (1947).

Scale enters as another consideration. At what level does the planner seek to impose a relatively regular or easily comprehensible pattern such as the gridiron or the radial street system? No one answer emerges from the Ideal Community literature though, almost without exception, one notes a proposal for one or another such pattern. Some writers feel that such form-giving circulation schemes are most appropriate at the regional or metropolitan level, with little attention paid to the character or shape of internal street networks. Others hold that the pattern is most appropriate at such levels as it defines and borders neighborhoods but not within the units. And still others would bring the formal design to the most intimate street scale. One can generalize that the earlier writers tended to be specific with regard to internal circulation systems. Examples can be found in Triggs's work (1909), Cauchon's (1927) and Kern's (1924) schemes. More recent writers think in terms of organizing principles at the metropolitan or even larger scale; this is exemplified in the proposals of N. Wiener (1950), Le Corbusier (ASCORAL) (1945), and the Goodmans (1947). A final group does not concern itself with a specific pattern of a geometric nature but applies certain propositions to circulation ways at the neighborhood, other subcity, or city level. Among these we find the works of Wolfe (1945) and Herrey

(1944). In this connection, it is important to note that the desirability of one or another pattern is not the same at all scales. The typical difficulties ascribed to the radial system in a small town may well disappear or be replaced by other problems when circulation is so organized on the regional or metropolitan level. The same may be said for most of the patterns. To be sure, this should cause no wonder, considering the various purposes that circulation ways and systems serve at the different levels of the urban environment.

POPULATION AND DENSITY

It is not surprising to find a high degree of interdependence between recommendations for optimum levels of population and suggested density standards. The population problem is usually presented as the quest for an ideal total population for a given city or metropolis or its subparts. Density standards are expressed either as so many people or so many households per given unit of land. When the design, due to other considerations, calls for a fixed land area devoted to residential uses, then, obviously, the density and total population become rigidly linked. In Ideal Communities, one of these two considerations is often presented simply as the dependent variable of the other. Even when this is not the case, it is recognized that demands of internal consistency require that close attention be paid to the effect of population and density considerations on each other.

Ideal Communities uniformly show that population size and levels of density are crucial elements of the physical environment. These two considerations, furthermore, are declared to have significant impact on the achievement of major aspects of the good life. This follows from the writers' environmental determinism. However, critics ought to pay greater attention to less obvious links which implicitly tie an author's assumptions and values to his urban ideal and the consequent population and density standards he selects and recommends.

Control of size

Ideal Communities reveal a belief that density and population size are proper subjects for planning predetermination and control. The typical scheme offers an appropriate population size for each hierarchical element in the total structure.[31] While control of population is an important element of almost all schemes, there is hardly the same unanimity when the size of

[31] Where a geographical restriction in size is also suggested, it is generally presented in terms of local walking-distance limits. The distribution of commercial, community, and transportation facilities at the local or neighborhood level may be fixed with this criterion as the crucial determinant.

the entire city or metropolitan area is at stake. Some of the designs, such as Le Corbusier's Cité Contemporaine (1924) and the Goodmans' Communitas proposals (1947), suggest that control of size is feasible at all levels. An opposing viewpoint is found in Howard's Garden City (1898), Comey's Regional City (1923), Neutra's Rush City (1934), and the more sophisticated linear-city models. While maintaining the validity of size controls at the neighborhood or community levels, these proposals find an over-all limit on population both inappropriate and impossible to accomplish. So we see Howard most anxious to limit the Garden City to 32,000 inhabitants, yet specifically recognizing England's over-all trend toward urbanization. The individual Garden City plan has its complement in the concept of Social Cities and the suggestion that neighboring garden cities be established. Similarly, those writers who identify themselves most strongly with concepts designed for growth, such as the ASCORAL group and other modern linearists, urge the adoption of a neighborhood pattern as the basis for the city. Although neighborhoods can be added indefinitely, each is to have a definite size limitation.

These conflicting views of the Ideal Community arise from considering the ideal either as a static or as a dynamic condition. They also reflect rather fundamental differences as to the role of planning and ideal-making. The first group of authors maintains that over-all controls are feasible and an essential part of the planning process. They further hold that ideal-making itself necessitates the anticipation of a fixed final size. Le Corbusier's Cité Contemporaine (1924) and Klein's scheme for an Israeli city (1947) are two of several works which state this quite explicitly. This viewpoint finds added support among a whole succession of English planners who maintain that unlimited growth, if not the cause of the ills plaguing modern urban life, is certainly one of its worst symptoms. The writers on the other side of this issue believe that there is virtue in designs permitting flexibility of arrangements and growth.[32] A similar approach holds that the Ideal Community, like any other plan, must incorporate dynamic elements as a necessary concession to inexorable urbanization or population pressures. Justement (1946) is one of many writers who would fall in this category. The argument favoring a dynamic approach is upheld by the sorry experience of attempts at over-all control, even under the most authoritarian of regimes. It also is consistent with the few technical studies that exist in this area, which disclose that there is no evidence that would point to an over-all ideal city size.[33]

[32] Interestingly, no proposal has come to light that speaks of the possibility of contraction, of planning for an eventual decrease in the size of the metropolis.

[33] See, for example, the articles by Chapin (1950), Duncan (1951), and Lillibridge (1952) and references cited therein.

Another weak support underlies the concept of controlled size. The justification for instituting ceilings is generally based on a rather restricted understanding of one or more phenomena, such as the service radius of one elementary school, the limits posed by the face-to-face acquaintance group, or the appropriate size of a town-meeting type of political action community. In the case of Perry's Neighborhood Unit (1929), there is an attempt to combine a large number of such factors. But Perry's essay points precisely to one of the limitations of the approach: when he seeks to determine the ideal, he relies on evidence culled from several unrelated residential areas which typify today's unreconstructed society. In a similar way, most of the other works, with the notable exceptions of the Goodmans' Communitas proposals (1947), lean heavily on such specific justifications from selected evidence. This procedure often gives the rational, normative aspects of the proposals a *post hoc* flavor and, at best, suggests the plausibility of the scheme. It does not provide the firm, conclusive evidence the authors seek to establish.

So far, we have only dealt with the authors' explicit intentions. But, here as elsewhere, the best-laid plans may have serious imperfections and give rise to unanticipated consequences. In execution, anything but the author's intention might be served. Thus, the Goodmans' City of Efficient Consumption, if the contemporary urban world has anything to teach us, would hardly fail to draw to itself a growing consuming population. However, it is unlikely that the design could accommodate these added numbers. This can also be said of the proposals presented by Sanders and Rabuck (1946) and Adams (1934). In general, linear, sector, and polynucleated proposals are more consistent with possibility of growth, while essentially ring patterns are better suited to a stable situation.

The optimum population

The optimum population per unit is derived by means of a number of approaches. It is no wonder that such a range of conclusions is reached.[34] We may summarize these approaches as follows:

1. Perhaps the most frequently used basis for determining population size of the Ideal Community is the economic level of operation of facilities and services. Reference is often made to the efficient working of the educational plant, particularly the elementary school. Note how Perry's work (1929)

[34] It should be noted that population and density standards refer to what is generally known as "nighttime" or residential population. Rare is the work (Le Corbusier's *Cité Contemporaine,* 1924, is one of few) which calculates the working or daytime population and density levels. Furthermore, data are generally given only in terms of people, not in terms of households or families. This is an area where a more sophisticated approach would prove fruitful.

hinges on the work of George D. Strayer and N. L. Engelhardt, school consultants. (*See* Appendix to Perry's Regional Plan proposal.) At a larger scale, the critical factor frequently is the reputed ability of a city of a certain size to support a variety of cultural and recreational institutions. Considerable effort is directed to the design of more efficient arrangements of facilities. However, often relatively superficial considerations can substantially change the conclusion (*see* Table 3).

The schemes are often quite liberal in their intention to serve a larger part of the population with a greater number of facilities. Nevertheless, there is not too much imagination shown in this matter. The society and environment that are envisaged are, on the whole, not visions of a new world. Rather, they seek to invest the existing order with a more equitable and efficient range of services and facilities. Wright (1945), with a car (and then some) in every garage, and Herrey (1944), with the P.T.A. on every superblock, fall in this category. The Goodman brothers' approach (1947) is relatively unique. Their Ideal Communities seek to satisfy basic human needs. The facilities they propose and population levels following from these vary in accordance with the needs under consideration.

2. A second approach to the determination of Ideal Community size stresses the need to establish a population range which can support or attract sufficient employment possibilities and variety of jobs. Then, generally, the smallest size which meets this requirement is selected.[35] Such is Osborn's way (1946). As does the preceding method, this rests on observation of the way in which existing cities function. Often the research referred to is of a high order, as in the P.E.P. report of the distribution of industry in England (1939). But at other times, the author rests his case on an unsophisticated selection of examples which are not rigorously limiting or on studies which are not reported in any detail. It is not so much the danger of "wrong" answers which should cause reflection and caution in the use of such schemes. It is the doubtful validity of binding one's conclusions as to the ideal state upon current or historical data and conditions.

3. Another method employed in setting the optimum population of an area is one that has a social basis. This generally has been confined to use at the neighborhood or small-town level. Certain criteria are established, such as the limits of face-to-face acquaintanceship (Wolfe, 1945) or the size of the group capable of acting together politically (this platonic ideal is reflected, for example, in Gropius and Wagner's New England New Town, 1943). The underlying notion is that people are happier and their lives

[35] It should be pointed out that the decision to select the smallest appropriate population grouping in itself reflects a value judgment regarding the relative merits of small or large urban units.

Table 3. Interrelation of Physical Planning Factors

The sketches below link, in a simplified manner, street pattern and school district radius. Depending on the way these are interpreted, neighborhoods of different size and form will arise.

Given that an Ideal Community scheme specifies a maximum walking distance of one-half mile to a school located at the center of the neighborhood, at least three models may be considered:

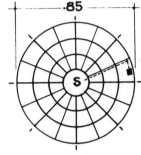

1. RADIAL STREET OR WALKING SYSTEM. No house on the periphery is to be more than one-half mile walking distance from school at the center. *Gross Unit area:* 0.55 square mile.

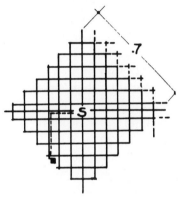

2. GRIDIRON WITH DIAGONAL ROAD SYSTEM. All houses on the periphery and one-half mile walking distance from school at center of the Unit. *Gross Unit area:* 0.5 square mile.

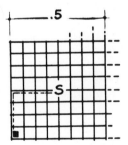

3. GRIDIRON AS USUALLY PRESENTED. Walking distance to school from the most remote house is one-half mile; other structures on the periphery are closer to the school at the center. *Gross Unit area:* 0.25 square miles.

With a fixed neighborhood density of (say) 25 people per acre, system 1 could accommodate about 9,000 people; system 2: 8,000; and system 3: 4,000. System 1 obviously runs into difficulties where units abut on each other (as in a city). System 3 would seem to be wasteful in the sense that neighboring districts overlap. System 2, although not depicted in the literature studied, would appear to be the best schematic representation.

[141]

more convenient when effective group life prevails, where control of group destinies exists, and where participants are conscious of their mutual interrelationships. It is also expected that, under such circumstances, individuals' contributions to society will be greater, both on a folkcraft, creative level and in productive efficiency. We note again the assumption that manipulation of the physical environment has consequences on the quality and efficiency of the personal and social milieu.

Two further approaches even less rigorous than the above deserve mention.

4. Optimum population is sometimes offered as the dependent variable, with density and geographical area as the independent variables. Thus, the population size may be based on considerations of dwelling unit or building size, the notion of a limited radius for the neighborhood in order to establish a walking distance to an elementary school, estimates of family size, and so forth. It should be emphasized that the resulting population figure obviously must meet the author's tacit approval. Therefore, it is at least implicitly weighed by him for plausibility and desirability.

5. Finally, there may be, as in Howard's Garden City (1898) and several more recent works, simply the assertion that a particular size is plausible and therefore adequate to develop the author's scheme. This may involve the selection of an existing city as the basis for comparison, with the Ideal Community then being designed to that size. Thus, Le Corbusier's Cité Contemporaine (1924), like Paris, has 3 million inhabitants. The City of Efficient Consumption (Goodman and Goodman, 1947) was designed, for obvious reasons, with New York's population in mind. Perry's Neighborhood Unit (1929) relied on confirming evidence provided by the success of certain residential developments. Handling the problem in this manner is consonant with the skills and inclination of the urban planner and his ability to reconcile a variety of considerations.

Density

Considerations of density in many ways reflect the thoughts on intensity of development (page 127, above). More specifically, such standards may be calculated from a study of housing types, as in Perry's formulation of the Neighborhood Unit (1929), as well as from a general view of the good life as a balance between urban and rural components. Density, as in the case of Gropius's new town (1945), is sometimes derived from already calculated area and population estimates.

The over-all pattern of densities receives considerable attention. Maintenance of uniform housing over a considerable area, as one view, is opposed by the wish to provide for a variety of dwelling types within each area.

Adams's (1934) design for a city largely composed of one-family homes may be cited as an example of the first approach, while the Goodmans' New Commune (1947) is perhaps the extreme solution in the second direction. Sanders and Rabuck (1946), on grounds of democratic heterogeneity, plan a mixture of densities throughout residential areas. There have been architectural designs for the Ideal Community which seek to enhance and communicate the central importance of one or another crucial institution by proposing a peaking of densities near this focus. Taut's city plans (1919) have this form and so do Ferriss's (1929), although with a less explicit mystique. To be sure, these density considerations are aesthetic in part only; they also contain significant connotations of a social, political, and economic nature.

Population and the total Ideal Community

Not only is there considerable variation in the methods used to reach density standards and optimum population levels; the conclusions show a wide range of ideal environments so far as these criteria are concerned. For Ideal Communities analyzed in Chapter III, the suggested range in standards is shown in Table 4. Note that writers whose visions of the ideal environment resemble each other suggest dissimilar standards. Conversely, there are proposals which urge the adoption of identical density and population levels, offered under the impression that each represents a view of the most individualistic or unusual style of life.

Urban forms proposed by means of Ideal Communities vary in the population range appropriate to them. The neighborhood proposals are limited to about ten thousand inhabitants. Polynucleated proposals tend to refer to agglomerations of several hundred thousand people upwards. Otherwise, it can be said that each of the basic forms has been found adaptable to a full range of population magnitudes. Linear cities run the gamut from the few thousand residents of the Madrid project of Soria y Mata (1882) to the several million possible in the more recent schemes. Ring-city designs have been prepared which would serve the needs of as few as 30,000 inhabitants (Howard's Garden City, 1898); but this is also the form selected to house the activities of the 6 million consumption-oriented inhabitants of the Goodmans' (1947) first paradigm.

LIFE STYLE

We have made repeated references to the Ideal Communities' "life style." This over-all environmental quality, whether explicitly or only implicitly

*Table 4. Population and Density Standards.**

Date	Author, title, subarea	Density per gross residential acre	Optimum population
1934	T. Adams		
	Design for Residential Areas		
	Residential Section	5–6 d.u.	1,000 families
1910	E. Chambless		
	Roadtown	20 d.u.	n.a.†
1923	A. Comey		
	Regional Planning Theory		
	"Sixth Class Size City"	±4 d.u.‡	10,000–30,000
1924	Le Corbusier		
	Urbanisme		3,000,000
	City	125 people	600,000
	Garden Cities	n.a.	2,400,000
1945	Le Corbusier—ASCORAL		
	Les Trois Établissements Humains		
	Linear Town		10,000–20,000
	High Density	±40 d.u.	
	Low Density	±10 d.u.	
1929	H. Ferriss		
	Metropolis of Tomorrow	±50 d.u.	n.a.
1896	T. Fritsch		
	Stadt der Zukunft		Several hundred thousand
	Inner ring ⎫ range	⎰ 4–10 d.u.	
	Outer ring ⎭	⎱ 30–46 d.u.	
1923	E. Gloeden		
	Inflation der Gross-Städte		100,000
	Inner ring	50 d.u	±80,000
	Outer ring	10 d.u.	±20,000
1947	P. Goodman and P. Goodman		
	Communitas		
	City of Efficient Consumption	100 d.u.	6,000,000–8,000,000
	New Commune		300,000
	Urban node	±75 d.u.	100,000
	Urban belt	¼ d.u.	100,000
	Semirural belt	¼ d.u.	100,000
	Production Center	n.a.	n.a.
1945	W. Gropius and M. Wagner		
	A Program for City Reconstruction		
	Small unit	10 d.u.	5,000
	Large unit	4 d.u.	5,000

Table 4 (cont.)

Date	Author, title, subarea	Density per gross residential acre	Optimum population
1944	H. Herrey, *et al.* Organic Theory Residential Unit	3–12 d.u.	500–2,000 families
1898	E. Howard Garden Cities	8–10 d.u.	32,000
1946	L. Justement New Cities for Old Inner ring Middle ring Outer ring	 ±35 d.u. 10 d.u. 2–3 d.u.	1,000,000+
1947	A. Klein Man and Town	25 d.u.	50,000–100,000
1934	R. Neutra Rush City Reformed (4 types of residential areas)	100, 15, 6, 3 d.u.	220,000 adults
1929	C. Perry Neighborhood Unit	5 d.u.	5,000–9,000
1946	S. Sanders and A. Rabuck New City Patterns Neighborhoods	5–60 d.u.	3,000–10,000
1944	J. L. Sert Human Scale in City Planning Residential Units	3–5 d.u.	5,000–10,000
1945	L. Wolfe The Reilly Plan Reilly Unit	10 d.u.	30–60 d.u.
1932	F. L. Wright Broadacre City	½–1 d.u.	n.a.

* Population is given in number of inhabitants, unless otherwise specified. Density is given in number of dwelling units per gross acre.

† n.a.: information not available.

‡ ±· approximately.

stated, is the goal to which the physical planning elements are instrumental. Without a keen appreciation of the life style, the actual form, circulation, and population considerations can hardly be analyzed. For, with different goals a given physical planning proposition need not have the same meaning or implications.

There are many possible ways of looking at the life style. One of the ways of organizing Ideal Communities in terms of their over-all context is shown in Table 5. Here we note the degree of urbanity as one variable. The other is what may be called the dimension of individualism, that is, the degree to which the entire model serves individual as opposed to group ends. Note what a variety of physical patterns fall in each cell.

Another way that is open to us is to look at Ideal Communities in terms of the size of the crucial or characteristic unit. Will the individual resident's identification be with a large urban mass, or would he be likely, if one reads the plan correctly, to consider himself predominantly part of a much smaller geographic aggregate? Ferriss's Metropolis (1929), Le Corbusier's Cité Contemporaine (1924), and the Goodmans' City of Efficient Consumption (1947) all emphasize a large scale of prime spatial and social organization. Turning to the Goodmans again, but this time to their proposal for a New Commune, and to the small "greens" of a few dozen houses envisaged in the Reilly Plan (Wolfe, 1945), we note an approach which anticipates that the individual's ties and identification will focus on a much more intimate spatial level. One finds several intermediate positions along this continuum, as well as proposals which mix these scales of emphasis.

Table 5.   Types of Ideal Communities

Dimension of urbanity in the environment	Degree of individualism stressed by the life style			
	Competition	Interaction	Cooperation	Direction
Rural	Wright	Fawcett	Chambless Wolfe	
Suburban or semiurban	Hilberseimer→ Adams→ Gropius and Wagner→ Justement↓ Comey↓	Perry Herrey Sert ←Osborn ←Howard↓		Köhler Miljutin↓
Urban	Goodman I Le Corbusier Sanders and Rabuck Ferriss Fritsch	Klein Neutra→	Goodman II	Goodman III↑

* The names of writers in the boxes refer to authors of Ideal Communities. Arrows show tendencies of a secondary nature.

The authors of Ideal Communities often have in mind an environment which is a purer, more organized version of an existing urban species or one that prevailed in the past. The reader of the ideal schemes, therefore, would do well to identify and understand these archetypes. Their fundamental differences in part account for the variety of forms and other physical planning recommendations found in Ideal Communities. As an example, let us take a group of writers, predominantly English, and see what prototype helps to structure their thoughts. With varying degrees of explicitness they seek to re-establish the semi-isolated, but close-knit, preindustrial small-town or village life. This seems associated with an existence far less weighted with problems and bitterness than is today's, even if it was not as rich or at times as creative. It is as if the Ideal Community were the answer to Blake's call not to rest "till we have built Jerusalem on England's green and pleasant land." In direct contrast is the marked idealization of New York: the city which Walt Whitman and countless others have seen, with its "numberless crowded streets, high growth of iron, slender, strong, light, splendidly up-rising toward clear skies. . . . a million people—manners free and superb—open voices. . . ." Between these two ideals lie others, for Wolfe and Ferriss or Howard and Le Corbusier only suggest the extremes. Some of the internal inconsistencies evident in Ideal Communities indeed stem from ill-starred attempts to incorporate virtues of more than one such ideal. This may take the form of an on-the-spot amalgam; such is the essentially nonurban neighborhood, whatever its density and whether located in city or suburb. Or it may be attempted in a design which seeks to accommodate two such ideals in different sections of the Ideal Community. It would seem that this type of dichotomy provided the basis for Communist enthusiasm for the linear city as a synthesis leading to a new, fuller, and more productive urban-rural life.[36]

The quality of urban living which the Ideal Community seeks to promote may also have a nonurban basis. Thus, the essential, worthwhile, and timeless aspects of the city have on occasion been characterized as the village —and even as the congregation, family, or other primary group—writ large. The picture of such an urban environment will naturally stress local autonomy in civic affairs. To a large extent, most of the activities in which residents participate will be limited to the geographic bounds of an area, and, often, one notes a tendency to do without some of the artifacts of modern technology. The plan for communal facilities does not place much emphasis on the exchange of services, little commuting is envisaged, and there is a rejection of the automobile, at least for the life in the neighborhood.

Among the writings we have reviewed, we can find just the opposite

[36] For further insights to this direction taken by Soviet planners, *see* Kampffmeyer (1932), Blumenfeld (1942), and Parkins (1953).

image. This is one best exemplified by the factory. In such works, we see an emphasis on exchange, enlargement of horizons, efficiency. This would clearly give rise to a planning basis which is sharply in contrast to the one previously described.

One finds repeated references to the *organic* nature of the city. This implies a certain way of looking at urban areas and thus deserves some comment. Organic, more specifically, is used as an adjective to characterize one ideal scheme in contrast to another, less desirable one. It is a value-laden word, which also has considerable bearing on the physical plans of Ideal Communities. Several meanings, not all entirely consistent with each other, can be discerned.

Organic, first, is a rather loose adjective implying that a particular scheme resembles some natural phenomenon or body. Specifically, this use of the word may refer to certain striking similarities disclosed by means of microphotography. Structures and processes of amoebae, cells, hair cross sections, or ferns and other plants are found to resemble some aspects of the urban pattern. Further analogies are drawn from botany or natural geography, from flowers, trees, or air views of river systems, to explain, justify, or analyze the city scene or some of its particular features such as the traffic system. Thus, the medieval street plan and town layout strike certain writers as of a higher order and worthy of imitation, because, by contrast to the unmitigated rectangular street grid, the former are more *organic*. Hilberseimer (1944) and Saarinen (1943) are among the many writers who use the term in this connection.

The word *organic* has also been used to describe a system which shows a process of growth whereby a desirable end results over a relatively extended period in consequence of a large number of discrete individual choices. These decisions and the actions which follow from them are essentially planless. There is no subjective recognition of an explicitly stated goal. The example from nature might be the balance of a forest at any one time. Tunnard (1953) and, again, Saarinen are among those who use *organic* with this meaning. This is a viewpoint which, in a sense, is critical of certain types of intervention in the natural course of events. As such, *organic* city building can be (though it is not necessarily so) profoundly antiplanning. That this need not be, one has only to return to the forest analogy. The balance that is the desideratum can be and often is affected and enhanced by a number of agents. The possibility of wise conscious management should not be excluded.

A third element of the *organic* concept stresses interrelationships. Thus, Fritsch (1896) uses the term to describe a system whose constituent parts are mutually consistent and are, according to certain stated criteria, in balance. *Organic* growth is a process marked by parallel development of components. As such, it is a contrast to the haphazard accretion or expansion of one or a few elements to the exclusion and detriment of others. For example, population increase to qualify as an instance of *organic* growth, as used in this sense, must be accompanied by provisions for schools and other facilities, housing, employment, and so forth.

The general content of the word *organic* then, points to a view of the desirable urban environment as a phenomenon arising from, or at least reflecting, the natural world. It has connotations of flexibility, naturalness, humanness and is used to contrast a proposal with another that is deemed to be rigid and mechanistic. Yet it must be said that the parallels to biology are poorly drawn or exaggerated, where they are not totally irrelevant. The literature fails to establish why an organic concept is, per se, more deserving of support than one that is not. It seems that, all too often, the view of the city in terms of an organic analogy boils down to an attempt to muster support for a particular concept by means of a value-laden word and image.

Can any general statement be made regarding life style or basic social environment? The only conclusion to be drawn from the study of Ideal Communities is that the form is a relatively neutral consideration and does not play too central a role. This is not to say that at times even vitriolic arguments have not raged around the question of the unique appropriateness of a particular form to a particular society. The pros and cons of linear or concentrated urban development, which were considered during the interwar years in the Soviet Union, or the unequivocal defense of the English way of life by means of Garden Cities are only two of several such disputes. For that matter, individual writers have maintained with utmost gravity and emphasis that only their approach was consistent with one or another way of life—Wright's defense of Broadacre City, as in *When Democracy Builds* (1945), comes to mind here. Yet, with more than half a century's perspective we can see that each of the urban forms suggested has at one time or another been found appropriate to a variety of life styles and economies and political structures. The linear city, for example, has had its communist adherents, who thought it would both maximize home-work integration and facilitate a much sought urban-rural synthesis. It has also found support in the most conservative circles, however, since this basic form could let each "city" dweller be of the rural gentry. It has flourished among the technologically oriented: witness the Corbusier (ASCORAL) machine town (1945) for efficient production and transport, set in salubrious surroundings. But it was also selected as an appropriate form for Chambless's Roadtown (1910), that quite reactionary withdrawal from the complex twentieth century with its vexing issues. A similar range of adherents could be found for the other

[149]

basic city forms as well as for the concept of the Neighborhood Unit within the city.[37]

[37] It has been suggested that certain fundamental relations do exist between urban form and society viewed in most general terms. For example, Blumenfeld (1943, 1949) has written that, on the basis of historical evidence, he finds all city plans fall into two categories: the rectangular and the radial. The rectangular, with its stress on easy lotification and unlimited growth, has been associated with a life style characterized by social plurality. The radial form has always been grounded on a static, centralized, and unified concept such as defense. However, both of these, as Blumenfeld himself has pointed out, have been adapted to a wide range of urban situations. Furthermore, the city of today and tomorrow, he implies, must incorporate both elements.

V

Summary Considerations

HAVING ANALYZED a number of Ideal Communities, a general evaluation of the subject is in order. We shall first consider the significance of some rather large areas of consensus which were observed in the review. What do these say about the way these planners, and others, look at the urban environment? Next, what is the value of Ideal Communities as a tool, and where do these models suggest planners should direct their attention in the future? Recognizing that Ideal Communities, as political and methodological constructs, are far from perfect, any evaluation must pay attention to their shortcomings. And, finally, this work will conclude with some thoughts as to what an Ideal Community should be. In other words, some of the criteria by which Ideal Communities have been judged in this essay will be made more explicit, and some suggestions will be offered to those sufficiently intrepid to take upon themselves the task of designing an Ideal Community.

AREAS OF CONSENSUS

Knowing an area of agreement is clearly not the same as knowing what is correct. It is not even necessarily the basis for developing principles or hypotheses, for consensus may exist in the domain of value statements which are not susceptible to further development. The selective nature of the group of works which comprise the Ideal Community proposals may bias the conclusion and suggest consensus where familiarity with other types of sources would show strong disagreements. It may well be that the very nature of the concept of the Ideal Community is such that certain propositions are inherently bound to arise, that one has to search for another approach to find divergent viewpoints. For instance, Ideal Communities as defined carry a built-in bias which favors describing and analyzing the city in terms of land-use considerations.

Looking at this problem from a different perspective, it may be suggested that in a given context it is precisely the exception which may make the

[151]

most significant contribution. For example, there is well-nigh uniform acceptance of the desirability of a plan based on functional separation of the parts of a city, with specific areas assigned to work, recreation, trade, etc. This is true save for the case of the Goodmans' second design, the New Commune (1947), which stresses the reintegration of the family and its members into the full range of urban activities. This scheme suggests that what is normally regarded as an absolute, a given, need not be so fixed when the values themselves are subject to analysis.

A general agreement may also reflect other factors, such as what is fashionable or salable at any one time. One needs only reflect on the tendency of both city plans and Ideal Communities prepared at the turn of the century to focus on majestic parks or monuments. Consensus may point to areas of shared ignorance, such as is caused by the absence of techniques which would measure densities or population during daytime hours. Consensus may, in more general terms, signify the acceptance of a broader scheme of values, of an understanding of what city life in the twentieth century is like and where it should head. Planners are part of their contemporary society and are as reluctant as most people to dissociate themselves from their environment. Were this study to have extended its scope (the schemes noted are, after all, largely selected from those of the present century and originating in Europe and North America), then the analysis of the proposals might well have shown greater diversity. Unfortunately, we have few examples which indicate the physical nature of Ideal Communities drawn from societies markedly different from our own. This is at least partly a consequence of the fact that development of Ideal Communities is, in general, bound up with the city-planning profession as it has existed for the last half century and consequently shares the field's geographic and cultural limitations.

Comparing areas of consensus with those where differences prevail, it is evident that the former tend towards a high level of generalization, while the points of disagreement center upon issues of the middle range. In Ideal Communities, the common ground, such as it is, is found in considerations which largely transcend the specifics of form, circulation pattern, population size, and density. This is not surprising, but it probably contributes but little to the making or the discovery of an existing body of "received doctrine."[1]

There are universal qualities to considerations of street width, as well as in the general attempt to use land sparingly and economically. It may not be possible to identify clearly characteristic features of a design or the life style to which the plan is directed if one is restricted to propositions at only one level of generality. It is when one looks beyond the graphic material,

[1] Higgins (1949) urged planners to build up such a professional foundation: not only knowledge shared by all planners but also the all-important identifying basis for their public activities.

below the surface of the verbal presentation, to see, for example, the home-work relationship, that one can detect significant differences between Ideal Communities. For example, what do the home-work relationships show about the integration of the job into a man's private life? Is this scheme one for a regimented or for a free life? Are the ultimate beneficiaries of the plan the residents of the area or are the benefits to accrue to a larger entity? And when one comes to analyze the assumptions, then the individual nature of the proposal becomes even more evident. These steps can, in outline, be applied to a prototype German industrial town of the Nazi era designed by Köhler (1939). At first blush, the scheme has few identifying facets and has much in common with the other proposals for cities of that scale and epoch. Only as one studies the design in its context does it become evident that work areas are separated from homes as a precaution against air raids, that the neighborhood structure is closely related to the activity of the Nazi Party, and that the entire living tone is keyed to preparation for and the conduct of war.

AREAS OF NO CONSENSUS

No clear pattern emerges by which it would be possible to say that, at any one time or in any one nation, Ideal Communities shared the same standards with respect to form, population, or densities. However, a few general observations can be made. In the United States, concern with circulation, as well as the manifest urban situation, has led to a wider range in proposed standards than in Europe. England, more specifically, has seen the development of a sequence of writers whose designs share qualities of compactness coupled with a wish to preserve rural amenities, values, and character. There has also been, over time, an increasing awareness of the large-scale impact of urbanization. The frame of reference for Ideal Communities has surpassed traditional municipal boundaries and has shown expanding perspective. Yet, in all fairness, one must note, after all, that Howard's Social Cities (*see* the last chapter of his *Garden Cities*, 1898) were a vision set in the broadest of geographic terms. This is yet one more instance of his wisdom and prescience.

Does the physical form of the ideal city reflect the political bias of the author? It may, but only on an individual basis, where each scheme must be analyzed separately. There are no designs nor physical propositions that show up as unequivocally liberal or conservative, laissez faire or reformist, nor, for that matter, designs which could be characterized in Mannheim's terminology as truly "utopian," with a built-in "nerve of failure" (Riesman, 1947), compared with those which profess to work within the framework of a given society. Thus, Mazet and Chauvin's design for a monolithic cone-

[153]

city for 100,000 inhabitants (1951) resembles structurally some aspects of the Goodmans' revolutionary first paradigm (1947). Nevertheless, it is as tied to existing society as is Ferriss's view of a highly efficient metropolis (1929). Schemes which have the most dramatic, extreme physical characteristics—Wright's (1945) or Le Corbusier's (1924), for example—are not necessarily those which suggest new ways of life or the possibilities of reorganizing society. Rather, they are the limits to the direction in which significant elements in our society head today. Truly "utopian" works are few in number. The category includes only the Goodmans' schemes and elements of certain other proposals: The life suggested in Wolfe's description of Reilly's community proposal (1945) has some elements of the Goodmans' New Commune, yet its physical form, density standards, and land-use patterns are of a decidedly different nature. A second example: Miljutin's linear city (*see* Parkins, 1953) without a doubt had reconstructionist motives behind it, since it sought to consolidate home and work, farm and factory, individual and society.[2] Yet it resembles, as a physical planning document, Kern's scheme (1924) for an essentially bourgeois American city. On the other hand, in some of its broadest aspects, the goals of Miljutin's city resemble the goals of Howard's Garden City (1898), to which it bears no immediate physical resemblance.

The same lack of consistency follows us when we seek to trace professional influence. Architecturally inclined planners present schemes as sharply contrasted as Wright's and Le Corbusier's. At another scale, we note the modest proposal of twelve houses to the acre, as developed and popularized by the English architect-planner Unwin (1909). The architectural planner stresses the highly individualist environment if he is Wright or several of the English writers, but the same profession has brought us the city characterized by extensive interaction. Such are the Goodmans' and Klein's approach. The person trained in the social sciences, when he is the other member of the Goodman team or Wolfe, can see as one possibility a most integrated society. But a similar background can result in the somewhat less close atmosphere of Perry's world and the quite individualistic proposals which emerged from the new village study for the Columbia Valley in Washington State which was prepared by the U.S. Department of the Interior (1947).

Some interest in climatic variation and the general physiographic environment is shown, particularly in those Ideal Communities which lean in the direction of master plans. Nevertheless, there does not appear to be a consistent relationship between kinds of physical environment and the physical propositions put forth. That is, there is not universal acceptance among these planners of particular urban forms as most appropriate, for example,

[2] But it was limited, as the Goodmans point out, in the degree to which it really departed from the normal city life it sought to replace.

to warm climates or cool, to dry rather than moist, to flat terrain rather than hilly. The intense cultivation of the soil which is possible and traditional in England no doubt has contributed to the emphasis on the small home with garden, but then again similar densities are proposed for quite alien surroundings. In general, the Ideal Communities share such faith in the successful control, domination, and exploitation of the natural environment that they do not reflect with any clarity the forces of nature. As a consequence, too, they lack what might be termed regional flavor, such as produced characteristically different urban types under varying climatic or geographic conditions. They most lamentably fail to give the planner a system of patterns whereby, given such different conditions, appropriate variations in density or distribution of structures could be suggested. Among the few exceptions is the attention given orientation with respect to sunlight and wind, particularly as the latter affects air pollution (*see* the works of Hilberseimer, 1944). Of course, this situation may in part reflect the very attempt to create models which are universally applicable. Some of the very same authors faced with the need to develop an actual master plan do pay considerable attention to climatological and geographic factors.

The physical planning propositions as developed by means of the Ideal Communities similarly are not at all clearly identified with some of the other major aspects of the environment. To be sure, linear cities tend to be considered most appropriate for an industrialized society, and there are at least implicit connotations of insularity and small-town existence in many of the polynucleated proposals. But so far as population and density standards, circulation schemes, and most of the other structural elements are concerned, these seem to reflect the particular interpretation given a problem by an author. Most important in this connection is that specific bundle of assumptions, values, and techniques, in unique combination, which each writer brings to bear on those problems he strives to resolve by means of an Ideal Community design.

SHORTCOMINGS OF IDEAL COMMUNITIES

Study of the Ideal Communities shows that, in certain crucial respects, limitations exist. This is not to say that each scheme shows weakness in these respects; it does suggest where the critic or reader may profitably direct his attention. Obviously, whatever the weaknesses of a particular plan, we do not mean to suggest that the proposals as a group lack merit nor that the Ideal Community approach should be abandoned.

The analysis has revealed that, at times, conclusions simply do not flow from assumptions. More often, a particular scheme is presented as *the one* appropriate design, whereas actually it is but one of several possible alternatives which could satisfy the stated conditions. This deficiency gives rise to yet greater concern when, as is often the case, neither assumptions nor goals are clearly presented or identified as such. Further, little attention is paid to the need to identify these as to their source and degree of certainty. As a result, ample grounds for misinterpretation exist. Contradictory aims need to be clearly stated and, once stated, understood and avoided.

While Ideal Communities are attempts to deal with the total environment, gaps often occur. Sometimes the omissions are in whole broad areas of basic information, such as economic or social conditions. At other times, the lack is in specific areas of direct concern to the planner, as in the failure to consider transportation facilities. Numerous, too, are examples where a proposal's soundness is impaired by a lack of knowledge of findings made by other planners or those in related disciplines or by unsophisticated reliance on achievements in related fields, such as economics and psychology.

There is often a confusion as to the purpose of the scheme. Is it to serve as an actual plan of action which includes means toward reaching the goals and which also considers but turns down alternative proposals? On the whole, this is what Howard's Garden City (1898) hopes to be. Is it a model of a grab-bag sort, containing a number of proposals, some of which are mutually inconsistent, from which one scheme or set of facilities may be selected? It would appear that, intentionally or not, Garnier's Cité Industrielle (1918) is of this nature. Or is it a study of the consequences on the rest of the urban environment when the satisfaction of one particular goal is overwhelmingly stressed. At worst, this results in the cultist's approach, such as is offered by Chambless's Roadtown (1910). At best, when a rich imagination runs riot, it produces schemes such as Wright's Broadacre City (1945) or the paradigms offered by Goodman and Goodman (1947). It is not the existence of fundamentally different alternatives which causes concern but rather the fact that the authors often do not appear to recognize the characteristic uniqueness and limitations of each of these approaches.

Value of Ideal Communities

The above-mentioned considerations lead one legitimately to ask: What are the values of Ideal Communities to planners? In Chapter I, we justified an interest in Ideal Communities by noting their use as models in the development of theory and substance and their place in the history and growth of the planning field. How close have these proposals come to realizing their potential?

As Stephenson notes, "I do not believe we can make worthy plans without having ideal conceptions" (1958, p. 28). These are an indispensable link leading to public understanding, acceptance, enthusiasm, and action. Ideal

[156]

Communities are prerequisites for many of the efforts to modify and improve the environment on more than a piecemeal basis. The numerous examples of efforts which border on the polemic suggest that, indeed, Ideal Communities do serve as symbols. The gravity of errors found in such works is at least partly mitigated by the success they have in awakening the world, in "stirring men's blood." They bring to the public's attention an awareness of alternative living patterns with their broad benefits and of the possibilities of manipulating the environment to accomplish these.[3]

Stephenson also speaks of the "necessity of ideal conceptions for every science" (p. 26, quoting Geddes, 1915, in this instance). We have found in this survey that the most imaginative works have, indeed, successfully pitted the elements which constitute an urban environment against such visions. Such Ideal Communities have become indispensable steps on the road to master plans and, eventually, to reality. But the Ideal Communities have also served to anticipate and illuminate problems to be faced by twentieth-century cities and have been instrumental in developing and popularizing particular solutions, standards, and techniques to be applied to such problems. As such problems have been resolved, the science of planning has expanded.

To the urban-planning student, the best of the Ideal Communities are examples of how broadly an unfettered mind can think and dream and how far the undimmed eye can see. Exposure to Ideal Communities is perhaps a part of the most vital element of a planner's education. For these are case studies, examples, which inculcate a spirit of healthy criticism towards the existing environment and society. They contribute to the systematic destruction of belief that all that is with us today is, of necessity, given, permanent, and at least bearable, if not good. Ideal Communities are exercises in creating alternatives, and it is the planner's job to discover and analyze their implications as they are applied to real situations. It is in such terms that they must, in the end, be judged.

Finally, the Ideal Community has a heuristic function. In the schemes' relatively rarefied conditions, problems and propositions are presented in simplified form and in such a manner as may suggest lines of research. The variety, significance, and validity of derived research stemming from an Ideal Community proposal is an appropriate criterion by which the usefulness of such a scheme may be judged. There follow a number of research areas drawn from this study of the Ideal Community literature.

RESEARCH AREAS

To start with, let us consider the problem of moving people and goods; Ideal Communities make much of the improvements to circulation which

[3] Both Clark and Bauer (*see* Fisher, 1955) discuss the contributions which Ideal Communities bring to rational public decision making.

would follow from adoption of the scheme. As the above review has shown, one of the most frequently held hypotheses, although it is often stated only implicitly, is that a circulation way serves to separate laterally to the degree that it links longitudinally. There is thought to be a relation between the capacity or the efficiency of a traffic route and its function as a boundary. Thus, we noted numerous proposals which employ motorways as boundaries between residential areas or betweeen residential and industrial and commerical districts. It should be possible to evaluate the existing conditions where this prevails, to see why a roadway or rail line is seen as a barrier, to make observations regàrding the quantitative scales involved, and to establish under what circumstances this pattern may be expected.

On a local scale, some definitive word is needed on how far people actually do walk to reach certain facilities. These observations need first to be analyzed in terms of the broad population groupings: male and female, child and adult, working and nonworking mother, etc. Attempts must also be made to link walking habits to living patterns, to such crucial factors as car ownership and use, as well as to attitudes toward the physical environment. Study of the last should include consideration of walking on green-set paths compared to streets, when all the destinations are grouped rather than scattered, and so forth. Obviously this is no place for armchair theorizing that one distance is more appropriately "human" than is another.

Safety, particularly for children, is a frequently voiced concern. All too often, this is stated in absolute terms. The result is that some of the proposals would almost certainly prove to be unreasonably costly. With this in mind, it might be valuable to find out how much children do use pedestrian walks, play spaces, and bicycle paths when these are provided. What design elements seem to be significant? What educational factors? Is there any danger that children growing up in a sheltered residential environment may lack the training necessary to care for themselves on busy streets elsewhere? Again, what role does family style of life have in determining patterns of outdoor play or whether the child will walk without an adult? Are there alternatives to construction of physical facilities, such as providing supervision or closing certain streets to traffic during off-peak hours? The answers to these questions will require data not only regarding play, supervision, etc., but also on car use, users, and so forth.

Another group of problems appropriate for research are those which center on questions of land use. As Lynch and Rodwin have asked (1958), is land use, as it is now classified and quantified, the appropriate measure of space utilization? Is there a more fundamental basis analogous to the performance standard suggested for zoning? How do we better incorporate into our city plans the concept of land-use intensity?

[158]

Secondly, with regard to land use, what are the real benefits which arise from a functional differentiation of areas? To what extent do the reasons offered reflect transient factors, such as the wish to quarantine factories on account of their smoke? What real advantages, besides those of "order" and "rationality," can one find? Perhaps of equal importance, how does one go about measuring this desired differentiation? At what scale does it make sense or achieve significance: at the level of the neighborhood, the superblock, the individual block? Or perhaps only when we reach the small cluster of houses or even the individual building? We also need to set up significant criteria by which costs and benefits can be rationally measured. Obviously, land value plays an important role. But what about the elements of health, safety, and welfare on which universal reliance is placed to justify such separation? Can these be broken down to measurable parameters? Can planners come to quantify such factors as amenity and, further, differentiate the amenity of residents, workers, and visitors? Are there operational criteria with respect to the intertwined factors of clarity, that is, communication to the passers-by, and identification, which is largely of interest to residents? Finally, are there elements of efficiency which can be separated from the question of land value, factors such as the distance the employee walks to work, the ease with which a facility may change its use, or the intensity of space utilization? Does the land market favor or inhibit separation of uses? Attention should also be directed to seeing how effective the market is in registering individual preferences with regard to land use. Finally, are there people whose choice is restricted, whose preferred style of life is refused recognition, by the wish to maintain an ordered separation of land uses?

With so much attention paid to the impact of the physical environment on the social organization of the inhabitants, it might be of value to investigate the characteristics of groups from a planning viewpoint. This requires, however, clarification of whether group activity is instrumental to the good life, or whether in itself it is something to be striven for as the aim of social endeavor. In other words, is neighborliness a step (cause or *sine qua non*) to the good life, or is it the indication that the ideal has been reached? This needs to be studied from the viewpoint of the client-resident as well as that of the planners. If it is concluded that interaction is an end in itself, then many of the neighborhood proposals themselves become instrumentalities rather than goals and deserve to be regarded with much greater flexibility.

In more specific terms, too, it is important to analyze the content of interaction within a neighborhood. Operational indices need to be developed and tested. Perhaps one index may be found in the rate of voting participation. Where neighboring or interaction becomes the end, criteria such as the success of local government, degree of mutual aid, and personal interaction need to be made specific. Where concern is with the neighborhood as an instrument, the specific criteria might include, again, the extent of political activity, the success of the neighborhood as a feed-back mechanism serving to improve the physical environment, or the extent to which participation in neighborhood affairs results in a more satisfied and satisfying personality.

Such considerations implicitly reflect the opinion that the existence or nonexistence of neighborhood organization or sentiment is the dependent variable, while the independent variable is to be found in changes in the physical environment. With this in mind, it becomes important to establish which aspects of the physical environment, if any, possess the ability to affect social organization.

Psychology can offer but the most tentative findings linking group size and processes. Even the terms used are far from definitive: friend, acquaintance, loneliness, anonymity, inner direction. Do the minutiae of planning and the type of housing affect channels of communications as crucially and as dramatically as Festinger's study (1950) suggests? Or is the style of life the predominant factor? Or does the quality of the social process reflect the type of problems faced by the community? Or, finally, can one shape institutions by the provision of ready-made facilities or leadership, be it provided or self-grown?

There is in the Ideal Community literature frequent reference to the economic criterion: a certain system, the author will claim, is more efficient than another. But until the planner learns to measure welfare against cost, present enjoyment against future and long-term satisfactions, this standard should be used only with extreme caution. This is a field where planners must, to a considerable extent, rely on others' findings and theories. Therefore the planner cannot realistically jump ahead of advances made elsewhere. The tendency of several Ideal Community authors to do so is regrettable. But the very fact that this is a central feature in the design of Ideal Communities should help planners focus on these economic issues and possibly to contribute to their solution.

Most works attempt to suggest an optimum size for the Ideal Community. This area, too, is one where there is room for research. While the schemes are properly concerned with proposition of general applicability, until now only the most rudimentary consideration has been given to how population characteristics should affect the size of the Ideal Community. Recent attempts to consider a number of factors, including that of economic efficiency, point up the difficulties which are faced by the planner in determining optimum size.

The Ideal Ideal Community

The content and form of the Ideal Communities have been subjected to extended review. What are the essential features of such a scheme which ought to be preserved in future efforts? What are the characteristics which identify a good Ideal Community?[4]

The major purpose of an Ideal Community, as was stated earlier, is to serve as a model by means of which the possibility of various propositions can be tested. The greater the number of elements that are considered in an intelligent manner, the better will this over-all purpose be served.

The development of an Ideal Community requires complete and clear identification of the assumptions and goals on which the entire structure is based. The standardized critiques (Chapter III, above) give an indication of what is involved in this. The failure to express and explain these ends and assumptions often leads to internal inconsistencies and, in any case, gives rise to misunderstandings. It may further lead a critic to assign false motives to the author. Moreover, the Ideal Community should distinguish, within the hierarchy of goals, which aim is more important than others. Those propositions which are instrumental should be so identified and the ends for which they are being employed pointed out.

The text of the proposal should show clearly how the scheme proceeds from the initial assumptions and goals. It should demonstrate how the scheme would satisfy the ends (it is surprising to find instances where duly noted goals are ignored shortly after the first pages). And some thought should be directed to the question of whether alternative solutions would satisfy the given criteria. Theoretically, all alternatives which would meet the conditions should be presented, and the reasons given for the selection of one particular scheme over another. This may involve setting up more restrictive criteria which exclude all solutions but one.[5]

It would be appropriate to indicate permissible deviations from the scheme as it passes from ideal to reality, in other words, to present the tolerance levels. The Ideal Community model is not a plan, and modifications would, naturally, follow in applying the scheme. However, a critic is entitled to maintain that beyond a certain point an essentially new concept would arise. Therefore, the author should identify the most es-

[4] This review of Ideal Communities—itself a value-laden undertaking—of necessity involved a definite concept of what is appropriate to such schemes. The following few paragraphs are an attempt to make explicit this writer's feeling on this matter. In this connection it may be noted that the quality of the analysis found in the Goodman brothers' *Communitas* (1947) at least partly stems from their decision explicitly to set forth their own values.

[5] Inadequacies in this respect suggest that on several occasions the aims and presuppositions have been introduced only after a particularly satisfying scheme had been developed.

sential elements, the irreducible minimum beyond which the ideal loses its identity. This applies not only to the recommended principles but also to the value judgments.

The likelihood that the scheme can actually be developed deserves consideration, but all too often is not mentioned in the work. This may indicate that the author expects that existing cities will more or less automatically turn into the proposed Ideal Community through the operation of trends already in evidence. It may imply, however, that techniques and steps will have to be utilized which he cannot or does not wish to identify. It may even be that the author feels that any attempt to pin down the proposal would only serve to dilute the force of the ideal and to build up opposition, although agreement presently exists on the plan's general desirability. It is also of value to know whether the Ideal Community is uniquely tied to current circumstances and their amelioration and can be expected to grow out of the present environment, or whether it is so general (or perhaps not even appropriate to existing conditions at all) that the scheme in its present state has well-nigh universal applicability.

Substantively there are certain indispensable elements which each Ideal Community should contain. One would expect to find a socioeconomic content: that is, an indication of what activity goes on and on whose part. There should also be consideration of the spatial relationships of these activities. Where and in what three-dimensional relationships to each other do the actions ideally take place. And there must be some concept of cost and benefit and of how the ideal may be achieved and evaluated. It cannot be expected that these substantive areas should be developed to any high degree of sophistication. For example, cost may be considered in terms of ordinal rather than cardinal numbers or even simply expressed as the wish to minimize certain expenditures with regard to each other.

Certain other matters would be appropriately included in a satisfactory Ideal Community scheme. There should be consideration of possibilities of growth or decline once the ideal has been reached. The scheme should be of such a nature as to accommodate some changes in technology, institutions, and patterns of behavior without rendering the entire proposal useless. In other words, we look for plans which do not involve a final commitment to the scheme.

These would appear to be the *sine qua non* of Ideal Communities. Examination of these models should facilitate the study of other planning schemes, and the very familiarity with Ideal Communities should give a better understanding of a larger portion of urban-planning literature.

VI

Bibliography

SECTION I

The items in this first section are works to which reference is made in the body of this book. An asterisk (*) precedes those Ideal Communities which are discussed at length in Chapter III. Others which are mentioned in the text are briefly described below. On pages 174 ff. below, numerous other Ideal Community schemes are listed.

*ADAMS, THOMAS. *The Design of Residential Areas: Basic Considerations, Principles, and Methods.* Cambridge: Harvard University Press, 1934. *See* "The Civic Pattern," chap. 9.

BAUER, CATHERINE. "Good Neighborhoods," *Annals of the American Academy of Political and Socal Science,* CCXLII (November, 1945), 104–115.

BELLAMY, EDWARD. *Looking Backwards.* Boston: Ticknor, 1888.

BERNERI, MARIE LOUISE. *Journey Through Utopia.* London: Routledge & Paul, 1950. First American edition, Boston: Beacon Press, 1951.

BLUMENFELD, HANS (1942). *See* MILJUTIN, N. A.

——— (1943). "Form and Function in Urban Communities," *Journal of the American Society of Architectural Historians,* III (January–April, 1943), 11–21.

——— (1949). "Theory of City Form, Past and Present," *Journal of the Society of Architectural Historians,* VIII (July–December, 1949), 7–16. The ideal city, reflecting inexorable growth trends, will be sector shaped. Wedges of green penetrate to the business center at the core.

BOESIGER, WILLY (ed.). *Richard J. Neutra: Buildings and Projects.* Zurich: Girsberger, 1951.

BUBER, MARTIN. *Paths in Utopia.* Translated by R. F. C. HULL. London: Routledge & Paul, 1949. American edition, New York: Macmillan, 1950.

BURGESS, ERNEST W. "The Growth of the City: An Introduction to a Research Project," *Publications of the American Sociological Society,* XVIII

(1923), 85–97. Reprinted in PARK, R. E., BURGESS, E. W., and McKENZIE, R. D., *The City*. Chicago: University of Chicago Press, 1925.

This is the classic formulation of the concentric-ring theory to explain the structure of cities. It is a dynamic model, for the zones are seen to grow outward with expansion and to contract with decline. Economic forces are seen as the basic factors forming the urban pattern.

CALVERTON, VICTOR F. *Where Angels Dared to Tread*. Indianapolis: Bobbs-Merrill, 1941.

CAUCHON, NOULAN. "Planning Organic Cities to Obviate Congestion," *Annals of the American Academy of Political and Social Science*, CXXXIII (September, 1927), 241–246.

A honeycomb pattern is suggested for the residential portion of a large city. This should facilitate accessibility among points in the city and encourage smooth traffic flow.

*CHAMBLESS, EDGAR. *Roadtown*. New York: Roadtown Press, 1910.

CHAPIN, F. STUART, JR. "How Big Should a City Be?" *Planning Outlook*, II (Autumn, 1950), 37–48.

*COMEY, ARTHUR C. "Regional Planning Theory: A Reply to the British Challenge," *Landscape Architecture*, XIII (January, 1923), 81–96. Reprinted, *ibid*. Augusta, Me: Printed by Nash & Son, 1923.

"Community: A Symposium," *Liberation*, I (January, 1957). Entire issue.

*LE CORBUSIER (Jeanneret-Gris, Charles Édouard); (1924). *Urbanisme*. Paris: Crès, 1924, American edition, *The City of Tomorrow and Its Planning*. New York: Payson and Clarke, 1929.

*——— (ed.); (1945). *Les Trois Établissements Humains*. (ASCORAL, Sections 5a and 5b.) Paris: Denoel, 1945.

——— (1947). *Oeuvre Complète*. Zurich: Girsberger, 1947. *See* vol. IV.

DAHIR, JAMES. *The Neighborhood Unit Plan: Its Spread and Acceptance. A Selected Bibliography with Interpretative Comments*. New York: Russell Sage Foundation, 1947.

DUNCAN, OTIS DUDLEY. "Optimum Size of Cities." In HATT, PAUL K. and REISS, ALBERT J. (eds.), *Reader in Urban Sociology*. Glencoe, Ill.: Free Press, 1951. Second edition, *Cities and Society: The Revised Reader in Urban Sociology. Ibid*, 1957.

EDITORS OF FORTUNE. *The Exploding Metropolis*. Garden City, N. Y.: Doubleday, 1958. *See*, particularly, chaps. 2, 5, and 6.

EDWARDS, A. TRYSTAN. *A Hundred New Towns for Britain: A Scheme for National Reconstruction Proposed by Ex-Serviceman J47485*. London: Simpkin Marshall, 1933.

Edwards's proposal combines two features for individual towns. One is a sector design par excellence; the other, a reform-based concept of dispersal of small towns. Each such unit is independent to all intents and purposes. For further references, *see* Section II of the Bibliography.

FAWCETT, CHARLES, B. *A Residential Unit for Town and Country Planning.* Bickley, Kent: University of London Press, 1944.

This is a geographer's search for an ideal urban settlement unit. In the absence of better criteria in sociology and psychology, a school-oriented neighborhood is proposed.

*FERRISS, HUGH. *The Metropolis of Tomorrow.* New York: Ives Washburn, 1929.

FESTINGER, LEON, *et al. Social Pressures in Informal Groups: A Study of Human Factors in Housing.* New York: Harper, 1950.

FIREY, WALTER I. *Land Use in Central Boston.* Cambridge: Harvard University Press, 1947.

FISHER, ROBERT M. (ed.). *The Metropolis in Modern Life.* Garden City, N. Y.: Doubleday, 1955. *See* CLARK, Sir GEORGE, "Ideal Cities of Past and Present," chap. 21, pp. 359–366. Also comment by BAUER, CATHERINE, chap. 22, pp. 369–372.

FOLEY, DONALD L. (1951). "The Use of Local Facilities in a Metropolis." In HATT, PAUL K. and REISS, ALBERT J. (eds.), *Reader in Urban Sociology.* Glencoe, Ill: Free Press, 1951. Second edition, *Cities and Society: The Revised Reader in Urban Sociology. Ibid,* 1957. Originally published in *American Journal of Sociology,* LVI (November, 1950), 238–243.

——— (1952). "Neighbors or Urbanites?" (Studies of Metropolitan Rochester, No. 2.) Mimeographed, Department of Sociology, University of Rochester, 1952.

*FRITSCH, THEODOR. *Die Stadt der Zukunft.* Leipzig: Hammer, 1896. Second edition, *ibid,* 1912.

GANS, HERBERT. "The Human Implications of Current Redevelopment and Relocation Planning," *Journal of the American Institute of Planners,* XXV (February, 1959), 15–25.

GARNIER, TONY. *Une Cité Industrielle: Étude pour la Construction des Villes.* Paris: Vincent, 1918. 2 vols. Second edition, *ibid.* Paris: Massin, 1929. A proposal for an industrial city with its major use areas clearly identified and well separated, this scheme saw to it that ample open space penetrated to the inner precincts. This led to the main defect of the proposal: the excessive distances which exist between places of frequent contact. It is hard to distinguish the normative from the descriptive, whether we are faced with the suggested city size (35,000 inhabitants) or with the rather rigid differentiation of residential areas by income.

GEDDES, PATRICK. *Cities in Evolution: An Introduction to the Town Planning Movement and to the Study of Civics.* London: Williams and Norgate, 1915. Revised edition, edited by the Outlook Tower Association, Edinburgh, and the Association for Planning and Regional Reconstruction, London, *ibid,* 1949. American edition, New York: Oxford University Press, 1950.

*GLOEDEN, ERICH. *Die Inflation der Gross-Städte und Ihre Heiligungsmöglichkeit.* Berlin: Der Zirkel, 1923.

*GOODMAN, PAUL., and GOODMAN, PERCIVAL. *Communitas.* Chicago: University of Chicago Press, 1947. Second edition, revised, New York: Random House, 1960.

*GROPIUS, WALTER. *Rebuilding Our Communities.* Chicago: Theobald, 1945.

GROPIUS, WALTER, and WAGNER, MARTIN. "A Program for City Reconstruction," *Architectural Forum,* LXXIX (July, 1943), 75–86.

GUTKIND, ERWIN A. *The Expanding Environment: The End of Cities, the Rise of Communities.* London: Freedom Press, 1953. A conscious attempt to provide a setting that is amenable to social reconstruction, *The Expanding Environment* seeks to place the city in a rural environment. A number of coequal cities, their sizes predetermined, fulfill characteristic functions in the national economy. An earlier work *(Creative Demobilization)* sought to relate the form of urban, metropolitan, and national development to the need to integrate man's basic functions. For further references, *see* Section II of the Bibliography.

*HERREY, HERMAN; PERTZOFF, CONSTANTIN A.; and HERREY, ERNA M. J. "An Organic Theory of City Planning," *Architectural Forum,* LXXX (April, 1944), 133–40.

HERTZLER, JOYCE ORAMEL. *The History of Utopian Thought.* London: Allen & Unwin, 1923. American edition, New York: Macmillan, 1923.

HIGGINS, BENJAMIN. "Towards a Science of Community Planning," *Journal of the American Institute of Planners,* XV (Fall, 1949), 3–13.

HILBERSEIMER, LUDWIG. *The New City: Principles of Planning.* Introduction by MIES VAN DER ROHE. Chicago: Theobald, 1944.
The need to provide healthfulness, order, and rationality in the city of tomorrow requires careful location of work and home areas with regard to each other and to climatic phenomena. Decentralization and decongestion are the main themes; the resulting urban region takes on a predominantly linear form. For further references, *see* Section II of the Bibliography.

HINE, ROBERT V. *California's Utopian Colonies.* San Marino, Calif.: Huntington Library, 1953.

HOLLOWAY, MARK. *Heavens on Earth: Utopian Communities in America, 1680–1880.* New York: Library Publishers, 1951.

*HOWARD, EBENEZER. *Tomorrow, a Peaceful Path to Real Reform.* London: S. Sonnenschein, 1898. Second edition, *Garden Cities of Tomorrow. Ibid,* 1902. New edition, edited by F. J. OSBORN, London: Faber and Faber, 1946.

HOYT, HOMER. *The Structure and Growth of Residential Neighborhoods in American Cities.* (Publication of the Federal Housing Administration.) Washington, D. C.: Government Printing Office, 1939.

The interplay between communication routes and high-rent districts is of significance in the determination of city structure. The resulting city form is essentially sectorial. The model on the whole is descriptive rather than normative. For further references, *see* ARTHUR M. WEIMER and HOMER HOYT in Section II of the Bibliography.

HUMBERT, RICARDO C. *La Ciudad Hexagonal.* Buenos Aires: Vasca Ekin, 1944.

This essay stresses the need to plan with the automobile in mind. A hexagonal grid is selected as most desirable from the viewpoint of circulation as well as the preservation of amenity and economy within residential areas. It is not clear whether the improved environment is not mainly the result of good superblock design rather than of a specifically hexagonal scheme. For further references, *see* Section II of the Bibliography.

HUXLEY, ALDOUS. *Brave New World.* Garden City, N. Y.: Doubleday Doran, 1932.

INGERSOLL, PHYLLIS, "Ideal Forms for Cities: An Historical Bibliography." (Committee of Planning Librarians, *Exchange Bibliography* No. 10.) University of California List No. 6, June, 1959.

ISAACS, REGINALD (1948). "The Neighborhood Theory," *Journal of the American Institute of Planners,* XIV (Spring, 1948), 15–23.

——— (1949). Statement in Symposium on "Frontiers of Housing Reform," *Land Economics,* XXV (February, 1949), 73–78.

*JUSTEMENT, LOUIS. *New Cities for Old: City Building in Terms of Space, Time, and Money.* New York: McGraw-Hill, 1946.

KAMPFFMEYER, HANS. *See* MILJUTIN, N. A.

KAPLAN, ABRAHAM. *On the Strategy of Social Planning.* A report submitted to the Social Planning Group of the Planning Board of Puerto Rico. Mimeographed, Puerto Rico Planning Board, September 10, 1958.

KERN, ROBERT R. *The Supercity: A Planned Physical Equipment for City Life.* Washington, D.C.: 1924.

A relatively rigid pattern (strict land-use separation and rectangular trafficways) is coupled with an early attempt to design standardized residential sections. These are provided with extensive communal services and are architectonic reflections of a highly cooperative way of life. The inconsistency between extensive provision of local shops and facilities and a sizeable central business district is not explained. Neither does the author face squarely the consequences of the very normative and personal social reconstruction measures he proposes. For further references, *see* Section II of the Bibliography.

*KLEIN, ALEXANDER. "Man and Town," *Technion Yearbook,* VI (1947), 72–90.

KÖHLER, PAUL, and WINKLER, RUDOLF. "Die Stadt der 22,000," *Monatshefte für Baukunst und Städtebau,* XXIII (May, 1939), Supplement, pp. 37–52. A dormitory town strongly focusing on a large civic center, this city is removed from its industrial area for protection against air raids. The size of the city is tied to the labor needs of the factory. This is an excellent example for the study of means and ends in the physical elements of the Ideal Community.

KORN, ARTHUR, and SAMUELY, FELIX J. "A Master Plan for London." Based on research carried out by the Town Planning Committee of MARS (Modern Architectural Research Group). *Architectural Review,* XCI (June, 1942), 143–50.

LANG, S. "The Ideal City from Plato to Howard," *Architectural Review,* CXII (August, 1952), 90–101.

LILLIBRIDGE, ROBERT M. "Urban Size: An Assessment," *Land Economics,* XXVIII (November, 1952), 341–352.

LYNCH, KEVIN (1954). "The Form of Cities," *Scientific American,* CXC (April, 1954), 20, 54–63.

——— (1958). "Environmental Adaptability," *Journal of the American Institute of Planners,* XXIV (1958, No. 1), 16–24.

LYNCH, KEVIN, and RODWIN, LLOYD, "A Theory of Urban Form," *Journal of the American Institute of Planners,* XXIV (1958, No. 4), 201–214.

MANN, PETER H. "The Socially Balanced Neighborhood Unit," *Town Planning Review,* XXIX (July, 1958), 91–98.

MANNHEIN, KARL (1934). "Utopia." *(Encyclopaedia of the Social Sciences,* Vol. XV.) New York: Macmillan, 1934.

——— (1936). *Ideology and Utopia: An Introduction to the Sociology of Knowledge.* Preface by LOUIS WIRTH. London: Paul, Trench, Trubner; New York: Harcourt, Brace, 1936. Harvest Book edition, New York: Harcourt, Brace, 1955.

MAZET, J. C., and CHAUVIN, ANDRÉ. "City for 100,000 Inhabitants," *Architectural Review,* CX (July, 1951), 56–58. An architectural tour de force and a *reductio ad absurdum:* Mazet and Chauvin propose a cone of gigantic proportions set in open country, with an industrial core and residential surface. The project's rationale resembles somewhat the Goodman's first paradigm.

MERTON, ROBERT K. *Social Theory and Social Structure: Toward the Codification of Theory and Research*. Glencoe, Ill: Free Press, 1949. Revised and enlarged edition, *ibid*, 1957.

MILJUTIN, N. A. *Socialist Towns*.

An attempt at a scientific and rational solution to societal and economic urban problems, the Soviet linear city had a period of popularity about thirty years ago. Parallel bands of different land uses give form to the industrial city and are justified on policy grounds. This proposal differs substantially from original linear city proposals in its treatment of transportation as a service to production rather than to consumers and in its placement of work areas: it resembles more the work of Sert and of the ASCORAL team. It has not been possible to locate Miljutin's original article. Journals available at the New York Public Library and the Library of Congress do not include his writings on the Linear City. Among the numerous references are:

BLUMENFELD, HANS. "Regional and City Planning in the Soviet Union," *Task,* No. 3 (1942), 33–52.

GOODMAN, PAUL, and GOODMAN, PERCIVAL. *Communitas*. Chicago: University of Chicago Press, 1947. *See* chap. 3.

GUTKIND, ERWIN. *Creative Demobilization*. London: Paul, Trench, and Trubner, 1943. *See* vol. I, pp. 291–297.

KAMPFFMEYER, HANS. *Wohnstätte und Arbeitsstätte; Homes Should Be Near Work Shops; L'Habitation et Sa Distance au Chantier*. (Frankfurt a.M.: Internationales Verband fur Wohnungswessen; International Housing Association; Association International de l'Habitation, Vol. VIII.) Stuttgart: Hoffman, [1932]. *See* "Town Planning in Soviet Russia," chap. 2.

LUBETKIN, BERTHOLD, "Russian Scene Builders," *Architectural Review,* LXXI (May, 1932), 201–14.

PARKINS, MAURICE, F. *City Planning in Soviet Russia*. Chicago: University of Chicago Press, 1953. *See* "The Initial Stage, 1922–1931," chap. 2.

MORGAN, ARTHUR E. *Nowhere Was Somewhere: How History Makes Utopias and How Utopias Make History*. Chapel Hill: University of North Carolina Press, 1946.

MORTON, ARTHUR LESLIE. *The English Utopia*. London: Lawrence & Wishart, 1952.

MUMFORD, LEWIS (1922). *The Story of Utopias*. Introduction by HENDRIK WILLEM VAN LOON. New York: Boni and Liveright, 1922. New edition, New York: P. Smith, 1941.

——— (1938). *The Culture of Cities*. New York: Harcourt, Brace, 1938.

———— (1945). "An American Introduction to Sir Ebenezer Howard's *Garden Cities of Tomorrow*," *Progressive Architecture Pencil Points*, XXVI (March, 1945), 73–78.

NEGLEY, GLENN R., and PATRICK, MAX J. (eds.). *The Quest for Utopia: An Anthology of Imaginary Societies*. New York: Schuman, 1952.

*NEUTRA, RICHARD J. (1926). *Wie Baut Amerika?* Stuttgart: Hoffman, 1926.

———— (1934). "Rush City Reformed," *La Cite*, XII (May, 1934), 71–82.

———— (1954). *Survival Through Design*. New York: Oxford University Press, 1954.

ORWELL, GEORGE. *1984*. New York: Harcourt, Brace, 1949.

OSBORN, FREDERICK J. *Green-belt Cities: The British Contribution*. London: Faber and Faber, 1946.

A contemporary restatement of the Garden City ideal, *Green-belt Cities* nevertheless makes little reference to any ties with an existing central city. Again, we note the search for an urban-rural synthesis appropriate to an industrial society. For further references, *see* Section II of the Bibliography.

PARKINS, MAURICE F. *See* MILJUTIN, N. A.

PARRINGTON, VERNON L. *American Dreams: A Study of American Utopias*. (Brown University studies, vol. XI.) Providence: 1947.

PARSONS, TALCOTT. *The Structure of Social Action: A Study in Social Theory with Special Reference to a Group of Recent European Writers*. Second edition, Glencoe, Ill.: Free Press, 1949.

PEP. *See* Political and Economic Planning.

*PERRY, CLARENCE (1929). "The Neighborhood Unit." In vol. VII, *Regional Survey of New York and Its Environs*. New York: Regional Plan of New York and Its Environs, 1929.

———— (1939). *Housing for the Machine Age*. New York: Russell Sage Foundation, 1939.

POLITICAL AND ECONOMIC PLANNING. *Report on the Location of Industry: A Survey of Present Trends in Great Britain Affecting Industrial Location and Regional Economic Development, with Proposals For Future Policy*. London: PEP, 1939.

PURDOM, CHARLES B. *The Building of Satellite Towns: A Contribution to the Study of Town Development and Regional Planning*. London: Dent and Sons, 1925. New edition, entirely rewritten, London: Dent, 1949.

RIESMAN, DAVID. "Some Observations on Community Plans and Utopia," *Yale Law Journal*, LVII (December, 1947), 174–200. Reprinted in RIESMAN, DAVID, *Individualism Reconsidered*. Glencoe, Ill.: Free Press, 1954. *Ibid*, Garden City, N.Y.: Doubleday, 1955.

RODWIN, LLOYD. "The Theory of Residential Growth and Structure," *Appraisal Journal*, XVIII (July, 1950), 295–317; replies, HOYT, HOMER

(October, 1950), 445–450, and FIREY, WALTER, *ibid*, 451–453; rejoinder, RODWIN, LLOYD, *ibid*, 454–457.

ROSENAU, HELEN. *The Ideal City and Its Architectural Evolution*. London: Routledge and Paul, 1959.

ROSS, HARRY. *Utopias Old and New*. London: Nicholson and Watson, 1938.

SAARINEN, ELIEL. *The City: Its Growth, Its Decay, Its Future*. New York: Reinhold, 1943.

The City includes a proposal for the section-by-section reconstruction of the present decaying metropolis. The ideal scheme would see the growth of relatively independent satellite units which would be closely linked by rapid transportation facilities. The work leans heavily on analogies drawn from the biological world. For further references, *see* Section II of the Bibliography.

*SANDERS, SPENCER E., and RABUCK, ARTHUR J. *New City Patterns: The Analysis of a Technique for Urban Reintegration*. New York: Reinhold, 1946.

SEELEY, JOHN R. "The Slum: Its Nature, Use and Users," *Journal of the American Institute of Planners*, XXV (February, 1959), 7–14.

SERT, JOSÉ LUIS (1942). *Can Our Cities Survive? An ABC of Urban Problems, Their Analysis, Their Solutions, Based on the Proposals Formulated by the CIAM* (International Congress for Modern Architecture). Cambridge: Harvard University Press; London: Milford, Oxford University Press, 1942.

*——— (1944). "The Human Scale in City Planning." In ZUCKER, PAUL (ed.), *New Architecture and City Planning, a symposium*. New York: Philosophical Library, 1944.

SORIA Y MATA, ARTURO. "Madrid Remendado y Madrid Nuevo," *El Progreso*, March 6, 1882.

The original linear-city proposal (modified and expanded in subsequent decades) was conceived both as a tentacle from existing cities and as a link between urban nuclei. The city form is determined by a major circulation way, with only a couple of blocks of development on each side. The social and economic reforms advocated by the author are applicable to suburban life in general more than to the linear city specifically. Several of the linear city writings speak of the essential similarity to the English Garden City proposals. Many of the publications served to promote the sale of land in the original linear city. For descriptions of the linear city concept, *see* the following:

LA COMPAÑÍA MADRILEÑA DE URBANIZACIÓN, *La Ciudad Lineal; Fórmula Española de Ciudad Jardín Como Sistema de Arquitectura de Ciudades y de Colonización de Campos: Memoria Presentada al XIII Congreso Internacional de Habitación y de Urbanismo*. Madrid: Ciudad Lineal, 1931.

COLLINS, GEORGE R., "The Ciudad Lineal of Madrid," *Journal of the Society of Architectural Historians*, XVIII (May, 1959), 38–53.

SPIRO, MELFORD E. *Kibbutz: Venture in Utopia.* Cambridge: Harvard University Press, 1956.

STEIN, CLARENCE. *Toward New Towns for America.* Liverpool: University of Liverpool, 1951. Revised edition, New York: Reinhold, 1957.

Towards New Towns for America summarizes Stein's thinking on planning over three decades. His schemes for Radburn, New Jersey, and for Greenbelt, Maryland, are the outstanding examples of the application of principles of neighborhood design. Superblocks, mixture of housing types, and a sensitive treatment of problems posed by the automobile are key design features. For further references, *see* Section II of the Bibliography.

STEPHENSON, GORDON. "Some Thoughts on the Planning of Metropolitan Regions," *Papers and Proceedings of the Regional Science Association,* IV (1958), 27–38.

TAUT, BRUNO. *Die Stadtkrone.* Jena: Diedrichs, 1919.

This is a design for a large city based on the premise that, for the good of society, the spiritual and political importance of civic institutions must be enhanced by the plan. Hence, the plan calls for the grouping of public structures at a magnificent scale at the city center. For further references, *see* Section II of the Bibliography.

TRIGGS, H. INIGO. *Town Planning: Past, Present and Possible.* London: Methuen, 1909.

A review of city planning, *Town Planning* summarizes, among others, the works of Adolph Müller and of Charles Lamb. Müller's hexagonal roadway grid is an early superblock design, though rather wasteful in land since triangular open or public spaces are left between hexagons so as to permit unbroken streets. Lamb's hexagonal grid serves to link portions of a metropolis, where concentrations of like activities created nuclei requiring efficient interaccessibility.

TUNNARD, CHRISTOPHER. *The City of Man.* New York: Scribner, 1953.

TYRWHITT, JAQUELINE. "Society and Environment: A Historical Review." In ASSOCIATION FOR PLANNING AND REGIONAL RECONSTRUCTION (eds.), *Town and Country Planning Textbook.* London: Architectural Press, 1950.

UNITED STATES DEPARTMENT OF THE INTERIOR, Bureau of Reclamation, Columbia Basin Joint Investigation. *Pattern of Rural Settlement.* Washington, D.C.: Government Printing Office, 1947.

This is a skillful study blending historical data, current examples, and theoretical proposals. The subject is the form that new rural and village developments should take as a heretofore barren area is settled. It can be considered an excellent example of the direction which could be taken by studies developing physical planning principles.

UNWIN, RAYMOND. *Town Planning in Practice: An Introduction to the Art of Designing Cities and Suburbs.* London: Unwin, 1909. New edition, *ibid,* 1919. American edition, New York: Century, 1932.

WIENER, NORBERT. "How U.S. Cities Can Prepare for Atomic War," *Life,* XXIX (December 18, 1950), 77–82+.

The aim of the M.I.T. research group is to find a scheme for decentralization appropriate to an age threatened with nuclear warfare, yet one which would also serve our needs in time of peace. An extended ring of secondary facilities surrounding the core of the metropolis is strongly tied to a new transportation network.

WILSON, EDMUND. *To the Finland Station: A Study in the Writing and Acting of History.* New York: Harcourt, Brace, 1940.

*WOLFE, LAWRENCE. *The Reilly Plan: A New Way of Life.* Introduction by SIR CHARLES REILLY. London: Nicholson & Watson, 1945.

WRIGHT, AUSTIN TAPPAN. *Islandia.* New York: Rinehart, 1942.

*WRIGHT, FRANK LLOYD (1931). *Modern Architecture.* Princeton: Princeton University Press, 1931. *See,* especially, chap. 6.

——— (1932). *The Disappearing City.* New York: Payson, 1932.

[———] (April, 1935). *Architectural Record,* LXXVII (April, 1935), 243–254.

[———] (May, 1935). *American Architect,* CXLVII (May, 1935), 55-62.

——— (1939). *An Organic Architecture: The Architecture of Democracy.* London: Lund, Humphries, 1939.

——— (1940). "Broadacre City," *Taliesin Fellowship Publication,* I (Oct. 1940), No. 1. Entire issue.

——— (1945). *When Democracy Builds.* Chicago: University of Chicago Press, 1945.

——— (1958). *The Living City.* New York: Horizon Press, 1958.

SECTION II

There exists no one definitive bibliography on the subject of Ideal Communities.[1] There are several reasons for this. First, a conceptual problem: Ideal Communities are hard to define. There are numerous works on the periphery which should be included in any work purporting to deal with the subject exhaustively. It is likely that such references would be so numerous as to swamp those more central to the concept.[2] Second, Ideal Community schemes often appear in short-lived periodicals, or under the imprint of little known publishers, or are given limited circulation. Thus, even were an omniscient reviewer to compile a lengthy and complete list, the would-be user of the designs would be hard put to locate many of the works indicated.

Although most of the significant schemes are included on the preceding pages, they are only some of the published examples of Ideal Communities. For the benefit of readers who wish to pursue this topic further, there follow a number of other references to Ideal Communities and to certain relevant works. Again, we should say that we are predominantly concerned with twentieth-century examples as these use and develop physical-planning propositions.

Part I. Ideal Communities

In addition to the Ideal Communities mentioned in the text of this book, a number of others have been designed during the past three quarters of a century. These are listed in this portion of the Bibliography. The reader should note that, for purposes of this compilation, a more generous definition of Ideal Communities was used than was the case in the text. In particular, there are a number of references to schemes which are

[1] However, three partial bibliographies were found helpful in the preparation of this book:
a. MCNAMARA, KATHERINE. "19th and 20th Century Proposals for Ideal Cities: A Selected List of References," *Books of the Month*, (January, 1946). Issued by Harvard University, Library of the Department of Landscape Architecture and Regional Planning.
b. INGERSOLL, PHYLLIS. *Op. cit.*
c. UMLAUF, JOSEF. *Deutsches Schrifttum zur Stadtplanung*. Düsseldorf: Werner, 1953.

[2] Most noteworthy are the numerous master plans of cities which develop concepts of general applicability. Parenthetically, one might add that there appears to be no publication evaluating these as a group. Work on this subject is now in progress at the Institute for Urban Studies at the University of Pennsylvania.

predominantly descriptive of an idealized urban structure. These seek to establish the essential characteristics of existing cities, rather than to establish normative criteria. Further, a number of schemes have been included which develop an optimum adaptation to inexorable technological trends or which seek an accomodation to the threat of atomic warfare.

ABEL, ADOLF. *Regeneration; der Städte; des Villes; of Towns.* Zürich: Verlag für Architektur, 1950. *See,* especially, "Ein Idealplan; Un Plan Ideal; An Ideal Scheme," chap. 4.

ACOSTA, WLADIMIRO. *Vivienda y Ciudad.* Buenos Aires: Aresti, 1936. *See* "Ciudad," part 2.

ADAM, C. G. M. "An Essay in Heresy," *Garden Cities and Town-planning,* XIII (November, 1932), 202–207.

ADSHEAD, STANLEY D. *Town Planning and Town Development.* London: Methuen, 1923. *See* "Town Extension," chap. 4.

AMERICAN PUBLIC HEALTH ASSOCIATION, Committee on the Hygiene of Housing. *Planning the Neighborhood.* Chicago: Public Administration Service, 1948.

ANDERSEN, OLIVIA C., and ANDERSEN, HENDRIK C. *Creation of a World Centre of Communication.* English edition, Rome, n.p., 1918. *See,* especially, HÉBRARD, ERNEST, and HÉBRARD, JEAN, "Architectural Execution of the Plans."

AUGUR, TRACY B. "The Dispersal of Cities as a Defense Measure," *Bulletin of the Atomic Scientists,* IV (May, 1948), 131–134.

AUSTIN, ALICE C. *The Next Step: How to Plan for Beauty, Comfort, and Peace.* Los Angeles: Institute Press, 1935.

BARDET, GASTON. *Pierre sur Pierre.* Paris: Editions L.C.B. Section Bâtiment, 1946. *See,* especially, "Fondations du Nouvel Urbanisme," chap. 6.

BARON, STANLEY (ed.). *Country Towns in the Future England.* London: Faber & Faber, 1944.

BEL GEDDES, NORMAN. "City 1960," *Architectural Forum,* LXVII (July, 1937), 57–62.

BLESSING, CHARLES A. "Rurbana: A Livable City for 200,000 People," *Coronet,* XIV (July, 1943), 143–145.

BOLL, ANDRÉ. *Habitation Moderne et Urbanisme.* Paris: Dunod, 1942. *See,* especially, "Éléments Techniques du Problème," part 2.

CARPENTER, J. E. R. (architect). "A Proposed Summer Capital and National Center for the United States of America; described by BROWN, FRANK C.," *The Architectural Review* [Boston], VI (April, 1918), 47–53.

CASTILLO, H. G. DEL. *Projet de Cité Linéaire Belge.* Madrid: Imprenta de la Ciudad Lineal, 1919.

CLAYTON, PHILIP. "Can We Plan for the Atomic Age?" *Journal of the American Institute of Planners*, XXVI (May, 1960), 111–118.

COMPAÑIA MADRILEÑA DE URBANIZACIÓN. *Ciudad Lineal*. Madrid: Ciudad Lineal, 1911. *See,* especially, "¿Que Es la Ciudad Lineal?" [chap. 2].

LE CORBUSIER (Charles Édouard Jeanneret-Gris). *Le Lyrisme des Temps Nouveaux et L'Urbanisme*. Paris: Le Point, 1939.

———. *La Ville Radieuse: Éléments d'une Doctrine d'Urbanisme pour l'Équipement de la Civilisation Machiniste*. Boulogne: Editions de L'Architecture d'Aujourd'hui, 1933.

LE CORBUSIER, and PIERREFEU, FRANCOIS DE. *The Home of Man*. London: The Architectural Press, 1948. Translation into English of *La Maison des Hommes*. Paris: Librairie Plon, 1942.

DENEKE, ALBERT. *Renaissance im Städtebau*. Münster: Regenberg, 1946. *See* "Die Neue Stadt," part 3.

DODI, LUIGI. *Elementi di Urbanistica*. Milano: Tambierini, 1953. *See,* especially, "La Fabbricazione-L'Abitazione," chap. 1: 4.

DOXIADIS, CONSTANTINOS A. "Dynapolis; The City of the Future," *Ekistics*, IX (January, 1960), 5–20. Abstracts from a report prepared for the Conference of the Polish Academy of Sciences and the Institute of History of City Planning and Architecture.

DREYFUSS, HENRY. "The City of Tomorrow at the New York World's Fair," *House & Garden*, LXXIV (November, 1938), sec. 2, pp. 28–29.

EBERSTADT, RUDOLF; MÖHRING, BRUNO; and PETERSON, RICHARD. *Gross-Berlin: Ein Programm für die Plannung der Neuzeitlichen Grosstadt*. Berlin: Wasmuth, 1910. *See* "Grundformen der Neuen Grosstadt," chap. 1.

EDWARDS, A. TRYSTAN. "A Hundred New Towns?" *Design for Britain*. Second series, No. 36 (1944). Entire issue.

———. "A 'Model' Town Designed for Traffic," *Town Planning Review*, XIV (May, 1930), 31–41.

EGLI, ERNST. *Die Neue Stadt in Landschaft und Klima; Climate and Town Districts; Consequences and Demands*. Zurich: Verlag für Architektur-Erlenbach, 1951. *See,* especially, "The New Town; The Town Development," part 1, chap. 3; "Town Structure and Climate; Deductions," part 2, chap. 2; and "Landscapes; Consequences and Demands," part 3, chap. 8.

FEDER, GOTTFRIED, and REICHENBERG, FRITZ. *Die Neue Stadt*. Berlin: Springer, 1939.

FOLLETT, MARY PARKER. *The New State*. New York: Longmans, Green, 1920. *See,* especially, "The Neighborhood Group," part 3: 1.

FRY, MAXWELL. *Fine Building*. London: Faber and Faber, 1944. *See,* especially, chap. 4.

GÖDERITZ, JOHANNES; RAINER, ROLAND; and HOFFMANN, HUBERT. *Die Gegliederle und Aufgelockerte Stadt.* Tübingen: Wasmuth, 1957.

GOLDBECK, MAXIMILIAN VON, and KOTZER, ERICH. "Die Stadt von Morgen, Ein Film vom Städtebau," *Wasmuth's Monatshefte für Baukunst & Städtebau,* XIV (May, 1930). In *Städtebau,* sec. 25 (May, 1930), 237–239.

GREAT BRITAIN, NEW TOWNS COMMITTEE (Lord Reith, chairman). *Final Report of the New Towns Committee,* Cmd. 6876. London: His Majesty's Stationery Office, 1946. *See,* especially, "Principles in Planning," part B.

GRUEN, VICTOR. "The Emerging Urban Pattern," *Progressive Architecture,* XL (July, 1959), 115–162. *See,* especially, "The Emerging Pattern," pp. 130–153.

———. "How to Handle This Chaos of Congestion, This Anarchy of Scatteration," *Architectural Forum,* CIV (September, 1956), 130–135.

GUTKIND, ERWIN A. *Creative Demobilization.* London: Paul, Trench, Trubner, 1943. 2 vols. *See,* especially, "Principles of National Planning," vol. I, and MEALAND, H. A., "Memorandum on the Development of a New Town," vol. II, pp. 204–207.

GUTTENBERG, ALBERT Z. "Urban Structure and Urban Growth," *Journal of the American Institute of Planners,* XXVI (May, 1960), 104–110.

HARRIS, CHAUNCY D., and ULLMAN, EDWARD L., "The Nature of Cities," *Annals of the American Academy of Political and Social Science,* CCXLII (November, 1945), 7–17.

HASTINGS, MILO. "A Solution of the Housing Problem in the United States," *Journal of the American Institute of Architects,* VII (June, 1919), 259–266.

HEILIGENTHAL, ROMAN F. *Deutscher Städtebau.* Heidelberg: Winter, 1921.

HERBÉ, PAUL. "Un Essai d'Urbanisme Colonial," *Architecture d'Aujourd' hui,* XIX (October, 1948), iv–v.

HILBERSEIMER, LUDWIG. *Grozstadt Architektur.* Stuttgart: Hoffman, 1927. *See,* especially, "Städtebau," [chap. 2].

———. *The Nature of Cities.* Chicago: Theobald, 1955. *See,* especially, "Planning Problems," chap. 3.

———. *The New Regional Pattern.* Chicago: Theobald, 1949.

HILLMAN, MAYER, *et al.,* "Project for a Linear New Town," *The Architect's Journal,* CXXV (April 4, 1957), 503–507. Reprinted in *Community Planning Review; Revue Canadienne d'Urbanisme,* VII (September, 1957), 136–140.

HOEBEN, J.-F. "Problème Urbanistique," *La Cité,* XII (October, 1934), 168–172.

HOYT, HOMER. *See* WEIMER, ARTHUR M., and HOYT, HOMER.

HUGHES, W. R. *New Town.* London: Dent, 1919.

HUMBERT, RICARDO C. "La Cité Hexagonale," *Technique et Architecture,* VIII (Nos. 3–4, 1948), 11–13.

———. "A Hexagonal Layout for Cities," *Traffic Engineering,* XVI (April, 1946), 266–268.

HURD, RICHARD. *The Structure of Cities.* New York: Alexander Hamilton Institute, 1910.

ILYIN, M. "Städtebauliches aus Russland," *Wasmuth's Monatshefte für Baukunst & Städtebau,* XV (May, 1931). In *Städtebau* section, XXVI (May, 1931), 237.

INTERNATIONALE BAUAUSSTELLUNG BERLIN, 1957. *Die Stadt von Morgen.* Berlin: Interbau, 1957.

KEEBLE, LEWIS. *Principles and Practice of Town and Country Planning.* London: The Estates Gazette, 1952. Second Edition, 1959. *See,* especially, in first edition: "The Regional Plan," chap. 11; "The Town Plan I—General," chap. 12; "The Town Plan IV—Preparation of the Plan," chap. 15; and "The Neighborhood Plan," chap. 16. *See,* especially, in second edition: "The Planning of Towns," chap. 7.

KERN, ROBERT R., and GESCHICKTER, CHARLES. "The New City, a Planned Physical Equipment," *Journal of the American Institute of Architects,* VIII (November, 1920), Supplement, pp. 1–8.

KOBBE, HERMAN. *Housing and Regional Planning.* New York: Dutton, 1941. *See* "Regional Plan," [chap. 6].

KOSMIN, MICHEL. *Ville Linéaire: Aménagement, Architecture.* Paris: Vincent Fréal, 1952.

KOSTKA, V. JOSEPH. *Neighborhood Planning.* Winnipeg. Published by the author at the University of Manitoba, 1957.

[LANCHESTER, H. V.] "An English Planner's Visualization of an Ideal City," *American City,* XXXV (September, 1926), 313.

LAPP, RALPH E. "The Hydrogen Bomb: IV," *Scientific American,* CLXXXII (June, 1950), 11–15. *See also* comment by MILTON SHAPIRO, *ibid.* (August, 1950), 2.

LAUGA, PIERRE. *La Révolution Urbaine.* Paris: Je Sers, 1946. *See,* especially, "Les Villes Nouvelles," part 2, and "Schèma . . . d'une Ville Nouvelle," appendix.

LEBRETON, JEAN. *La Cité Naturelle: Recherche d'un Urbanisme Humain.* Paris: Dupont, 1945.

"Louis Kahn and the Living City," *Architectural Forum,* CVIII (March, 1958), 115–119.

MACKAYE, BENTON. *The New Exploration.* New York: Harcourt, Brace, 1928. *See,* especially, "Regional City vs. Metropolis," chap. 11 and "Controlling the Metropolitan Invasion," chap. 12.

McKenzie, Roderick D. *The Metropolitan Community.* New York: Mc-Graw-Hill, 1933.

Malcher, Fritz. "A Traffic Planner Imagines a City," *American City,* XLIV (March, 1931), 134–135.

Mayer, Albert W. "A Technique for Planning Complete Communities," *Architectural Forum,* LXVI (January, 1937), 19–36, and (February, 1937), 126–146.

Meier, Richard L. *Science and Economic Development: New Patterns of Living.* Cambridge: Technology Press of Massachusetts Institute of Technology; and New York: Wiley, 1956. *See,* especially, "New Patterns of Living—Characteristics of the New Urbanization," chap. 4:3.

"Motopia," *Housing Review,* VIII (November–December, 1959), 202–204.

Mouvement Ville Radieuse. *V. R.: Maisons et Villes Radieuses.* Paris: Mouvement Ville Radieuse, 1956.

National Council of Social Service. *The Size and Social Structure of a Town.* London: Allen & Unwin, 1943.

New Townsmen. *New Towns after the War.* London: Dent, 1918.

Osborn, Frederic J. *New Towns after the War.* London: Dent, 1942. First edition, 1918. *See,* especially, "The Solution," [chap. 4].

Otto, Karl (ed). *Die Stadt von Morgen: Gegenwartsprobleme für Alle.* Berlin: Mann, 1959.

Perkins, G. Holmes. "The Regional City." In Woodbury, Coleman (ed.), *The Future of Cities and Urban Redevelopment.* Chicago: University of Chicago Press, 1953.

Persitz, Alexandre. "A Twentieth Century Architect [Richard J. Neutra]," *L'Architecture d'Aujourd'hui,* XVI (May–June, 1946), 8–13.

Petavel, J. W. "The Town Planning of the Future," *Westminster Review,* CLXXII (October, 1909), 398–405.

"Planned Neighborhoods for 194X," *Architectural Forum,* LXXIX (October, 1943), 65–142. Entire issue. *See,* especially, Englehardt, N. L., Jr., "The School-Neighborhood Nucleus," pp. 88–90.

Pope, Robert A. "A Solution of the Housing Problem in the United States," *Journal of the American Institute of Architects,* VII (July, 1919), 305–314.

"Principios Fundamentales de la Ciudad Lineal," *La Ciudad Lineal,* XXIX (October 10, 1925), 389–392.

Principios Fundamentales de la Ciudad Lineal. Madrid: Imprenta de la Ciudad Lineal, 1925.

Project East River. Part V: Reduction of Urban Vulnerability. New York: Associated Universities, 1952. *See,* especially, "Reduction of Urban Vulnerability by Space," sec. 2, and WHEATON, WILLIAM L. C., with the help of HAMILTON, CALVIN S., "Minimum Density and Spacing Standards for Metropolitan Dispersal," appendix 5:B, sec. 1. Appendix 5:B was also issued in mimeographed form under the title *Reports on Metropolitan Dispersal for Project East River* by Harvard University, Department of Regional Planning. *See also* MONSON, DONALD, "City Planning in Project East River," *Bulletin of the Atomic Scientists,* IX (September, 1953), 265–267; and NORTON, C. McKIM, "Report on Project East River; Part II: Development of Standards," *Journal of the American Institute of Planners,* XIX (Summer, 1953), 159–167.

RADING, ADOLF. "The Garden Village; a New Method of Developing Suburban Land," *National Municipal Review,* XII (April, 1923), 168–171.

RAYMOND, JEAN. "La Cité du Rail. Projet de Ville Nouvelle Coloniale," *L'Ingénieur-Constructeur,* XXIII (November–December, 1931), 1433–1500; and XXIV (January-February, 1932), 1587–1600.

———. *L'Urbanisme à la Portée de Tous.* Paris: Dunod, 1925. Second edition, 1938. *See,* especially, "Les Différents Quartiers de la Cité Moderne," chap. 8.

———. *Précis d'Urbanisme Moderne.* Paris: Dunod, 1934. *See* "La Cité Linéaire; La Ville de Demain," chap. 7.

REICHOW, HANS B. *Organische Stadtbaukunst; von der Gross-stadt zur Stadtlandschaft.* Braunschweig: Westermann, 1948.

REIFENBERG, H. J. "Cities Built for Traffic," *Housing Review,* VIII (November-December, 1959), 200–201.

REY, A-AUGUSTIN; PIDOUX, JUSTIN; and BARDE, CHARLES. *La Science des Plans de Villes.* Lausanne: Payot; and Paris: Dunod, [1929?]. *See* "Les Plans de Villes Nouvelles," part 3.

RIC-WIL COMPANY, *Industrial Destiny.* Cleveland: Ric-Wil, 1950.

RIGOTTI, GIORGIO. *Urbanistica di Guerra? No. . . . Urbanistica di Pace.* Torino: Rattero, 1944. *See,* especially, "La Città Solare Isocrona," chap. 6.

[SCHOOL FOR PLANNING AND RESEARCH OF NATIONAL DEVELOPMENT.] "Wilson Midgley Visits the Perfect Town," *Town and Country Planning,* VII (April–June, 1939), 58–59.

SCHWAGENSCHEIDT, WALTER. *Ein Mensch Wandert durch die Stadt.* Bad Godesberg-Mehlem: Die Planung, 1957.

SCHWARZ, RUDOLF. *Von der Bebauung der Erde.* Heidelberg: Schneider, 1949.

SCHWEIZER, OTTO E. *Die Architektonische Grossform.* Karlsruhe: Braun, 1957.

SEGAL, WALTER. *Planning and Transport: Their Effects on Industry and Residence.* London: Dent, 1945.

SENNET, ALFRED R. *Garden Cities in Theory and Practice*. London: Bemrose, 1905. 2 vols. *See,* especially, vol. I, "On the Laying-out of Garden Cities," chap. 2, and "Proposal for Plan of First Garden City," chap. 3.

SHARP, THOMAS. *Town and Countryside: Some Aspects of Urban and Rural Development*. London: Oxford University Press, 1932. *See,* especially, "Urban Growth," chap. 8.

SIERKS, HANS L. *Grundriss der Sicheren; Reichen; Ruhigen Stadt*. Dresden: Kaden, 1929.

SMITHSON, PETER, and SMITHSON, ALISON. "The Cluster City," *Architectural Review, CXXII* (November, 1957), 333–336.

SMYTHE, WILLIAM E. *City Homes on Country Lanes*. New York: Macmillan, 1921. *See* "The Farm City and the Garden City," chap. 2:4.

STEIN, CLARENCE. "City Patterns, Past and Future," *New Pencil Points,* XXIII (June, 1942), 52–56.

———. "Education and the Evolving City." In vol. 17, *The American School and University*. New York: American School, 1945. Summarized in "The City of the Future—A City of Neighborhoods," *The American City,* LX (November, 1945), 123–125.

STEPHENSON, GORDON. *Greenbelt—A New Town*. London: Town and Country Planning Association, 1944.

TYRWHITT, JAQUELINE. "Culture and Cities," *Information Bulletin of the Association for Planning and Regional Reconstruction,* Sheet 193, (June, 1949), p. 1.

———. "The Size and Spacing of Urban Communities," *Journal of the American Institute of Planners,* XV (Summer, 1949), 10–17.

UNIÓN DE ARQUITECTOS SOCIALISTAS [MEXICO]. *Proyecto de la Ciudad Obrera en Mexico, D.F.* Mexico: XVI° Congreso Internacional de Planificación y de la Vivienda, 1938.

UNWIN, SIR RAYMOND. *Nothing Gained by Overcrowding*. London: Garden Cities and Town Planning Association, 1912. Third edition, 1918.

VACCARO, GIUSEPPE. "La Casa a Collina e la Città con Case a Collina," *Architettura,* XVI (November, 1937), 656–666.

VOGLER, PAUL (ed.). *Medizin und Städtebau*. München: Urban & Schwarzenberg, 1957. 2 vols. *See,* especially, vol. 2, "Sinngebung der Grossstadt," [part ii]; and GÖDERITZ, JOHANNES, "Auflockerung und Gliederung der Grossstadt," and HILBERSEIMER, LUDWIG, "Die Umformung einer Grossstadt," [part iii].

VÖLCKERS, OTTO. *Dorf und Stadt*. Leipzig: Staackmann, 1942. *See* "Dorf und Stadt im 19. und 20. Jahrhundert," [chap. 6].

WAGNER, MARTIN. *Die Neue Stadt im Neuen Land*. Berlin: Buchholz, 1934.

WATERHOUSE, PAUL, and UNWIN, SIR RAYMOND. *Old Towns and New Needs,* and *The Town Extension Plan*. Manchester: University Press, 1912.

WECHS, THOMAS. *Die Stadt Ypsilon*. Augsburg: Brigg Ausburg, 1957.

WEIMER, ARTHUR M., and HOYT, HOMER. *Principles of Real Estate*. New York: Ronald Press. Revised edition, 1948. Third edition, 1954. *See* "Location Factors and Property Incomes," chap. 5 in 1948 edition, chap. 17 in 1954 edition.

WHITTEN, ROBERT. "The Economics of Land Subdivision," part 3, of Monograph Three, "Problems of Planning Unbuilt Areas," in vol. VII, *Regional Survey of New York and Its Environs*. New York: Regional Plan of New York and Its Environs, 1929. *See,* especially, "Comparison of Neighborhood Plan and Standard Layout," chap. 14.

———. "How a Self-Contained Neighborhood Unit Might Be Planned," *American City*, XXXVI (March, 1927), 287–293.

———. "The Organization of a Metropolitan Community," *Landscape Architecture*, XIV (January, 1924), 77–80.

———. *Regional Zoning*, National Conference on City Planning, 1923.

WHITTEN, ROBERT, and ADAMS, THOMAS. *Neighborhoods of Small Homes*. Cambridge: Harvard University Press, 1931. *See,* especially, "Summary and Recommendations," chap. 9.

WILENSKI, HARRY, and FERRISS, HUGH. "Toward the Regional City," *American City*, LXIX (February, 1954), 9–10. Summary of article by authors in 75th Anniversary Issue, St. Louis *Post Dispatch*, 1953.

WOLF, PAUL. *Wohnung und Siedlung*. Berlin: Wasmuth, 1926. *See,* especially, "Die Privatwirtschaftlichen, Volkswirtschaflichen, und Organisatorischen Grundlagen," chap. 2:3.

———. *Städtebau: Das Formproblem der Stadt in Vergangheit und Zukunft*. Leipzig: Klinkhardt und Biermann, 1919. *See,* especially, "Die Grundform der Neuen Stadt," chap. 5.

WOOLDRIDGE, CHARLES W. *Perfecting the Earth: A Piece of Possible History*. Cleveland: Utopia Publishing Co., 1902. *See* chap 4.

WRIGHT, HENRY. *Rehousing Urban America*. New York: Columbia University Press, 1935. *See,* especially, "The Blight of Our Cities," chap. 1, and "The Case for Group Housing," chap. 5.

YEOMANS, ALFRED B. *City Residential Land Development: Studies in Planning; Competitive Plans for Subdividing a Typical Quarter Section of Land in the Outskirts of Chicago*. Chicago: University of Chicago Press, 1916. Includes WILHELM BERNHARD, first prize; ARTHUR COMEY, second prize; entry by FRANK LLOYD WRIGHT; and others.

Part 2. Descriptions of Ideal Communities

Planning texts usually describe a number of Ideal Communities as part of their overview of the field. In addition, several articles have been dedicated to the study of a particular class of Ideal Communities. Reference to some of these has been made in the body of this book; these are noted in the first section of this Bibliography. Among the numerous other works falling in this category are the following:[3]

ABENDROTH, A. "Die Grossstadt als Städtegründerin," *Der Städtebau*, II (No. 2, 1905), 24-27; (No. 3, 1905), 32-38; and (No. 4, 1905), 49-51.

ABERCOMBIE, PATRICK. *Town and Country Planning*. London: Oxford University Press, 1933. Second edition, 1943. *See*, especially, "The Practice of Town Planning," part 2 in second edition.

————. "The Rise and Decline of Neighborhood Planning," *Housing Review*, V (September–October, 1956), 143–145.

ARESI, A. E. *Urbanistica*. Milano: Hoepli, 1949. *See*, especially, "Direzione e Sistemi dell'Espansione Urbana," chap. 5.

ASHWORTH, WILLIAM. *The Genesis of Modern British Town Planning*. London: Routledge and Paul, 1954.

AUCKENTHALER, KURT. *Architektur Menschbezogen*. Wels: Amt der O.-Ö. Landesregierung, 1954.

BARDET, GASTON. *Le Nouvel Urbanisme*. Paris: Vincent, Fréal, 1948.

————. *Problèmes d' Urbanisme*. Paris: Dunod, 1948. *See*, especially, "Problèmes de Circulation," chap. 2, and "Problèmes Intellectuels et Spirituels," chap. 6.

BARLOW, RALEIGH. *Land Resource Economics*. Englewood Cliffs, N.J.: Prentice Hall, 1958. *See* "Location Factors Affecting Land Use," chap. 9.

BARRET, MAURICE. "Urbanisme; II. Les Théories," *Techniques et Architecture*, VII (March–April, 1947), 117–134.

BAUER, CATHERINE. "First Job: Control New City Sprawl," *Architectural Forum*, CIV (September, 1956), 105-112.

BENOIT-LÉVY, GEORGES. *La Cité-Jardin*. Paris: Bibliothèque de Museé Sociale, H. Jouve, 1904. Second edition, *ibid*. Paris: Cités-Jardins de France, 1911. 3 vols. Third edition, *Cités-Jardins*. Nice: The Author, 1932. 4 vols.

————. "Las Ciudades Lineales del Porvenir," *La Ciudad Lineal*, XXX (March 10, 1926), 99–101.

BLUM, OTTO. *Städtebau*. Second revised edition, Berlin: Springer, 1937. *See*, especially, "Städtebau Schemata," part 2, chap. 3.

BOILEAU, IVAN. "La Ciudad Lineal: A Critical Study of the Linear Suburb of Madrid," *Town Planning Review*, XXX (October, 1959), 230–238.

BROWN, ALFRED JOHN, and SHERRARD, H. M. *Town and Country Planning*.

[3] It should be mentioned that often works presenting original Ideal Communities do so after evaluation of other such schemes. Consequently, many of the items listed in earlier sections of this bibliography contain description of one or several other Ideal Communities. Critical book reviews, although rare, are still another category which the diligent student of the topic may wish to explore.

Carlton, Victoria: Melbourne University Press, 1951. *See,* especially, "Neighborhood Planning," chap. 13; "Planning New Towns," chap. 14; and "Garden Cities and Satellite Towns," chap. 15.

BRUNNER, KARL H. *Manual de Urbanismo.* Bogotá: Imprenta Municipal, 1939–1940. 3 vols. *See,* especially, "Edificación, Urbanización, Vialidad Urbana," vol. II.

BUNIN, ANDREI VLADIMIROVICH, *et al. Gradostroitel'stvo.* Moskva: Akademiia Arkhitektury SSSR, 1945. *See,* especially, "Gradostroitel'stvo XIX v. i Nachala XX v. v Zarybezhnykh Stranakh," chap. 11, and "Gradostroitel'stvo v SSSR," chap. 12.

CHAPIN, F. STUART. *Urban Land Use Planning,* New York: Harper, 1957. *See,* especially, "Land Use Determinants," part 1.

CHIODI, CESARE. *La Città Moderna: Tecnica Urbanistica.* Milano: Hoepli, 1935. Reissued, 1945. *See,* especially, "La Città del Passato e le Tendenze Moderne," part 1, and "Le Organizzazioni Urbane nel Loro Complesso," part 3.

CHURCHILL, HENRY S. *The City Is the People.* New York: Reynal & Hitchcock, 1945. *See,* especially, "Approach," chap. 3, and "Trends," chap. 6.

COLLINS, GEORGE R. "Linear Planning Throughout the World," *Journal of the Society of Architectural Historians,* XVIII (October, 1959), 74–93.

COLLISON, P. "British Town Planning and the Neighborhood Idea," *Housing Centre Review,* V (December, 1956), 190–192.

LE CORBUSIER (Charles Édouard Jeanneret-Gris). *Concerning Town Planning.* New Haven: Yale University Press, 1948. Translated from *Propos d'Urbanisme. See,* especially, "One Takes the Opportunity to Reply to an Enquiry," part 3.

DAHIR, JAMES. *Communities for Better Living.* New York: Harper, 1950. *See,* especially, "How American Communities Are Being Developed Today: In Urban Areas," [chap. 3]; "Encouragement from the Past," [chap. 5]; and "New Local Institutions and Patterns of Life," [chap. 6].

DAVIE, MAURICE R. "The Pattern of Urban Growth." In MURDOCK, GEORGE P. (ed.), *Studies in the Science of Society.* New Haven: Yale University Press, 1937.

DICKINSON, ROBERT E. *City Region and Regionalism: A Geographical Contribution to Human Ecology.* London: Paul, Trench, Trubner, 1947. *See,* especially, "The Structure of the City," part 2.

DOGLIO, CARLO. "L'Equivoco della Città-giardino," *Urbanistica,* XXIII (No. 13, 1953), 56–66.

DREIER, JOHN. "Greenbelt Planning; Resettlement Administration Goes to Town," *Pencil Points,* XVII (August, 1936), 401–419.

DUNCAN, OTIS D., *et al. Metropolis and Region.* Baltimore: John Hopkins

University Press, for Resources for the Future, 1960. *See,* especially, "Urban Location and Function," chap. 2.

EDEN, W. A. "Studies in Urban Theory—II. Ebenezer Howard and the Garden City Movement," *Town Planning Review* (Joint Nos. 3–4, 1947), pp. 123–143.

GALLION, ARTHUR B., AND EISNER, SIMON. *The Urban Pattern.* New York: Van Nostrand, 1950. *See,* especially, "The Industrial City," part 2; "The Neighborhood Unit," part 5, chap. 21; and "New Horizons," part 6.

GIBBERD, FREDERICK. *Town Design.* New York: Reinhold; London, Architectural Press, 1953. Third edition, *ibid.* New York: Praeger, 1959. *See* "Design of the Complete Town," part 1.

GIBBON, SIR GWILYM. *Reconstruction and Town and Country Planning.* London: The Architect & Building News, 1943. *See* especially, "The Regional Authority," chap. 22.

GIEDION, SIGFRIED. *Space, Time and Architecture.* Cambridge: Harvard University Press, 1941. Third edition, 1954. *See,* especially, "City Planning as a Human Problem," part 8, and "Space-Time in City Planning," part 9.

GOODMAN, PAUL. "Some Remarks on Neighborhood Planning," *Journal of the American Institute of Planners,* XV (Summer, 1949), 40–43.

"Greenbelt Towns," *Architectural Record,* LXXX (September, 1936), 215–234.

GROPIUS, WALTER. "Organic Neighborhood Planning," *Housing and Town and Country Planning, Bulletin No. 2* (April, 1949), pp. 2–5.

HALLMAN, HOWARD W. "Citizens and Professionals Reconsider the Neighborhood," *Journal of the American Institute of Planners,* XXV (August, 1959), 121–127.

HARRISON, HENRY R. "Richard J. Neutra: A Center of Architectural Stimulation," *Pencil Points,* XVIII (July, 1937), 410–438.

HAWLEY, AMOS. *Human Ecology: A Theory of Community Structure.* New York: Ronald Press, 1950. *See,* especially, "Spatial Aspects of Ecological Organization," chaps. 13 and 14, and "Expansion; the Growth of the City," chap. 19.

HEGEMANN, WERNER. *City Planning, Housing.* New York: Architectural Book, 1936–1938. 3 vols. See vols. II and III, *passim.*

HUDSON, ROBERT B. *Radburn: A Plan for Living.* New York: American Association for Adult Education, 1934. *See,* especially, "The Place," chap. 1.

INGERSOLL, PHYLLIS. *Concepts of Ideal Urban Form.* Unpublished MCP thesis, University of California, Berkeley, June, 1958.

KABEL, ERICH. *Baufreiheit und Raumordnung.* Ravensburg: Maier, 1949. *See,* especially, "Erkenntnisse," chap. 3, and "Die Umkehr," chap. 4.

[185]

KANTOROWICH, ROY. "Architectural Utopias: The City Planning Theories of Frank Lloyd Wright and Le Corbusier," *Task*, (No. 2, 1941), 30–35.

KAUFMAN, E. C. "Neighborhood Units as New Elements of Town Planning," *Journal of the Royal Institute of British Architects,* XLIV (December 19, 1936), 165–175.

KORN, ARTHUR. *History Builds the Town.* London: Lund Humphries, 1953. *See* "Theory and Practice," chap. 6.

KRIESIS, PAUL. *Speculations on Town Planning.* Athens: Printed by Christou & Sons, 1953. *See,* especially, "On the Relation of Town Patterns to Sociopolitical Milieus," [chap. 5].

LAVEDAN, PIERRE. *Histoire d'Urbanisme.* Paris: Henri Laurens, 1926, 1941, 1952. 3 vols. *See,* especially, vol. III: "La Ville Malade," chap. 2:3; "L'Urbanisme Constructeur. La Cité-Jardin. La Cité-Satellite," chap. 2:5; and "Création des Villes au XIXᵉ et au XXᵉ Siècles," chap. 3:2.

LEWIS, HAROLD MACLEAN. *City Planning: Why and How.* New York: Longmans, Green, 1939. See "Planning's Future," chap. 24.

———. *Planning the Modern City.* New York: Wiley, 1949. 2 vols. *See,* especially, vol. II, "Neighborhood and Community Planning," chap. 13, and "Decentralization of Industry and Residence," chap. 18.

McALLISTER, GILBERT, and McALLISTER, ELIZABETH G. *Town and Country Planning. A Study of Physical Environment: the Prelude to Post-war Reconstruction.* London: Faber & Faber, 1941. *See,* especially, "Towns for Healthy Living and Industry," chap. 8.

MACFADYEN, DUGALD. *Sir Ebenezer Howard and the Town Planning Movement.* Manchester: Manchester University Press, 1933.

McLEAN, MARY (ed). *Local Planning Administration.* [Third edition], Chicago: International City Managers' Association, 1959. *See,* especially, HAND, IRVING, "Planning of Residential, Commercial, and Industrial Areas," pp. 106–148.

MAUL, ALFRED. "Idealstadt," *Städtebau,* XXIV (November, 1929), 313–314.

MAY, ERNST. "L'Urbanisme en U.R.S.S.," *La Cité & Tekhne,* X (January, 1932), 77–84 of *Tekhne* and 65–78 of *La Cité.*

MEYERSON, MARTIN D., and MITCHELL, ROBERT B. "Changing City Patterns," *The Annals of the American Academy of Political and Social Science,* CCXLII (November, 1945), 149–162.

MORA, SANTIAGO ESTEBAN DE LA. *Planeamiento vs. Arquitectura.* Bogotá: Iqueima, 1952. *See,* especially, chaps. 8 and 9.

MORAND, FRANÇOIS C. *Urbanisme.* Paris: Morancé, 1956.

MUMFORD, LEWIS. "The Neighborhood and the Neighborhood Unit," *Town Planning Review,* XXIV (January, 1954), 256–270.

NELSON, LOWRY. *The Mormon Village: A Pattern and Technique of Land*

Settlement. Salt Lake City: University of Utah Press, 1952. *See, especially,* "Basic Pattern," chap. 1.

NOLEN, JOHN. *New Towns for Old.* Boston: Marshall Jones, 1927.

ORTMANN, WOLF. *Städtebau Früher und Heute.* Düsseldorf: Werner, 1956. *See* "Stadtbild der Gegenwart," [chap. 2] and "Planen," [chap. 5].

OSBORN, FREDERICK J. "The Country-Belt Principle: Its Historical Origins," *Town and Country Planning,* XIII (Spring, 1945), 10–19.

PAULSSON, THOMAS. *Ny Stad.* Stockholm: Gebers, 1958.

PEARSE, INNES H., and CROCKER, LUCY H. *The Peckham Experiment.* London: Allen and Unwin, 1943. American edition, New Haven: Yale University Press, 1946.

PICCINATO, LUIGI. *Urbanistica.* Roma: Sandron, 1947. *See, especially,* "La Città Moderna," [chap. 3:2].

RAINER, ROLAND. *Städtebauliche Prosa: Praktische Grundlagen für den Aufbau der Städte.* Tübingen: Wasmuth, 1948.

RASMUSSEN, STEEN EILER. "Neighborhood Planning," *Town Planning Review, XXVII* (January, 1957), 197–218.

————. *Towns and Buildings.* Liverpool: University Press of Liverpool, 1951. *See, especially,* "Functionalism," [chap. 16].

RATCLIFF, RICHARD U. *Urban Land Economics.* New York: McGraw-Hill, 1949. *See, especially,* "City Growth and Structure," chap. 13.

"Rebuilding Britain," *Architectural Review,* XCIII (April, 1943). Entire issue.

RIGOTTI, GIORGIO. Urbanistica: La Composizione. Torino: Unione Tipografico, 1952. *See, especially,* "La Composizione del Piano Regolatore," part 2.

RODWIN, LLOYD. *The British New Towns Policy.* Cambridge: Harvard University Press, 1956. *See, especially,* "The Garden City Idea: A Historical Appraisal," part 2, and "A Perspective on New Towns; Implications and Prospects," part 4.

————. "Garden Cities and the Metropolis," *Journal of Land and Public Utility Economics,* XXI (August, 1945), 268–281.

SCHNEIDER, WOLF. *Überall Ist Babylon: Die Stadt als Schicksal des Menschen von Ur bis Utopia.* Düsseldorf: Econ-Verlag, 1960. *See, especially,* "Die Stadt der Zukunft," chap. 7.

SCHWAN, BRUNO (ed.). *Städtebau u. Wohnungswesen der Welt; Town Planning and Housing Throughout the World; L'Urbanisme et l'Habitation dans Tous les Pays.* Berlin: Wasmuth, 1935.

SERT, JOSÉ LUIS. "And Town Planner," In STAMO PAPADAKI, (ed), *Le Corbusier.* New York: Macmillan, 1948.

SHAPIRO, MEYER. "Architect's Utopia," *Partisan Review,* IV (March, 1938), 42–47. Review of FRANK LLOYD WRIGHT, *Architecture and Modern Life.*

SHARP, THOMAS. *Town Planning.* Harmondsworth, Middlesex: Penguin, 1940. Revised edition, *ibid.,* 1945. *See,* especially, "Town and Country— or Neither?" chap. 2, and "The Town," chap. 3.

Städtebau und Stadtwirtschaft. Berlin: Deutsche Bauakademie, 1955. Translation into German of "Gradostroitel'stvo" and "Gorodskoe Khoziastvo," two articles in *Bol'shaia Sovetskaia Entsiklopediia,* vol. XII, 1952 edition.

STEWART, CECIL. *A Prospect of Cities.* London: Longmans, Green, 1952. *See,* especially, "A Pillar of Salt," chap. 8, and "Rus in Urbe," chap. 9.

STILLMAN, SEYMOUR. "Comparing Wright and Le Corbusier," *Journal of the American Institute of Architects,* IX (April, 1948), 171-178, and (May, 1948), 226–233.

Survey Graphic, VII (May, 1925). *See,* especially SMITH, ALFRED E., "Seeing a State Whole," pp. 158–160; WRIGHT, HENRY "The Road to Good Housing," pp. 165–168, 189; and PURDOM, C. B., "Garden Cities—What They Are and How They Work," pp. 169–172.

TEAGUE, WALTER D. *Land of Plenty: A Summary of Possibilities.* New York: Harcourt, Brace, 1947. *See,* especially, "In Gracious Communities," chap. 12.

THABIT, WALTER. "Planning and Civil Defense," *Journal of the American Institute of Planners,* XXV (February, 1959), 35–39.

TOMBOLA, GIUSEPPE. *Urbanistica; Storia e Technica.* Padova: CEDAM, 1958. *See,* especially, Genesi delle Città, chap. 1, and "Sviluppo della Città Moderne," chap. 2.

TYLOR, W. RUSSELL. "The Neighborhood Unit Principle in Town Planning," *Town Planning Review,* XVIII (July, 1939), 174–186.

"Villes Nouvelles," *Urbanisme,* XXII (Nos. 25 and 26, 1953). Entire issue.

WHITE, LEONARD E. *New Towns: Their Challenge and Opportunity.* London: National Council of Social Service, 1951. *See,* especially, "Why New Towns?" chap. 1.

WOOD, EDITH E. "The Spanish Linear City," *Journal of the American Institute of Architects,* IX (May, 1921), 169–174.

WRIGHT, HENRY. "The Autobiography of Another Idea," *Western Architect,* XXXIX (September, 1930), 137–141, 153.

ZEVI, BRUNO. *Storia dell'Architettura Moderna.* Torino: Gulio Einaudo, 1950. *See,* especially, "La Genesi dell'Architettura Moderna," chap 1; "Il Movimiento Organico in Europa," chap. 6; and "Il Rinnovamiento degli Studi Storici di Architettura," chap 12.

ZUCKER, PAUL. "Space Concept and Pattern Design in Radio-centric City Planning," *Art Quarterly,* VIII (Spring, 1945), 99–115.

Part 3. Utopias

A number of books reviewing utopias in general have been discussed in the text, together with a few references to works relating utopian communities and planning concepts. The following items, although not mentioned heretofore in this book, should be studied by those interested in this aspect of planning.

ABERCOMBIE, PATRICK. "Ideal Cities," series in *Town Planning Review.* "No. 1—Christianopolis," VIII (April, 1920), 99–104; "No. 2—Victoria," IX (March, 1921), 15–20.

ADAMS, THOMAS. "Model Towns and Communities," series in *Garden Cities.* "Plato's Republic, Owen's Harmony," I (February, 1906), 16–18; "Buckingham's Victoria," I (March, 1906), 33–34, and (April, 1906), 56–58; "The Influence of Carlyle, Ruskin, and Emerson," I (May, 1906), 77–80; and "Early Co-operative Communities in the United States," I (July, 1906, 130–131.

ALYEA, PAUL E., and ALYEA, BLANCHE R. *Fairhope, 1894–1954: The Story of a Single Tax Colony.* University of Alabama Press, 1956. *See* "Some Problems of Policy," chap. 17.

BAUER, CATHERINE. *Modern Housing.* Boston and New York: Houghton Mifflin, 1934. *See,* especially, "Gathering Forces," part 2.

BESTOR, ARTHUR E., JR. *Backwoods Utopias: The Sectarian and Owenite Phases of Communitarian Socialism in America, 1663–1829.* Philadelphia: University of Pennsylvania Press, 1950.

BISHOP, CLAIRE HUCHET. *All Things Common.* New York: Harper, 1950.

COLE, GEORGE D. H. *A History of Socialist Thought.* London: Macmillan, 1953–1958. 4 vols. See vol. I, *passim.*; vol II: "Belgian Socialism in the 1850's—Colius, Kats, and de Keyser," chap. 4; "Anarchists and Anarchist-Communists—Kropotkin," chap. 12; "The Revival of British Socialism —William Morris," chap. 14; vol. III: "Great Britain—Socialism before the Labour Party," chap. 3; "Great Britain—The Labour Party and the Great Unrest," chap. 4; "Theodor Hertzka," appendix to chap. 12.

COMEY, ARTHUR C., and WEHRLY, MAX S. "Planned Communities." In *Urban Planning and Land Policies,* part 1, vol. II of the Supplementary Reports of the Urbanism Committee, U.S. National Resources Committee. Washington: Government Printing Office, 1939.

DAHL, ROBERT A., and LINDBLOM, CHARLES E. *Politics, Economics, and Welfare.* New York: Harper, 1953. *See,* especially, "Some Social Processes for Rational Calculations," chap. 3.

DAHRENDORF, RALPH. "Out of Utopia: Toward a Reorientation of Sociological Analysis," *American Journal of Sociology,* LXIV (September, 1958), 115–127.

DONNER, HENRY W. *Introduction to Utopia.* London: Sidgwick and Jackson, 1945. *See,* especially, "Utopian Society," chap. 7.

DOOB, LEONARD W. *The Plans of Men.* New Haven: Yale University Press, for the Institute of Human Relations, 1940. *See* "The Nature of Planning," chap. 1, and *passim.*

EAVES, CHARLES DUDLEY, and HUTCHINSON, C. A. *Post City, Texas.* Austin: Texas State Historical Association, 1952.

EGBERT, DONALD D., and PERSONS, STOW (eds.). *Socialism and American Life.* Princeton: Princeton University Press, 1952. 2 vols. *See* vol. I, *passim;* and in vol. II, "Bibliography: Descriptive and Critical," *see,* especially, "Socialism, Housing, and City Planning," part 4, special topic 11.

Encyclopaedia of the Social Sciences. New York: Macmillan, 1930–1934. *See* DOUGLAS, DOROTHY W., and LUMPKIN, KATHERINE DUP., "Communistic Settlements," vol. IV; MASON, EDWARD S., "Fourier and Fourierism," vol. VI; COLE, G. D. H., "Owen and Owenism," vol. XI; and LARRABEE, HAROLD A., "Saint-Simon and Saint-Simonianism," vol. XIII.

FULMER, OTIS KLINE. *Greenbelt.* Introduction by LEWIS MUMFORD. Washington: American Council on Public Affairs, 1941.

FUZ, J. K. *Welfare Economics in English Utopias: From Francis Bacon to Adam Smith.* The Hague: Nijhoff, 1952.

HEILBRONER, ROBERT L. *The Worldly Philosophers.* New York: Simon and Schuster, 1953. *See,* especially, "The Beautiful World of the Utopian Socialists," chap. 5.

HUNTINGTON, CHARLES W. *Enclaves of Single Tax.* Harvard, Mass.: Fiske-Warren, 1921. *See* "Fairhope Town Planning Scheme," [chap. 3:1].

INFIELD, HENRIK F. *The American Intentional Communities.* Glen Gardner, N.J.: Glen Gardner Community Press, 1955.

———. *Cooperative Communities at Work.* New York: Dryden, 1945.

———. *Cooperative Living in Palestine.* New York: Dryden, 1944.

KAUFFMANN, RICHARD. "Planning of Jewish Settlements in Palestine," *Town Planning Review,* XII (November, 1926), 93–116.

KRIESIS, PAUL. *Approach to Town Planning.* Athens: Printed by Christov, 1952. *See,* especially, "The Utopian Approach," chap. 1.

LAIDLER, HARRY W. *Social-economic Movements: An Historical and Comparative Survey of Socialism, Communism, Co-operation, Utopianism, and Other Systems of Reform and Reconstruction.* New York: Crowell, 1927. Second edition, 1944. *See,* especially, "Utopianism and Its Precursors," part 1.

LANDAUER, CARL, in collaboration with ELIZABETH KRIDL VALKENIER and

HILDE STEIN LANDAUER. *European Socialism: A History of Ideas and Movements from the Industrial Revolution to Hitler's Seizure of Power.* Berkeley and Los Angeles: University of California Press, 1959. 2 vols. *See* "The Three Anticapitalistic Movements," chap. 1, and "The Revival of the Analysis of the Desirable Society," chap. 46.

MANNHEIM, KARL. *Man and Society in an Age of Reconstruction.* New York: Harcourt, Brace, 1940. *See,* especially, "Thought at the Level of Planning," part 4.

MONTOLIU, C. "Fairhope—A Town-Planning Scheme for Its Development into an Organic City," *American City,* XXIV (April, 1921), 355–359.

PARAF, PIERRE. *Les Cités du Bonheur.* Paris: Editions du Myrte, 1945. *See* "Le XIXe Siécle et la Marche au Bonheur," chap. 7.

QUINT, HOWARD H. *The Forging of American Socialism: Origins of the Modern Movement.* Columbia: University of South Carolina Press, 1953. *See,* especially, "Marxism Comes to America," chap. 1, and "Bellamy Makes Socialism Respectable," chap. 3.

RUYER, RAYMOND. *L'Utopie et les Utopies.* Paris: Presses Universitaires de France, 1950. *See,* especially, "Les Utopies Socialistes après 1850," chap. 14, and "Les Grandes Anticipations Contemporaines," chap. 15.

SHARON, ARIEH. "Collective Settlements in Israel," *Town Planning Review,* XXV (January, 1955), 255–270.

WARNER, GEORGE A. *Greenbelt: The Cooperative Community.* New York: Exposition Press, 1954.

WEBBER, EVERETT. *Escape to Utopia: The Communal Movement in America.* New York: Hastings House, 1959.

Part 4. Models

There is a growing literature on the subject of so-called urban models. These have been developed to solve problems arising largely out of the transportation crisis afflicting North American cities. The end product represents an ideal not unrelated in content to the Ideal Communities studied in this book.[4] Methodologically, the linear programming models hold perhaps the greatest promise with respect to the problems studied in this book, for they express most clearly the function to be optimized, and they show one way to be explicit regarding the goals. Such urban models involve the interaction of economics, land-use and transportation planning, and statistics. The following items, although demanding a background in mathematics,

[4] These models should be distinguished from other attempts originating in economics (as well as other disciplines) which attempt to distill the essential elements of urban structure. Section I and Section II, Part 1, of this bibliography include items in this category.

should be consulted by the interested reader. Each reference contains an extensive and helpful bibliography.

HERBERT, JOHN D., and STEVENS, BENJAMIN H. "A Model for the Distribution of Residential Activity in Urban Areas," *Journal of Regional Science,* II (Fall, 1960), 21–36.

ISARD, WALTER. *Location and Space-Economy.* Cambridge: Technology Press of Massachusetts Institute of Technology, and New York: Wiley, 1956. *See,* especially, "Some Empirical Regularities in Space-Economy," chap. 3, and "Partial Graphic Synthesis and Summary," chap. 11.

————. *Methods of Regional Analysis: An Introduction to Regional Science.* Cambridge: Technology Press of Massachusetts Institute of Technology, and New York: Wiley, 1960. *See* "Gravity, Potential, and Spatial Interaction Models," chap. 11.

"Land Use and Traffic Models: A Progress Report," *Journal of the American Institute of Planners,* XXV (May, 1959). Entire issue. *See also* discussion by WEISMANTEL, WILLIAM L., "Dante's Inferno: The First Land Use Model," *ibid.,* (November, 1959), 175–179; and CREIGHTON, ROGER, "Comment on 'Dante's Inferno: The First Land Use Model:' " *ibid.* (February, 1960), XXVI, 67.

STEVENS, BENJAMIN H. "A Review of the Literature on Linear Methods and Models for Spatial Analysis," *Journal of the American Institute of Planners,* XXVI (August, 1960), 253–259.

STEWART, JOHN Q., and WARNTZ, WILLIAM. "Physics of Population Distribution," *Journal of Regional Science,* I (Summer, 1958), 99–123.

WARNTZ, WILLIAM, and NEFT, DAVID. "Contributions to a Statistical Methodology for Area Distribution," *Journal of Regional Science,* II (Spring, 1960), 47–66.

Index of Authors*

Adams, Thomas, 20, 24, 64-68, 121, 139, 143, 144, 146
ASCORAL,
See Le Corbusier

Bauer, Catherine, 120n.
Bellamy, Edward, 19n.
Berneri, Marie Louise, 17n.
Blumenfeld, Hans, 21n., 30n., 116n., 147, 150n.
Buber, Martin, 16n., 17n., 18n.
Burgess, Ernest W., 28

Calverton, Victor F., 18n.
Cauchon, Noulan, 136
Chambless, Edgar, 43-47, 134n., 144, 146, 149, 156
Chapin, F. Stuart, Jr., 138n.
Comey, Arthur C., 30n., 47-49, 114, 135, 138, 144, 146
Le Corbusier, 24, 34, 54-57, 60, 85-87, 114, 118, 118n., 122, 124, 126, 127, 129n., 132n., 133, 134, 135, 136, 138, 139n., 142, 144, 146, 147, 149, 154, 156

Duncan, Otis Dudley, 138n.

Editors of *Fortune,* 123
Edwards, A. Trystan, 114, 116n., 122, 125

Fawcett, Charles B., 146
Ferriss, Hugh, 31, 57-60, 116n., 120n., 133, 143, 144, 146, 147, 154

Festinger, Leon, 25n., 160
Firey, Walter I., 28n.
Fisher, Robert M., 157n.
Foley, Donald L., 25n., 119n.
Fritsch, Theodor, 23, 36-39, 127n., 129, 129n., 134, 144, 146, 148

Gans, Herbert J., 120
Garnier, Tony, 22, 133, 156
Geddes, Patrick, 157
Gloeden, Erich, 50-54, 114, 122n., 123, 126, 134n., 144
Goodman, Paul, and Percival Goodman, 21, 31, 57, 97-106, 122, 125, 133, 134, 135, 136, 138, 139, 140, 142, 143, 144, 146, 152, 154, 154n., 161n.
Gropius, Walter, 142
Gropius, Walter, and Martin Wagner, 75-78, 114, 140, 144, 146
Gutkind, Erwin A., 118, 121n.

Herrey, Herman, Constantin A.Pertzoff, and Erna M. J. Herrey, 78-81, 114, 135, 136, 140, 145, 146

Hertzler, Joyce Oramel, 17n.
Higgins, Benjamin, 24, 152n.
Hilberseimer, Ludwig, 34, 108, 124, 126, 146, 148, 155
Hine, Robert V., 18n.
Holloway, Mark, 18n.

Howard, Ebenezer, 21, 28, 28n., 39-43, 53, 112, 114, 115, 123, 125, 126, 127, 134n., 138, 142, 143, 145, 146, 147, 153, 154, 156
Hoyt, Homer, 28, 28n.
Humbert, Ricardo C., 133
Huxley, Aldous, 30

Ingersoll, Phyllis, 21n.
Isaacs, Reginald, 120n.

Jacobs, Jane, *See* Editors of *Fortune*
Jeanneret, Gris, Charles Édouard, *See* Le Corbusier
Justement, Louis, 20, 22, 91-94, 114, 126, 138, 145, 146

Kampffmeyer, Hans, *See* Miljutin, N. A.
Kaplan, Abraham, 28n.
Kern, Robert R, 57, 136, 154
Klein, Alexander, 106-109, 136, 138, 145, 146, 154
Köhler, Paul, and Rudolf Winkler, 146, 153
Korn, Arthur, and Felix J. Samuely, 22

Lang, S., 21n.
Liberation, 18n.
Lillibridge, Robert M., 138n.
Lynch, Kevin, 116n., 122, 126n.
Lynch, Kevin, and Lloyd Rodwin, 113, 113n., 158

Mann, Peter H., 119

* Bibliographic citations will be found in Chapters III and VI. The reader is also referred to the analytical Table of Contents at the beginning of this volume.